T0341374

A Commentary on
1 and 2 Corinthians

SPCK International Study Guide 42

A Commentary on 1 and 2 Corinthians

J. Ayodeji Adewuya

First published in Great Britain in 2009

Society for Promoting Christian Knowledge
36 Causton Street
London SW1P 4ST

British Library Cataloguing-in-Publication Data
A catalogue record for this book is available from the British Library

ISBN 978–0–281–06199–0

10 9 8 7 6 5 4 3 2 1

Typeset by Manila Typesetting Company

Produced on paper from sustainable forests

Contents

Contributors   vii
The SPCK International Study Guides   viii
Acknowledgements   ix
Using this Commentary   x
Further reading   xii

Introduction   1

1 Corinthians

1 Corinthians 1.1–9: Greetings and thanksgiving   9

1 Corinthians 1.10—4.21: Divisions in the Church   14

1.10–31: A plea for unity   14

2.1–16: Human wisdom versus God's wisdom   20

3.1–23: The nature of Christian leadership Part 1   26

Special note A: The flesh   31

4.1–21: The nature of Christian leadership Part 2   33

1 Corinthians 5.1—6.20: Moral problems in the Church   39

5.1–13: Discipline and purity   39

6.1–20: Pagan courts and Christian purity   43

1 Corinthians 7.1–40: Purity, sexual relations, divorce and marriage   50

1 Corinthians 8.1—11.1: Food sacrificed to idols   57

8.1–13: Christian freedom and the common good   57

9.1–27: Use and abuse of Christian freedom   61

10.1—11.1: Flee from idolatry   67

Special note B: Case studies   72

1 Corinthians 11.2—14.40: Christian worship   75

11.2–34: Head covering and the Lord's Supper   75

12.1–31: Many members, one body   82

Applied theology essay 1: The Holy Spirit and spirituality   88
Kirsteen Kim

13.1–13: The way of love   94

Contents

14.1–40: Spiritual gifts and edification 99

Applied theology essay 2: Women in Corinthians 105
Lisa Meo

1 Corinthians 15.1–58: The resurrection 112

Special note C: The kerygma of the early Church 114

Special note D: Resurrection and reincarnation 118

1 Corinthians 16.1–24: Finance and farewell 120

2 Corinthians

2 Corinthians 1.1—7.16: Paul's visit, tearful letter and
apostolic ministry 129

1.1–24: Greeting, prayer, thanksgiving and travel plans 129

2.1–17: Paul's defence 135

Special note E: Lessons on church discipline 138

3.1–18: A ministry of the new covenant 141

4.1–18: Treasure in jars of clay 146

5.1–21: Ambassadors for Christ 153

Special note F: The new creation 157

Applied theology essay 3: Reconciliation 160
Daryl Balia

6.1–18: Christian relationships 164

7.1–16: Urgent appeals 170

2 Corinthians 8.1—9.15: The collection 176

8.1–24: Grace of giving 176

9.1–15: More about giving 183

Special note G: Paul's vocabulary of giving 185

2 Corinthians 10.1—13.14: Paul's self defence and preparation for visit 188

10.1–18: Paul's apostolic defence 188

Special note H: Spiritual warfare 191

11.1–33: Paul's foolish boasting 194

Special note I: Further reflection on 2 Corinthians 11.21–33 202

12.1–21: Foolish boasting and heavenly visions 205

Special note J: Paul's thorn in the flesh 209

13.1–14: Concluding appeal 211

Index 215

Contributors

Author

Dr Ayodeji Adewuya is Professor of New Testament at the Church of God Theological Seminary, Cleveland, Tennessee, USA. Originally from Nigeria, he and his family were missionaries in the Philippines from 1984 to 2001. They remain involved in ministry to that country. He is an active member of the Society of Biblical Literature, Wesleyan Theological Society and the Society of Pentecostal Studies. He is the author of *Holiness and Community in 2 Corinthians 6:14–7:1 – A Study of Paul's View of Communal Holiness in the Corinthian Correspondence* and *Transformed by Grace: Paul's View of Holiness in Romans 6–8*.

Essay contributors

Daryl Balia, a native South African ordained in the Methodist Church, was Scholar in Residence at the Selly Oak Centre for Mission Studies in Birmingham before taking up his current position as International Director of the Edinburgh 2010 project at New College, University of Edinburgh.

Dr Kirsteen Kim is Associate Senior Lecturer at Leeds Trinity and All Saints, where she brings experience from living in Korea and India to bear on teaching theology. She was formerly Chair of the British and Irish Association for Mission Studies and is now Vice-moderator of the Commission for World Mission and Evangelism of the World Council of Churches. Kim is the author of *The Holy Spirit in the World: A Global Conversation* (Orbis/ SPCK, 2007) and, with Sebastian Kim, of *Christianity as a World Religion* (Continuum, 2008).

Originally from Fiji, Lisa Meo has taught theology since 1963, devising innovative Bible study methods and promoting theological education for women in the Pacific through the South Pacific Association of Theological Schools and the World Association of Theological Schools. She has written on Pacific and feminist theologies. She is married with four children and thirteen grandchildren and has retired to Sydney, Australia.

The SPCK International Study Guides

The International Study Guides (ISGs) are clear and accessible resources for the Christian Church. The series contains biblical commentaries, books on pastoral care, church history and theology. The guides are contextual and ecumenical in content and missional in direction.

The series is primarily aimed at those training for Christian ministries for whom English is an alternative language. Many other Christians will also find the ISGs useful guides. The contributors come from different countries and from a variety of church backgrounds. Most of them are theological educators. They bring their particular perspectives to bear as they demonstrate the influence of other contexts on the subjects they address. They provide a practical emphasis alongside contemporary scholarly reflection.

For over forty years, the ISG series has aided those in ministerial formation to develop their own theology and discern God's mission in their context. Today, there is a greater awareness of plurality within the universal Christian body. This is reflected in changes to the series that draw upon the breadth of Christian experience across the globe.

Emma Wild-Wood
Editor, International Study Guides

Acknowledgements

Over the years, both in the Philippines and the USA, I have enjoyed teaching Paul's Letters to the Corinthians at graduate level. But nothing compares with writing a commentary on those two books at this level. I wish to express my gratitude to various people for their assistance and suggestions. Thanks are due especially to: Dr Emma Wild-Wood, whose constructive editorial comments and stimulating queries have immensely contributed to the final form of the book; Dr Lee Roy Martin, my colleague and a seasoned pastor, and Dr Emerson Powery, whose careful reading and detailed comments on an early version were of great help; Dr Dean Flemming and Dr Jerry Sumney, who read portions of the book; Shannon and Debra Mimbs who, as the 'first readers' of the commentary, asked probing questions and were of great help in reformulating the questions at the end of every chapter; my students at the Church of God Theological Seminary, who are probably unaware of their role in the project, but on whom all the material has been tried out, and whose response to it has largely contributed to the final form in which it appears; and above all, my wife, Grace, who during the entire process of writing the commentary has been a source of encouragement.

J. Ayodeji Adewuya

Using this Commentary

In planning this book, much the same pattern has been followed as for earlier biblical guides in the series. There is a preliminary note on the background to Paul's Letters to the Corinthians, and on ways of studying them. Then the Letters themselves have been divided into fairly short sections for study. The treatment of each section consists of:

 1 A **summary** of the Bible passage, briefly indicating the subject matter it contains. Of course, the summary is not intended as a substitute for the words of the Bible itself, which need to be read very carefully at each stage of our study.

 2 An **introduction** to the passage, summarizing what Paul was trying to say and his reasons for saying it, and showing how it fits into the rest of the Letter and Paul's teaching as a whole.

 3 An **interpretation** of the passage as it applied to Paul's hearers at the time, and how we should understand and apply its teaching to our own lives as Christians today. **Notes** on particular words and points of possible difficulty are included as part of the interpretation, so that readers can make sure of understanding them as they arise.

 ## Special notes

Separate special notes deal in more detail with some of the main themes and problems which Paul was wrestling with. They explain some ideas of his time which we may find helpful in order to understand his teaching more fully, and apply it to our own situation today. They are, however, not essential, and readers with limited time may skip them.

 ## Applied theological essays

Topics that warrant extended attention because of their implication for theology and the current situation of many churches today are covered as 'Applied theological essays'. The essay contributors show one way in which a theme, a biblical text and a particular context can be read together to discern God's will in our world today.

 ## Study suggestions

Questions for further study are provided throughout the guide. Besides enabling students working alone to check their own progress, they provide topics for group research and classroom discussion, and will help all readers to understand Paul's teaching more clearly. They are of four main sorts:

1 **Word study**, to help readers check and deepen their understanding of important words and phrases.

2 **Review of content**, to help readers check the work they have done, and make sure they have fully grasped the ideas and points of the teaching given.

3 **Bible study**, to link the ideas and teaching of the biblical passage with related ideas and teaching in other parts of the Bible.

4 **Discussion and application**, to help readers think out the practical significance of the passage being studied, both to those to whom the biblical author was writing, and for the life and work of the churches and of individual Christians in the modern situation. Many of these are suitable for use in a group as well as for students working alone.

The best way to use these study suggestions is: first, reread the Bible passage; second, read the appropriate section of this commentary once or twice; and then do the work suggested, either in writing or in group discussion, without looking at the commentary again unless instructed to do so.

Please note that all these are only **suggestions**. Some readers may not wish to use them. Some teachers may wish to select only those most relevant to the needs of their particular students, or may wish to substitute questions of their own.

A list of books for **further reading** is provided on pp. xii–xiii.

Index

The Index includes only the more important names of people and places and the main subjects treated in the Letters or discussed in this commentary.

Bible versions

The English translation of the Bible used in this commentary is the New Revised Standard Version (NRSV). Reference is also made to the following versions, where these help to show the meaning more clearly:

• the New International Version (NIV)

• the Revised Standard Version (RSV)

In a few cases, reference has also been made to the Authorized (King James) Version (AV).

Further reading

Arrington, French L. *The Ministry of Reconciliation: A Study of 2 Corinthians*. Cleveland: Pathway Press, 1988.

Barnett, Paul. *1 Corinthians: Holiness and Hope of a Rescued People*. Rossshire: Christian Focus Publications, 2000.

Barrett, C. K. *The First Epistle to the Corinthians*. Harper's New Testament Commentaries. Peabody: Hendrickson, 1968.

Barrett, C. K. *The Second Epistle to the Corinthians*. Black's New Testament Commentaries. Edited by Henry Chadwick. London: A. & C. Black, 1973.

Belleville, Linda L. *2 Corinthians*. IVP New Testament Commentary Series. Edited by Grant R. Osborne. Downers Grove: InterVarsity Press, 1996.

Bruce, F. F. *I and II Corinthians*. The New Century Bible Commentary. Edited by Matthew Black. Grand Rapids: Eerdmans, 1971.

Fee, Gordon. *The New International Commentary on the New Testament*. Edited by F. F. Bruce. Grand Rapids: Eerdmans, 1987.

Garland, David E. *1 Corinthians*. Baker Exegetical Commentary on the New Testament. Grand Rapids: Baker Academic, 2003.

Hays, Richard B. *First Corinthians*. Interpretation: A Bible Commentary for Teaching and Preaching. Edited by James Luther Mays. Louisville: John Knox Press, 1997.

Johnson, Alan F. *1 Corinthians*. IVP New Testament Commentary Series. Edited by Grant R. Osborne. Downers Grove: InterVarsity Press, 2004.

Keener, Craig S. *1–2 Corinthians*. The New Cambridge Bible Commentor. Edited by Ben Witherington III. Cambridge: Cambridge University Press, 2005.

Kistemaker, Simon J. *II Corinthians*. New Testament Commentary. Grand Rapids: Baker Book House, 1997.

Talbert, Charles H. *Reading Corinthians: A New Testament Commentary for Preachers*. London: SPCK, 1987.

Thiselton, Anthony C. *1 Corinthians*. A Shorter Exegetical and Pastoral Commentary. Grand Rapids: Eerdmans, 2006.

Watson, Nigel *The First Epistle to the Corinthians*. Epworth Commentaries. Edited by Ivor H. Jones. London: Epworth, 1992.

Watson, Nigel. *The Second Epistle to the Corinthians.* Epworth Commentaries. Edited by Ivor H. Jones. London: Epworth, 1993.

Witherington III, Ben. *Conflict and Community in Corinth: A Social-Rhetorical Commentary on 1 and 2 Corinthians.* Grand Rapids: Eerdmans, 1995.

Introduction

There are perhaps no other New Testament Letters that offer such a variety and wealth of material touching on Christian conduct, both for the individual and for the local church, as do 1 and 2 Corinthians. Many of the church problems in these books are rooted in the background and surrounding of the Corinthian believers. Their need was to be established and grounded in God's Word and, consequently, to live as befitted their calling as God's people.

Authorship

Paul's authorship of 1 and 2 Corinthians is hardly contested. As a matter of fact, both Letters are among those generally known as the 'undisputed Letters of Paul'.

The city of Corinth: its location and history

Location

Corinth was a cosmopolitan city, a principal city of Greece and the capital of the province of Achaia. It was strategically located on the isthmus, that is, the narrow strip of land which connected northern and southern Greece and separated the Saronic Gulf from the Corinthian Gulf. It was the crossroads of east–west trade. It boasted two major harbours: Cenchreae in the east and Lechaeum in the west. It controlled the north–south overland commercial traffic and the west–east sea route between Italy and Asia. Merchants preferred to unload their ships and to transport their goods across the isthmus, while the empty ships went around the Peloponnese, the southern part of Greece, rather than to get caught by one of the frequent dangerous storms and risk losing both their ships and cargoes. Corinth was a natural shipping and trading centre.

History

The history of the city of Corinth has two parts. First it was a city-state in the golden years of Athens. It flourished until it was destroyed by the Romans in 146 BC. Second, it was rebuilt in 44 BC by Julius Caesar as a Roman colony. From 29 BC onward it was the capital of the senatorial province of Achaia and seat of the proconsul. That was the status it retained till the time that Paul visited it several years later. Several things stand out about the city:

- *Major commercial centre* Corinth was one of the busiest international ports of the ancient world.

- *Political centre* As the seat of the proconsul of Achaia, Corinth was a mini-Rome.

- *Cultural diversity* Prosperity returned to the new Corinth almost immediately after it was rebuilt, attracting many people from both East and West. However, the Romans were dominant.

- *Religious diversity* The Romans brought with them their culture and religions. Since Corinth was traditionally Greek, it maintained many ties with Greek religion, philosophy and the arts. The mystery cults were brought from Egypt and Asia in the East, while the Jews worshipped in their synagogues and continued their unique belief in one God.

Corinth: a city of religion and vice

Religion, it has been noted, was as diverse as Corinth's population in Paul's day. There were as many as 26 sacred places devoted to the 'many gods' and 'many lords', that is, the Graeco-Roman pantheon, and 'lords many', that is, the mystery cults (cf. 1 Corinthians 8.5, AV), and the centre of worship was Aphrodite, the goddess of love, to whom many immoral priestesses were consecrated. As in many cosmopolitan cities, then and now, vice and religion prospered side by side in Corinth. Drunkenness and sexual immorality were rampant. The city became a byword for moral corruption and synonymous with immorality. To live like a Corinthian meant to have extremely low moral standards and loose conduct. The Greek word *korinthiazesthai*, taken from the name of the town, meant to have a drunken, immoral, perverted lifestyle.

The Christian community: ethnic and social diversity

Based on the facts from Acts, 1 Corinthians and Romans, the Corinthian community was in many ways a reflection of the city (Acts 18.1–8; 1 Corinthians 1.10–17; 16.15–17; Romans 16.23). It was an ethnically and socially diverse community comprising Jews, Gentiles, slaves and free (1 Corinthians 1.28–30; 12.13). There were wealthy people in the community. But according to 1 Corinthians 1.26, not many of them came from the upper strata of society, and 1 Corinthians 7.20–24 suggests that some were slaves. Some of the tensions in the community were between the rich and the poor (1 Corinthians 11.17–34). Although there were some Jews in the community (Acts 18.6), passages such as 1 Corinthians 6.10–11; 8.7 and 12.2 clearly indicate that the community was primarily Gentile. So 1 Corinthians was written to readers with a pagan past, who were once 'led astray to dumb idols' (1 Corinthians 12.2, RSV; cf. 8.1—10.22) and who were in need of a reminder to avoid typically pagan sexual vices (6.9–20). The same is implied in the discussion about litigation before Gentile magistrates in 1 Corinthians 6.1–11 and the attitude towards marriage in 1 Corinthians 7, issues that were naturally at odds with the Judaism of the day.

Paul's relationship with the Corinthians

The relationship between Paul and the Corinthians is a complex one. It may be reconstructed as follows.

1 The pioneer visit: Paul plants the church at Corinth (Acts 18.1–17).

2 Paul writes a Letter to the Corinthians (1 Corinthians 5.9) in which he tells the Corinthians not to associate with immoral people.

3 Two delegations come to Paul from Corinth. They bring the news about the problems: factions, pride in wisdom, a case of incest, legal proceedings and immoral behaviour.

4 A letter is sent from Corinth seeking clarification from Paul on various issues: marriage, eating meat offered to idols, behaviour in the church assembly, charismata, the resurrection, and the collection of money.

5 Paul writes 1 Corinthians, an occasional response to problems at Corinth.

6 Paul makes a visit to Corinth and the visit does not go well. Hence, it is commonly known as the 'painful visit'.

7 Paul writes a sorrowful/severe letter in lieu of another visit. The letter is sent through Titus.

8 Titus reports to Paul in Macedonia (2 Corinthians 7.5–16).

9 Paul writes 2 Corinthians.

The purpose of 1 and 2 Corinthians

Paul's first Letter to the Corinthians is an occasional one, where 'occasional' means it is a real letter to real people who faced real problems. These problems had developed between the time Paul left the city at the end of an 18-month stay (cf. Acts 18), and the time of the writing of the letter approximately three years later. Paul wrote 1 Corinthians due to three major factors. First, it was a response to reports from Chloe's household about divisions as well as other reports about sexual immorality (1 Corinthians 1.11; 5.1; 11.18), and to a letter sent by the Corinthians (1 Corinthians 7.1). Second, it was written in response to a delegation sent from Corinth to Paul (1 Corinthians 16). The Letter shows that Paul addressed different, somewhat disparate, issues; all of which, with the exception of 1 Corinthians 15, are behavioural. Even in the case of the latter, Paul's discussion on the resurrection is interspersed with ethical warnings and imperatives (1 Corinthians 15.33–34, 58).

Scholars agree that 2 Corinthians is perhaps the most personal of Paul's Letters. It provides a window into Paul's heart. It is clear that at the time he wrote, there was a strained relationship between Paul and the Corinthians. This is due to several factors such as his change in travel plans and the infiltration of the church by various intruders. The goal of Paul's opponents was to undermine his apostolic authority and seduce the Corinthians. Paul wrote the Letter primarily to effect reconciliation between himself and the Corinthians. As part of his strategy, he vigorously defends his apostleship and personal integrity. The main issues addressed by Paul in 1 and 2 Corinthians can be summarized as follows.

1   *Divisions* That there was some form of internal division in the community is evident from 1 Corinthians 1.10–12; 3.4–5 and 11.18–19. The division appears to be along socio-economic lines as indicated by Paul's response in 1 Corinthians 11.17–34 (see also 1 Corinthians 1.26; 7.20–24; 12.13). Perhaps at the core of the problems that plagued the Corinthian church is how members should relate to one another. There was much selfishness and individualism.

2   *Holy living* There were serious ethical problems in the church. Their Christian faith was considerably influenced by a Hellenistic world view and attitude toward moral behaviour. They were the Christian community in Corinth, but in many things their attitude was more determined by their social location than by their Christian faith. It was not too long until the Corinthian church began to bear the marks of the surrounding Corinthian lifestyle that they had known before their conversion. The church began to mirror the city in which it was based. An old saint once said of the Corinthian church, 'I looked for the church and I found it in the world; and I looked for the world and I found it in the church.' They began to resemble and assimilate the city in which they lived, and all the sins that went along with it. Paul's concern for holiness among God's people permeates the two Letters even though they are separated by time in terms of writing. This commentary affirms that although new problems have surfaced by the time Paul wrote 2 Corinthians, the behavioural aberrations that Paul addressed in 1 Corinthians were not completely removed at the time he wrote the second Letter.

3   *Christian freedom* What is Christian freedom and how should it manifest itself in daily living? Answers to these questions propel Paul's handling of the issue of food sacrificed to idols (1 Corinthians 8—10). Located in a pluralistic society, the Corinthians were faced with problems of how to relate to those who were of opposite convictions, particularly with regards to issues of idolatrous food.

4   *Theological/doctrinal issues* Several theological issues stand out in the two Letters and are related to the daily living of Christians as well as to the corporate testimony of the worshipping church. The practical

problem of whether Christians should marry and how they should conduct themselves in a married or unmarried state is adequately discussed. There were problems concerning the place of women, abuse of the Lord's Supper and wrong use of spiritual gifts. There are several doctrinal issues interspersed within the two Letters. What is the role of women in the assembly? How about the exercise of spiritual gifts? Paul also addressed the interconnected problems of church discipline and restoration.

5 *Paul's apostolic authority* Who is an apostle? What are the marks of a true apostle? The opponents of Paul who infiltrated the community seemed to have succeeded in casting doubts on Paul's apostleship and authority. They raised questions not only about the authenticity of Paul's ministry but also concerning his integrity as it related to his message, handling of finances and other areas. It appears that some members of the congregation had been swayed. This is a major issue that Paul addresses in the Letters.

6 *Reconciliation* As noted above, the relationship between the Corinthians was not a smooth one. Paul found it necessary to write to the Corinthians to resolve the problems between them.

7 *The Jerusalem collection and Christian giving* An offshoot of the problem between Paul and the Corinthians is the desire of the latter to stop their collection of money for the church at Jerusalem, a project that was important to Paul. In addressing that problem Paul takes time to address the problem of Christian giving.

Many years separate us from first-century Corinth. Churches through the centuries may appear to have changed significantly. However, the conditions and issues we face in our times link us unmistakably both to the time in which Paul wrote 1 and 2 Corinthians and to the church to which he wrote.

1 Corinthians

1 Corinthians 1.1–9

Greetings and thanksgiving

 Summary

1.1–3: Greetings: Paul introduces himself and the church and prays for grace and peace.

1.4–9: Paul's thanksgiving for the giftedness and hope of the Corinthian church.

 Introduction

The Corinthians have sent delegates and written to Paul asking for clarification on various issues (see Introduction). Paul replies to them in this Letter. He begins with a customary greeting (1.1–3) in which he introduces himself and establishes common ground between himself and the Corinthians. He then expresses his thanksgiving to God for the manifestation of spiritual gifts among the Corinthians. This is followed by Paul's expression of his confidence that the Lord will complete the work that he has begun in them (1.4–9). The words of thanksgiving are not mere rhetorical flourish. Paul really did pray for his congregations and thanked God for them. In this regard he serves as a model for pastors and church leaders in the way he regularly prayed for those to whom he ministered. The thanksgiving section also prepares the way for some of the main issues that Paul will address later.

Interpretation and notes

1.1. Paul, called to be an apostle of Christ Jesus by the will of God: The statement contains two notable elements:

1 Paul understood his call to be a divine appointment. An African proverb says, 'You need only be afraid of the person who sent you on an errand, and not the person to whom you are sent.' Paul's ultimate accountability was to God and he could always, regardless of whatever

he faced, count on the assurance that he was in the will of God. Paul's statement undermines the popular saying that I heard as a young convert in Africa in the early 1970s that 'if God does not call you, call yourself'. Although such a statement was motivated by commitment and was a challenge to get involved in God's work, it is a wrong thing to do. Believers ought to make sure of their calling through prayer, studying the Word, listening to the Holy Spirit and godly advice from mature believers.

2   Paul's call is specific. He was called to be an apostle, that is, an emissary or representative of Christ. It mattered how he lived. Our character and relationships are of greater importance to God than our actions and employment. Being precedes doing.

1.2a. Church of God that is in Corinth: Paul now mentions the addressees.

1   Although the message of the Letter is applicable today in many ways, its primary audience was the Corinthians. It is important to remember context when we examine specific practices and issues, such as head covering (11.2–16) and women (1 Corinthians 14.33–35), that Paul addresses.

2   The whole Church belongs to God. The members of the Corinthian congregation belong to God and, as such, should behave responsibly. Division among church leaders, as Paul will soon address, is absurd.

3   God has a church at Corinth despite its reputation for immorality. God used Paul to plant a church in an unlikely place. It is like having a church in Las Vegas, Nevada, the gambling capital of the world.

4   For Paul, the church was primarily a 'people' who live, worship and work together for God's purposes. It was not just a building. Today, it is not uncommon to find competition among denominations about who has the largest edifice. Churches are defined by their seating capacity or the numbers that attend. People talk of 'the largest church' in Africa, Asia or elsewhere. Paul was more concerned about the character and mission of God's people in their environment.

1.2b. Sanctified in Christ Jesus, called to be saints: How could the Corinthian Christians be called saints, given the problems in the church? What does holiness or sanctification mean? The word derives from the Greek word *hagios* and has two general meanings:

1   To be set apart or dedicated to a holy use;

2   To be made holy.

However, it is possible to suggest a third meaning, which is 'belonging-ness'. Israel was considered holy, not because of the way it behaved but because it belonged to God as a people (Exodus 19.5–6). So when Paul says that the Corinthians are sanctified and called to be holy, he is not thinking of their being sinlessly perfect. Paul begins by reminding them of their identity in Christ. Although Paul will later address the ethical obligations and holy living that must follow their relationship with God, he refers here to the entire group of Corinthians as saints who, despite their moral shortcomings, belong to God.

1.2c. Together with all those who in every place call on the name of our Lord Jesus Christ, both their Lord and ours: Paul expands his audience to include all those who call on the name of the Lord everywhere. God's Church is much bigger than any lone individual or even a particular denomination. Although there are different denominations it is wrong to assume that our denomination represents the whole body of Christ.

1.3. Grace to you and peace: Paul wishes the Corinthians grace and peace. Grace has to do with both the favour that God bestowed upon the Corinthians at salvation and the continuing power to sustain their Christian lives. Peace is the result of the believer's relationship with God. Peace does not necessarily imply the absence of trouble but the calmness and assurance that derive from the knowledge that God is always in charge.

1.4–6. I give thanks: First, Paul gives thanks to God for the grace of God that was given to the Corinthians.

In Christ Jesus: From the outset, in emphasizing God's grace, Paul makes the important point that whatever they have or are is due to God's grace. Second, God has enriched them in everything. Their enrichment is a confirmation of the apostolic witness to Christ, into whose fellowship they have been called (v. 9).

1.7a. You are not lacking in any spiritual gift: The words grace (Gk. *charis*, v. 5) and gift (*charismata*, v. 7) both derive from the same root. Paul must be alluding to the discussion of spiritual gifts he will have later in 1 Corinthians 12—14. The Greek text has only the word *charismata*, which has a wider meaning than 'gifts of the Spirit'. It could include:

1   Capabilities to be used in service (cf. 1 Peter 4.10); and

2   General gifts such as justification (cf. Romans 5.15, 16), eternal life (Romans 6.23), ability for ministry (1 Timothy 4.4; 2 Timothy 1.6), and vocation (1 Corinthians 7.7).

As such, the meaning of gifts here must not be restricted to the gifts that Paul later mentions in 1 Corinthians 12. The relationship between grace and gift is also clear. In today's world, as it was in Corinth, there seems to be more emphasis on charisma than character and on gifts than grace. For Paul, the one presumes the other. Character and grace should be at the foundation of the gifts.

11

1.7b. You wait for the revealing of our Lord Jesus Christ: Christians wait for the revealing of Christ. The word 'revealing' denotes a future public disclosure of Christ's glory. This verse prepares the way for 1 Corinthians 13.9–10. Although we presently know in fragmentary ways, and prophesy in part, when the completed whole comes, that which is in part will be done away with.

1.8. Strengthen you to the end . . . blameless on the day of our Lord Jesus Christ: The phrase 'day of the Lord' comes from the Old Testament, where it refers to those occasional points in time when God would judge his people in a momentous way (Amos 5.18). Although we have earlier mentioned that Paul uses the word 'holiness' in terms of belongingness, he now introduces another term, 'blameless', a word that is also used in 1 Timothy 3.10 and Titus 1.6, 7. Paul is using the word in a way that shows that God really wants us to live above sin as both communities and individuals.

1.9. God is faithful: Paul ends the section with a powerful truth: God is faithful. Paul's expectation and confidence for the future well-being of his converts did not rest on them but on God's faithfulness both to them (1 Corinthians 10.13) and to his Son Jesus Christ (Ephesians 1.18).

 ## STUDY SUGGESTIONS

Word study

1 (a) What are the two general meanings of the Greek word, *hagios*?

   (b) What is offered as a third meaning of *hagios*?

   (c) How might Paul's establishing the initial definition of holiness as 'belongingness' prepare the way for the ethical imperatives he will bring later?

2 The word 'saint' in a Nigerian dialect is translated *eniyan mimo*, that is, a clean or pure person. In Filipino, it is the word *kabalanan*, which also means clean in an ethical sense. What word best describes the word 'saint' in another language that you know and how close is it to Paul's understanding and usage in this passage?

3 People say such things as, 'I do not like that church', or 'That church is good', or 'The Church of God is marching on'. Which of these statements accurately reflect the meaning of the Church?

Review of content

4 What prompted Paul's writing of 1 Corinthians?

5 (a) Who called Paul to be an apostle, and to whom was he ultimately accountable in ministry?

(b) How might the assurance that a call is from God impact how we handle ministry?

(c) What does it mean to be an apostle? Is this merely a job or position? If not, what is it?

Bible study

6   Read 1 Timothy 3.8–10 and Titus 1.5–9. How does Paul use the word 'blameless' in these contexts, and how do these passages inform the understanding of being 'blameless on the day of our Lord' (1 Corinthians 1.8)? According to 1 Corinthians 1.8, what (or who) is the source of the believers' strength to live blamelessly?

Discussion and application

7   (a) What is to the detriment of the body of Christ in churches competing for the 'largest' congregation in an area? How might such competition detract from the mission and witness of the Church?

(b) Is there a tendency in our local congregations to be unaware of our church family around the world? How might the witness of the Church be impacted by such a myopic view?

(c) Have you ever experienced a situation in which people's 'gifts' contradicted their 'character'? How would Paul address this issue? What role should the community of faith play in addressing such contradictions? What is the danger of allowing such contradictions to go unchecked, and what does that say about the necessity of accountability within the local church?

1 Corinthians 1.10—4.21

Divisions in the Church

1.10–31: A plea for unity

 Summary

1.10–17: Quarrels and divisions

1.18–25: The message of the cross versus human wisdom

1.26–31: God's wisdom versus human foolishness

 Introduction

Paul arrives at the main point of the first section of the Letter (1.10—4.21), an exhortation for the Corinthians to put an end to all squabbles (vv. 10–17). He first states his theme of unity (1.10), and proceeds to tell them about the indivisibility of Christ (1.11–12), and the essence of the gospel (1.13–17). He then moves on to discuss the underlying problems behind the divisions in the church. These are the Corinthians' pride in human wisdom and an inadequate understanding of God's wisdom as manifested through the cross of Christ (1.18–31).

 Interpretation and notes

1.10. Now I appeal to you: Paul uses familial language, 'brothers and sisters', rather than issuing a command as an apostle. His appeal is that they all **should be in agreement and that there should be no divisions** among them. To underscore the importance of his appeal, Paul makes it in the name of the Lord Jesus. Paul urges the Corinthians to do away with all 'divisions' or, literally, 'schisms' (Gk. *schismata*), a metaphor related to clothing. There is to be no ripping apart in the community. Rather, as one piece of cloth, the people of God should be perfectly united. In turn, such unity is to be evidenced in their confession – they are to speak with one voice. To be united in the same mind is to share the same convictions about God and Jesus Christ. It is important that Paul is addressing a house church and not a denomination or a group of denominations. Thus, the call for unity does not mean a call for a super-denomination in the twenty-first century, as some in the ecumenical movement have advocated. Nevertheless, Paul would have argued that it is possible to have different views that underlying convictions are able to unite. The reason for the appeal is further provided in 1 Corinthians 3.3 where Paul states that if the Christians are divided they are no different from other people. In that case it is impossible for them to do the special work to which God has called them. So deep is Paul's concern for the Corinthians that he reiterates his plea for unity three times over in this verse: they are to be in agreement; there should be no divisions among them; and they must be united in the same mind and purpose.

1.11–12: Paul has received a report from Chloe's people that there have been quarrels among the Christians. The gravity of the divisions is shown in the use of the word **quarrels**, which refers to a hot dispute, the emotional flame that ignites whenever rivalry becomes intolerable. It is listed in Galatians 5.20 as one of the 'works of the flesh' of which Christians should have no part. The mistake of the Corinthians was to put a human leader in the place of God. They were divisively forming particular allegiances to various leaders within the early Church. Each group in the congregation used the name of a particular leader – Paul, Peter, Apollos and even Jesus – as a justification for sticking to their point of view. They gave their loyalties to human leaders instead of Jesus Christ. Somehow, as they magnified the human instruments, they lost sight of the Saviour. It is a mistake Christians continue to make. There are still many groups and religious organizations that honour human beings, particularly the founders, as if they were a sort of second Christ. There are many denominations where the words of the leaders are final. But Paul would have none of it.

1.13: Paul asks three rhetorical questions that underline the absurdity of the state of affairs in the Corinthian church that he has just sketched in v. 12. The answer to each question is an emphatic 'No!' **Has Christ been divided?** Implicit in this question is the notion of the Church as the body of Christ, which Paul will later develop in 1 Corinthians 10—12. Christ cannot be divided for he is one (1 Corinthians 12.12). So, no one group may claim to follow him. Rather all of the Corinthians are supposed to follow Christ. **Was Paul crucified for you?** Paul was not crucified for them nor were they baptized into his name. The point is, the Corinthians were in danger of giving to mere human leaders that ultimate allegiance which belongs to Christ alone, as their only Saviour. As Paul will put it in 4.1, the Corinthians should think of Paul and his fellow apostles simply as servants of Christ, to whom the mysteries of God are committed and who are responsible to God. **Were you baptized in the name of Paul?** Some Corinthians were probably touting the name of the person who baptized them, suggesting that such persons were either more spiritual or exhibited greater wisdom. Once again Paul uses his own name to show up the error of the Corinthian factionalism. The phrase 'in the name', literally, 'into the name', when used with baptism implies that the person baptized is the exclusive property of Christ.

1.14–17. I baptized none of you except Crispus . . . I did baptize also the household of Stephanas: Realizing how the Corinthians could easily have distorted the implications of their baptism, Paul, with gratitude, recalls that he has baptized very few of them. Thus, he diminishes the danger of anyone being tempted to think that they were baptized into Paul's name (v. 15). Paul's preoccupation is the proclamation of the gospel, **not with eloquent wisdom, so that the cross of Christ might not be emptied of its power.** With this statement, Paul strikes at the heart of the Corinthian divisions. Had they understood the cross, they would not have exalted human leaders. Paul is not saying that baptism is unnecessary in vv. 14–17. He simply places the proper emphasis where it belongs, that is, the preaching of the gospel (see v. 17). Paul lays the groundwork for what he will immediately say about his evangelizing (1.18—2.5).

1.18: In vv. 18–25 Paul shows the incompatibility of the cross and human wisdom. Paul says that **the message about the cross is foolishness to those who are perishing,** but to those who are being saved it is the power of God. To some of the Corinthians, a crucified Saviour is a contradiction in terms. It is in fact perceived as 'foolishness' (v. 18). To associate salvation with weakness made no sense to both the Greeks and Jews. Not so for Paul and the Corinthian believers whose lives have been changed by the gospel message. Ultimately, for Paul, it is the response to the cross that determines eternal destiny. Those who reject the cross are on the road to eternal death. But those who embrace it display the power of God and are assured of eternal salvation. Note that Paul speaks of only two classes of people: the perishing and the saved.

1.19: When people accept the gospel, it entails a radical adjustment of their understanding of wisdom. It leads people to understand that God's ways are not human ways. Paul quotes Isaiah 29.14 and 33.18: **'I will destroy the wisdom of the wise',** in order to show both the limitation and overturning of human wisdom. God's plans often unravel the plans of those who think themselves wise. God's action through the cross transcends all human calculation and wisdom.

1.20: The four rhetorical questions in v. 20 further affirm Paul's claim that human wisdom is of no use with regard to the salvation of humankind. God's action in Christ has turned worldly wisdom on its head. The 'wise' were not hard to find in Paul's day. There were many itinerant philosophers about, but by and large they were not part of the Christian movement. If such non-Christians were really the measure of wisdom, then why were they not Christians? This is a question that Paul could have legitimately asked, given the value that the Corinthians placed on human wisdom. Some years ago, there was a self-styled, well-known 'Jesus of Oyingbo' who lived in Lagos, Nigeria. Though uneducated himself, he had learned university professors, lawyers and professionals among his followers. Obviously, though wise, they did not possess the right kind of wisdom to enable them to discern between the true and a false 'Christ'.

1.21: The world with all its claims of wisdom has not known God. The wisdom of the wisest philosopher cannot bring him or her to the knowledge of God. The concepts of sin, guilt and atonement were totally foreign and repugnant to Greek philosophy. Therefore, there was no need for salvation. But for Paul, Christ's crucifixion is the crux of his message and his own understanding of God's matchless wisdom. God's ways are not human ways and his thoughts are higher than human thoughts (cf. Isaiah 55.8). Paul's fundamental theological point is that if the cross is God's saving event, all human standards and evaluation are overturned. Instead of being instruments of salvation, the signs demanded by the Jews and the wisdom sought after by the Greeks are a stumbling-block and foolishness respectively.

1.22: The Jews demanded signs (cf. Numbers 14.11; Matthew 16.1–4), something that implies distrust of God, and also the Jews' false expectation of a spectacular messiah. Even at the time of Paul there were many self-proclaimed messiahs who appealed to the Jews and beguiled them with the promise of miraculous signs. For example, in AD 45, a man called Theudas convinced thousands of Jews to follow him to the Jordan river, promising that the water would divide at his command and he would lead them across. The seeking of wisdom by the Greeks illustrates the effort to discover God through human speculation.

1.23: A **crucified** messiah was unthinkable to the Jews (Deuteronomy 21.23; cf. Galatians 3.13) while for God to take human form and then to be put to death was incomprehensible to the Greeks. That the message of the cross continues to be an offence to many people cannot be doubted. For example, Muslims respect Jesus very highly as a 'prophet' but they cannot accept his death on the cross. They do not believe that someone they regard as an important prophet would be allowed by God to suffer in that way.

1.24–25. To those who are called: that is, those who respond to God's call, the cross makes available **the power of God** to overcome sin, and manifests the true wisdom of God in offering humanity its only effective way of salvation. God's **foolishness**, that is, God's foolish acts and God's weakness shown in allowing Jesus to be crucified, is **stronger** and more effective than human effort and wisdom.

1.26: To further bolster his claim that God's wisdom surpasses human folly, Paul appeals to the social location of the Corinthian Christians. Not many of them were wise, powerful or of noble birth by human standards. The contradiction of God's method to human wisdom is illustrated by the kind of people that he has called.

1.27–28: Although the Corinthian church must have comprised people from different walks of life including some rich and knowledgeable people, Paul says that many of them were indeed poor and not 'schooled' (vv. 27, 28). Yet, it is to those people who are regarded as foolish and weak that God has demonstrated his power as they embrace the message of the cross. So, for Paul, God has turned the standards of the world upside down.

1.29: God does not show favouritism to people because of what they have, what they know, who they are and where they come from. All are equal before him and saved the same way. Therefore no one may boast in the presence of God.

1.30–31: Paul presents the benefits of Christ to the Corinthians in particular and to all believers at large, in a fourfold, but not necessarily sequential manner (v. 30). First, he is the true wisdom of God as opposed to the human wisdom of which the Greeks boasted. Second, Christ is the believer's righteousness. There is nothing else. In the words of the hymn writer Augustus Toplady, 'Nothing in my hand I bring, simply to Thy cross I cling.' Third, Christ is the believer's sanctification. The holiness of believers is grounded in both the work of Christ and their relationship with him. Fourth, Christ is the believer's redemption. The word 'redemption' as used here seems to summarize all that Paul has just said. Christ paid it all. Hence, Paul concludes, 'Let the one who boasts, boast in the Lord' (v. 31). Thus, believers are cautioned to avoid any reliance on worldly wisdom.

 ## STUDY SUGGESTIONS

Word study

1 (a) What is the Greek word that is translated 'divisions' in 1 Corinthians 1.10, and what is the literal meaning of that word?
   (b) What is the significance of Paul's usage of this word in light of the current Corinthian situation?

Review of content

2 What does the phrase 'in the name' mean when used with baptism (e.g. 'baptized in the name of Paul')? How might Paul be faulting the Corinthians' allegiance to certain leaders by the rhetorical question, 'Were you baptized in the name of Paul?'

3 In vv. 30 and 31, Paul presents the benefits of Christ in a fourfold manner. What are the four benefits believers reap from a relationship with Christ according to this passage?

Bible study

4 Read Galatians 5.16–21. The word Paul uses in 1 Corinthians 1.11 to talk about the 'quarrels' among the people of the Corinthian congregation is the same as that used in Galatians 5.20. In light of Galatians 5.16–21, what implications might this have concerning the gravity of the divisions among the Corinthian congregation? Moreover, what are the ramifications of such quarrels existing in our local congregations today?

5 Read Deuteronomy 21.22–23 and Galatians 3.10–14. Discuss the unique plan of salvation that God has for us. How does this plan show the 'wisdom' and 'foolishness' which has been discussed in 1 Corinthians 1?

Discussion and application

6 Does Paul's plea for unity in the Corinthian congregation necessarily imply uniformity? Explain why or why not, and discuss the possible consequences of your answers for your local congregation and for fellowship with other denominations.

7 Have you ever been in a situation where you found yourself (or someone else) overly impressed with a church leader? What are the dangers of such a situation? How might we safeguard our allegiance to Christ and not fall prey to what is popularly known as 'hero worship'?

8 Why is the cross an embarrassment to many people, and why is it so important to Christian identity? Are there ways in which the Church today superimposes worldly categories of wisdom and power upon the gospel message? What are the possible results of such an imposition?

Given the levelling effect of the cross, what does this say to the intended constituency of the Christian community? Does your local congregation reflect the fact that in salvation all people are equal?

9 Are there ways in which the apparent foolishness of the cross might seem to impede our efforts of evangelism today? How might we emphasize the importance of a crucified Saviour to a twenty-first-century world?

10 Given the groups of people which Paul discusses – 'those who are perishing' and 'us who are being saved' – do you view the world through these categories or have you maintained secular categories in describing people based on race, education, socio-economic status, gender, etc.? How might contemporary walls of division be set aside by viewing the world through the two classes that Paul suggests?

2.1–16: Human wisdom versus God's Wisdom

 Summary

2.1–5: Paul's dependence on the power of the Holy Spirit

2.6–16: God's wisdom

 Introduction

Paul continues to address the problem of 'wisdom' and its relation to preaching in Corinth. Some people were placing undue emphasis on the wisdom of the Greeks. They liked to make impressive speeches to show off their wisdom. But Paul must have been a great disappointment to the philosophers of Corinth when they first heard him. He did not try and impress them by clever speaking. He presented the gospel in simple words. Paul uses himself as an illustration of the difference between divine and human wisdom. The conversion of the Corinthians was a testimony to the power of God and not the persuasion of logic. Paul shows that the content of his message is indeed wisdom, but wisdom not of this age.

 Interpretation and notes

2.1. When I came to you: Paul alludes to his first visit to Corinth (cf. Acts 18.1–18), when the Corinthians first heard the message and believed. When Paul first visited Corinth, he did not move the people with outstanding oratory and concise logic. So, Paul contrasts himself with some other preachers by using a Greek word which means, '*I* for *my* part' (as opposed to others). His manner of presentation matched his message. He maintains that his message was simple. He refused to take any credit as an orator. He did not compete with his opponents who used their clever speeches to impress the worldly wise Corinthians. He did not proclaim the mystery of God to them **in lofty words or wisdom**. To do so would have emptied the cross of its power. He seeks to remind the Corinthians that his own preaching to them conformed to what he has said about the 'foolishness' of the gospel. As such, Paul restates what he said in 1 Corinthians 1.17. It was not his own clever preaching or oratorical skill which led the Corinthians to believe in Jesus Christ. It was the experience of the power of God's Spirit as demonstrated by Paul that impressed them as he explained the mystery of God.

In many Eastern religions, as well as African traditional religion, people are fascinated with 'mysteries' as something that is unexplainable and unreachable. The Yoruba, for example, use the word, *a-wa-ma-ri-di*, that is, something that can never be understood despite investigations. But for Paul, the **mystery of God** refers to the counsel of God, unknown to humans except by revelation, especially his saving work and ultimate purposes in history. Mystery does not mean something esoteric or something necessarily unknown, but something not as fully understood at one time as it was at another (see Daniel 2.18ff.; 4.9; Romans 16.25, 26). It is the message that the Corinthians did not understand before, but is now explained by Paul and illuminated by the Holy Spirit (1 Corinthians 2.10–14) and relates to Christ and the cross.

2.2: Paul states his normal practice. He was concerned only with what he considered as the central truths of the gospel: Christ and his crucifixion. The content of his proclamation was **Jesus Christ, and him crucified**. It was the power of God through the gospel of Christ that changed the Corinthians. So, there was no reason for Paul to change his focus.

2.3: Paul goes on to describe further the manner of his coming. He did not come to the Corinthians as an accomplished orator. Paul came before them **in weakness and in fear and in much trembling**. He did not come to Corinth in his own strength and power. Instead he preached with the power of the Holy Spirit. Here is a contrast between Paul's human weakness and the power of the gospel supported by the Holy Spirit. Paul is not referring to physical weakness here (cf. Galatians 4.13; 6.10; 2 Corinthians 12.7–10). He is referring to his utter helplessness in convincing his hearers with ordinary human persuasive ability. Unlike some other preachers in the Corinthian congregation, Paul did not attempt to use 'enticing words' (v. 4, AV), nor did he attempt to speak human wisdom. While, on the one hand, Paul preached with fear and trembling, on the other hand he preached with the power of the Holy Spirit. Paul's preaching was not validated by eloquence and sophistication, but with demonstrations of the Spirit's power. The term used for demonstration carries a legal sense of irrefutable proof. The Corinthians must place their faith in the work of the Spirit rather than human wisdom.

2.4. My speech and proclamation were not with plausible words of wisdom: With regard to presentation, Paul reaffirms that the content of his preaching was purely and simply the wisdom of God. He did not depend on plausible or persuasive words of human wisdom, that is, overpowering oratory or philosophical argument or human wisdom. Paul came to them without any pretensions to eloquence or wisdom in declaring the truth about God.

The story is told of the Moravians, a people committed to Jesus Christ and moved by God to take the gospel right across the world. When they began their mission in Greenland they did not know how to share the gospel with the natives. They decided that they would first teach the people

21

of Greenland to read and write. It was a dismal failure. The results were terribly disappointing. They decided to give up and pack up and leave Greenland. While one of the missionaries was awaiting a ship to take him home, he began to translate a portion of the Gospels in the New Testament. After he had finished translating that portion, he decided that he would test the translation by reading it to the native people. He read to them about the death of our Lord Jesus Christ. After hearing the portion of Scripture in their own tongue there was silence for a period. Then the head of the tribe asked the missionary to read the portion of the Gospel again. After he finished reading it again the chief said: 'Is what you read true?'

When the missionary replied: 'It is true,' the man asked: 'Then why didn't you tell us this in the first place? Why did you have to leave it until now? We will listen now to the words of this man who suffered for us! You cannot go; you will have to stay and tell us more about him.'

This story illustrates the point of 1 Corinthians 2: simple proclamation of the gospel conquers where human wisdom fails. The cross trumps human wisdom!

2.5: Paul's overriding aim was to avoid drawing attention to himself so that the faith of the Corinthians might rest on the power of God rather than human persuasiveness. Paul's example provides a useful lesson for preachers today. Think of preachers you hear. Do they like to show off, use fancy words and clever techniques? Is their delivery more important to them than their content? Or do they speak simply and explain things clearly? But Paul chose a simple delivery of a powerful message. Christian history is replete with men and women who, despite lack of great pedigree or extraordinary academic achievements, were effective preachers and missionaries who led many people to Christ. Joseph Ayo Babalola (1904–59) of Nigeria is an example. He was a famous revivalist that God used in powerful ways to lead thousands to Christ through proclamation of the gospel that was attended by miracles, signs and wonders. Isaac Pelendo, also known as God's Prophet in the Congo, was an unlearned man whom God used to establish churches in the remote northwestern area of the Democratic Republic of Congo.

2.6. Yet among the mature we do speak wisdom: Some Corinthians might have come to the wrong conclusion that the gospel is devoid of wisdom. So Paul states that he speaks wisdom but it is intelligible only to those who are 'mature'. The mature here refers to the saved – those enlightened by the Holy Spirit – in contrast to the unsaved. Paul insists that his teaching is not the product of human intellectual activity; it is the gift of God and it came into the world with Jesus Christ. This wisdom, Paul says, does not come from this age of time and space and certainly not from the **rulers of this age**. It is a widely held view that the 'rulers', referred to here and in v. 8, are demonic powers or, that if Paul has in mind earthly rulers, he sees them as the tools of such demonic powers. However, in

Romans 13.3 the same word clearly refers to earthly rulers. Moreover, in the Gospels, the demons are the only ones who do in fact recognize Jesus. So the rulers here and in v. 8 are to be understood as earthly rulers.

2.7. But we speak God's wisdom, secret and hidden, which God decreed before the ages for our glory: Paul's presentation of God's eternal plan of salvation (v. 7) is based, through the Holy Spirit, on the wisdom of God revealed to him and to others.

'Wisdom' here therefore must mean God's plan of salvation. It is God's wise way of bringing humankind to fulfilment. It is not something apart from the gospel; it is rather that same gospel seen in greater depth. God's wisdom is contained in a mystery and has been planned before the beginning of the ages. God's plan of salvation is no afterthought. That plan, although revealed in the Old Testament, is not as fully explained and understood there as it is in the New Testament. It demands explanation, just as the Ethiopian, in response to Philip's question, 'Do you understand what you are reading?' says, 'How can I unless someone guides me?' (Acts 8.30, 31).

2.8. None of the rulers of this age understood this: God's secret remains veiled until it is revealed. As in v. 6, the reference to 'rulers of this age' seems to be an allusion to earthly rulers, but here Paul is thinking primarily of those, like Pilate and Herod, who were responsible for the death of Jesus. The secular and religious rulers (Acts 4.25–28) of Jesus' day revealed their ignorance through the way they treated him. By crucifying Jesus, they demonstrated their blindness to the wisdom of God. To amplify the depth of their blindness, Paul describes Jesus as the Lord of glory, or the glorious Lord. He brings together the divinity and humanity of Christ. God the Son, as incarnate human, died on the cross. Glory, an attribute of God, also belongs to Jesus Christ. Though the crucifixion was, at one level, the work of blind unbelief, it also made it possible for God's wise plan to come to fulfilment. By doing their worst, the rulers of this age gave God the opportunity to do his best.

2.9. Things which no eye has seen, nor ear heard: Paul appeals to Scripture (Isaiah 52.15; 64.4) to support his claim that the truth and blessings of the gospel are inconceivable to the natural person. The 'hidden wisdom' he has been preaching is the wisdom referred to in the Old Testament. In saving his people by means of the gospel, God surpasses their expectations, and does for them things unheard before. But to Paul, to the other apostles and their fellow workers, in contrast to the unsaved rulers of the world, God revealed them through the Spirit (v. 10). The Greek verb Paul uses is also used in Matthew 16.17 and Luke 10.22 to indicate divine revelation of certain supernatural secrets. It is also used in an eschatological sense of the revelation connected with certain persons and events (Romans 8.18; 1 Corinthians 3.13) for the Spirit reveals everything, even the depths of God.

2.10–12: Paul provides an illustration showing that the spiritual wisdom and truths of God can be understood only through the Holy Spirit, just as human wisdom needs the human spirit to understand it. In contrast to some other kind of spirit through which some might try to know God's wisdom and truth – such as the spirit of the wisdom of this world (1 Corinthians 1.20; 2.6; 3.19) – believers have received the Spirit who is from God. They can now understand and know the gifts that are bestowed on them by God.

Paul's argument in this section brings to mind the story of an incident that occurred in the USA during the Christmas season in 1879. An agnostic reporter saw three little girls standing in front of a store window full of toys. One of them was blind. He heard the other two describing the toys to their friend. He had never considered how difficult it was to explain to someone without sight what something looks like. That incident became the basis for a newspaper story. Two weeks later the reporter attended a meeting held by the famous evangelist, Dwight L. Moody. His purpose was to catch the evangelist in an inconsistency. He was surprised when Moody used his account of the children to illustrate a truth. 'Just as the blind girl couldn't visualize the toys,' said Moody, 'so an unsaved person can't see Christ in all his glory.' The reporter was speechless. Today many are unaware of the true identity of Jesus Christ and are ignorant of the saving power of the gospel. It requires the Spirit of God to illuminate a person's heart (Romans 8.9b).

2.13–14: Paul reverts to the nature of his own ministry (cf. vv. 4, 5). He wants it known that he speaks **in words not taught by human wisdom but taught by the Spirit**, as he and other associates express spiritual truths in words conveying the real spiritual truth. Human nature does not accept illumination and truths from the Spirit of God. Humans consider those truths to be foolish and, therefore, do not receive the gifts of God's Spirit, for they are foolishness to them. Paul makes it even stronger when he says that such people are unable to understand them (the things/gifts of God), because they are spiritually discerned. Such people cannot make spiritually intelligent decisions.

2.15–16: In contrast to the unspiritual people in v. 14, the ones who are spiritual, being guided by the Spirit, discern all things. Paul appeals to Isaiah 40.13, at the beginning of v. 16, to reinforce the idea that no one can fully grasp the mind of God. To receive the Spirit is to be gifted with discernment. Paul says that a spiritual person can judge the worth of everything, but he is no doubt thinking of the evaluation of spiritual phenomena. At the same time such a person is not subject to judgement by others. For those who do not have the Spirit to sit in judgement on those who do is presumptuous.

The central thought of this section has been that it is only through God's Spirit that we are able to know God or the truths of God. The point of the quotation in v. 16 appears to be that God must remain unknown until he takes the initiative and makes himself known. But God has made himself known. He has given us of himself, in order that we may know him. Through most of the paragraph Paul has used the term Spirit to describe this self-giving activity of God, but here he speaks of **the mind of Christ.**

 STUDY SUGGESTIONS

Word study

1 In v. 6, to whom is Paul referring when he says, 'among the mature'? Also, to whom is he referring when he mentions the 'rulers of this age'?

Review of content

2 What are some problems that arose due to the persistence of 'wisdom' preaching in Corinth?

3 In v. 3, Paul says that he came before the Corinthians 'in weakness and in fear and in much trembling'. Was Paul referring to his physical state or something different? Explain.

Bible study

4 Read Acts 18.1–18. This is the account of Paul's founding the church in Corinth.

   (a) How long did Paul minister in Corinth on his initial visit?
   (b) What trials did Paul endure because of his preaching, and what did the Lord say to Paul as encouragement?

Discussion and application

5 List several characteristics of a 'good' sermon.

   (a) In light of this chapter, how many of those characteristics listed are in fact congruent with Paul's perspective on preaching?
   (b) Does Paul's emphasis upon the simplicity of his proclamation mean that the delivery of the sermon is not important altogether?
   (c) Based on 1 Corinthians 2, how should one evaluate preaching?

6 What are some ways in which you can discern whether someone is preaching in the power of the Spirit rather than merely with enticing words or eloquent wisdom?

7 The story of the Moravians illustrates the power of the simple proclamation of God's word.

   (a) What are some ways in which you have experienced the simple proclamation of God's word?

(b) In what ways might this influence the way in which your local congregation evangelizes your community?

8 In this chapter, Paul is revealing the key to true wisdom.

(a) If human wisdom is insufficient in determining the things of God, what (or who) is the source of one's discernment concerning the gifts of God?

(b) How do you understand the ministry of the Holy Spirit in revealing the deep things of God?

3.1–23: The nature of Christian leadership Part 1

 Summary

3.1–4: Babes in Christ

3.5–9: Ministers are servants. Therefore there must not be rivalry among members.

3.10–15: Paul, the skilled master builder, shows the need for care in building the Church.

3.16–17: The Church: the temple of God

3.18–23: Warning about reliance on human wisdom

 Introduction

Paul continues to deal with the problem of divisions that plagued the Corinthian church. Paul shows that the problem is due to the Corinthians' lack of spiritual maturity. They were babes in Christ, like children at the breast, requiring to be fed with milk, and not with meat. They were different from mature people, described as 'spiritual'. They did not act as people who were 'in the spirit' or 'spiritual'. Furthermore, Paul describes them as 'people of the flesh'. Some were for setting up Paul, others Apollos, as their sole teachers (v. 4). Paul shows that he and his fellow apostles were only instruments which God used to bring the Corinthian church to the knowledge of the truth; and even their sowing and watering the seed was effective only because God gave the increase (vv. 5–8). He goes on to picture the Church as God's field, and as God's building, the foundation of which is Christ Jesus (vv. 9–11). Therefore ministers must beware how and what they build on this foundation (vv. 12–15). The Church is also God's temple, and those who defile it shall be destroyed (vv. 16, 17). People should not depend on their own wisdom; for the wisdom of the world is foolishness with God (vv. 18–20). People should not glory in human teachers; God gives his followers every good thing, both for time and eternity (vv. 21–23).

 Interpretation and notes

3.1–2. People of the flesh . . . infants in Christ: Paul overturns the Corinthians' estimation of themselves. To show the extent of their immaturity, Paul says that he fed them with milk. The apostle shows them the absurdity of their conduct in pretending to judge between preacher and preacher, while they only had a 'baby's' knowledge of the first principles of Christianity. Paul also uses the word 'infants' (also in 1 Corinthians 13.11; Galatians 4.1; 1 Thessalonians 2.7) to heighten his description of their immaturity. He could not feed them with 'solid food', because as babies in Christ they could not spiritually digest it.

Imagine adults that behave like babies! They have never developed – growing old, but not growing up! What would it be like to see a 50-year-old woman turning up for work wearing a bib? Or a 65-year-old man surrounded by toys? Ridiculous, one would say. And so it is. What Paul says in 1 Corinthians 3 is worse than these examples. The Corinthians have the power of God, the gifts of the Spirit and the riches of grace all at their disposal. But they refuse to grow and to mature. They choose to remain as babes and so are incapable of judging what is most suitable for themselves. They are unqualified to discern between one teacher and another. They have no right judgement and this springs from their lack of knowledge in spiritual matters.

3.3: Paul describes the Corinthians again as being **of the flesh, and behaving according to human inclinations**. They have been living in a way that is sub-Christian in selfishness, pride and envy. They are conforming to a human rather than a godly standard. Paul illustrates this self-orientation by reminding them of the jealousy and quarrelling which plagued the Christian community. He puts his assessment in question form, suggesting that the Corinthians, if honest with themselves, should admit their failing. Their immaturity led to contentiousness. The behaviour of the Corinthians shows that they were all too human, despite their claim of spirituality.

3.4: Verse 4 brings us back to the actual state of the Corinthian Christians, with their divisive preferences for individual apostles and ministers. Paul's example of himself and Apollos who shared in the ministry at Corinth (Acts 18.1–28) was needed to show the Corinthians that they had a distorted view of the Lord's work. Whenever they thought of God's work in terms of belonging to or following a particular Christian worker, they were simply acting on the human level and taking sides just as the world does. There still are thousands of such people in the Christian Church. Some follow particular leaders because of their charisma and eloquence while others prefer preachers who are deemed successful because of their financial prosperity. In either case, the main consideration is not the spirituality of the leaders as Paul indicates below. In Brazil, people follow a popular preacher, Edir Macedo, both for his charisma and eloquence in spite of documented wrong teachings. The sad story of Jim Jones of the People's Temple Church also comes to mind. The members of the church believed that their movement was the solution to the problems of society, and many did not distinguish Jones from the movement, something that led to following him into mass suicide in 1978.

3.5. What then is Apollos? What is Paul?: Paul responds to the implicit question of how the Corinthians should view him and Apollos. He wants to impress the Christians with the fact that he and Apollos are simply servants, so he uses 'what' instead of 'who'. No Christian worker is ever to be idolized. Indeed, those who are idolized can become instruments for fragmenting the work of God. Believers are to realize that Christian workers are simply God's servants – agents through whom people believe in Christ. The word *diakonoi*, 'servant', from which we get 'deacon', has also been translated 'minister'. It is properly used for attendants and waiters, those who serve others. God did not call Paul and Apollos to be masters of the Corinthian Christians. They were to serve them and meet their needs.

3.6. I planted, Apollos watered, but God gave the growth: Paul goes on to make a twofold emphasis. On the one hand, Paul and Apollos, though exercising different roles, are both engaged in the one mission – both have been commissioned to propagate the gospel. They are both to labour to promote the glory of God in the salvation of the Corinthians. The Corinthians should not be divided with respect to Paul and Apollos, while both are intimately united in spirit and purpose. Here again we see the self-effacing attitude of Paul. He was the one who sowed the seed of the gospel in the region. However, he neither overestimates his own labours nor detracts anything from the labour of Apollos. It is neither the sower nor the one who waters that produces the inexplicable multiplication of the seed; it is God alone. Ministers are instruments in God's hand. They depend on God's blessing to make their work fruitful. Without this they are nothing; with it their part is so small that they hardly deserve to be mentioned.

3.7–8. Common purpose: Although the functions of ministers are different, they are united in purpose. Moreover, ministers will receive according to their labour. They are responsible to God. There is therefore no need for competition. Growing up in a farming community, I have observed people working together either at the time of planting or harvesting. Some workers are stronger than the others and are able to get more done within a shorter period of time. It is never about competition. Rather, it is about getting the job done, and each person will be adequately compensated. The picture of a building that Paul is about to employ demonstrates the same truth. In erecting a building, there is always need for various workers: carpenters, bricklayers, electricians, plumbers, etc. The purpose of all these workers is not to outshine one another. The common goal is to put up an edifice that is good and adequately represents the master plan.

3.9: Paul states once more that he and Apollos are simply **God's servants, working together.** Then, picking up once more the dominant picture of the paragraph, Paul declares the Corinthians to be **God's field.** In elaborating the point that he and Apollos have been simply God's agents in bringing the Corinthians to faith, Paul has likened the Church to a field, and himself and Apollos to gardeners. Now he chooses a different image: **God's building.**

3.10. A skilled master builder: As a wise master builder and experienced man in architecture, Paul has laid the foundation by preaching Christ through the Grecian provinces. Each builder must choose with care how to build on it. Those who come after him are to build according to the plan and grand design of the temple – a design or plan that is from God; making it imperative that all things must be done according to the pattern that he has exhibited. One thing that Paul seeks to make clear in the verse is that building up the Church is not the work of any one evangelist, preacher or even an apostle. It is teamwork. Although God has used Paul to lay the foundation, he acknowledges that others, such as Apollos, also build on the foundation of Christ. Then he gives a warning: Each builder – Paul, Apollos and whoever works for God – must be careful how he builds. The shift in thought is now from the worker to the work.

3.11. That foundation is Jesus Christ: The Corinthians had preference for different leaders. But as Paul has previously said in 1 Corinthians 1.17 and 2.2, Jesus, rather than his followers, is the one irreplaceable foundation of the Church. No church leader must be seen as having more than a strictly subordinate role. Leaders are to be respected but not to be worshipped.

3.12–15. Gold, silver, precious stones, wood, hay, straw: Although the workers cannot lay a foundation other than Christ, they are warned to be careful how they build on him. Some understand the passage as the judgement of believers in general. But the overall tenor of the paragraph is more applicable to Christian workers. Paul wanted the preachers and teachers in Corinth to build a superstructure with the same material as the foundation. So, instead of talking about the details of the building itself, Paul turns his attention to the kind of materials Christian workers are using: the materials of preaching the cross for salvation, building up believers (cf. 1.18), and living a Christian life that reflects their preaching (2.2–4).

Those contractors who employ inferior materials, such as wood, hay and straw, will have the quality of their work exposed by the fire of God's judge-ment (v. 13). It shall be made clear what kind of materials every spiritual builder uses. God will test whether the doctrines preached produce genuine repentance, faith and holiness in the hearers. There are numerous instances of the serious consequences that careless builders have had to face in the case of the collapse of buildings, particularly when it results in the loss of lives. Builders are sometimes taken to court and are subsequently required to pay heavy penalties and effect settlement to the plaintiffs who sue for wrongful death. God will hold leaders accountable for the type of preaching and teaching in which they engage. As fire tries metals, and finds out and separates whatever dross is mixed with them, so shall the strict process of the final judgement test the work of every minister to see whether it comes up to the standard established by Scripture. But 1 Corinthians 3.12–15 is neither about 'purgatory' nor about individuals. It is concerned with the Church's or community's wholeness and holiness. With the eschatological framework that permeates Paul's writings (cf. Romans 2.5, 16; 13.12; 1 Corinthians 1.8; 2 Corinthians 1.14; Philippians 1.6), it is clear that the 'day' refers to the day of the second coming of Christ (cf. 2 Thessalonians 2.2).

In the modern Church there is an aversion to preaching and hearing about God's judgement. Such an attitude fails to grasp the truth that judgement and grace are inseparable parts of the gospel message. A popular televangelist in the USA recently said in an interview that he has nothing to do with the preaching of repentance and judgement. It is not surprising that 1 Corinthians 3.12–15 is left out by some when this chapter is read in worship. But the message of the passage is clear. God will not tolerate divisiveness and pride.

3.16–17. The temple of God: Paul has compared the Christian congregation at Corinth to a field (3.6–9) and then to a building (3.10–15). Now he compares them to a temple. When Paul says, 'You are the temple of God', he is speaking corporately, rather than individually. Although made up of individuals, it is the Church, corporately, that constitutes the temple or the body of Christ, a metaphor that Paul later expands on in 1 Corinthians 12. The import of this verse is to show the danger that awaits people who tear apart or destroy the Church. God will not save such people. The Corinthians must understand how special they are, and how their status as the temple of God demands a particular kind of leadership. Furthermore, the imagery of the metaphor drives home the point that the divisive loyalties that plagued the church at Corinth were not only contrary to the nature of leadership that is required in the Church, but were also contrary to the nature of the Church itself. The Church is God's project. The imagery of the temple should force the Church to think about how the presence of God is experienced when its members gather together and to reflect seriously on what it means to be a holy community in an unholy world.

3.18–23: Paul returns again to address the underlying problems of the church at Corinth – foolishness and wisdom. The Corinthians' immaturity prevented them from understanding the nature of God's work. It moved them away from the foundation of their faith. Quoting Job 5.13 and

Psalm 94.11, Paul reinforces what he has previously said in 1 Corinthians 3.1–3. The climax of Paul's discussion about the problem of division in the church ends with his exhortation to the Corinthians to focus on God. In our days, denominationalism is a great problem and often a hindrance to the proclamation of the gospel.

The question is always asked, to whom do you belong? Paul has made it clear to the Corinthians that they belong neither to him nor to Apollos. It is not right for a church to replace the Word of God with human wisdom and leaders. Men or women, committees, executives or board members must never be allowed to take over the leadership of the Holy Spirit. God provides human leaders to build up the whole Church in a spiritual way. However, when churches or individual believers become enslaved, as it were, to human leadership, not only do they miss the blessing of God, but also they mar the work of the churches, and this cannot be done with impunity. A Japanese student of mine told me of how his family was controlled and manipulated by the pastor of the congregation to which they belonged. It was a trying time for the members of the congregation. They took the pastor's words to be the final authority for their lives and sold their business at his command. However, after about five years of servitude, they sought counsel with other believers who prayed with them and helped them out of the situation. The church eventually split and the pastor was jailed.

 Special note A

The flesh

'Flesh' is one of the key words in Paul's vocabulary. As used by biblical authors in general, it primarily refers to the whole person regarded as a creature. However, the precise shade of meaning varies considerably in different contexts. The Greek word, which the NRSV translates as 'people of the flesh', is an adjective derived from *sarx*, flesh, and means, literally, fleshy or fleshly. In v. 3 Paul uses another adjective derived from the same noun.

1   'Flesh' can be used in a wholly neutral sense to denote what is outward and visible. It simply means 'human' (cf. Romans 4.1; 1 Corinthians 1.26).

2   'Flesh' can be used to refer to humanity in its distance and difference from God and therefore as mortal, frail and vulnerable (Romans 6.19; 8.3; 2 Corinthians 4.11).

3   Since human beings in their frailty are in fact sinners, 'flesh' can also be used in a sense to refer to humanity in its opposition to God (cf. Romans 7.5, 18; 8.3–12).

The range of meanings conveyed by the word *sarx* is therefore a very wide one. So also is the range of meanings conveyed by the adjectives derived from it. Paul is using 'flesh' in the present passage in the second sense, since in order to corroborate the charge that the Corinthians are 'fleshly' he points simply to their immaturity. His point is that they are acting as if they had not received the Spirit at all.

 STUDY SUGGESTIONS

Word study

1 What does *sarx* literally mean?

 (a) Describe three ways that the term (and its derivatives) may be understood.

 (b) Does Paul's usage of the term differ within 1 Corinthians 3?

2 Paul refers to himself and Apollos as *diakonoi*.

 (a) What does this term literally mean?

 (b) How does such a definition counter the Corinthians' current mind-set regarding leaders?

Review of content

3 In light of Acts 18.24–28 and 1 Corinthians 3, why were the Corinthians possibly drawn to Apollos over against Paul?

4 What is the significance of Paul using the word 'what' (in '*What* then is Apollos? *What* is Paul?') as opposed to 'who' in 1 Corinthians 3.5?

5 What are the two metaphors Paul uses to describe the Corinthian congregation? In each metaphor, what image represents Paul or Apollos? What image represents the Corinthian congregation? What is God's role in each metaphor? Can you think of a different metaphor that would accurately depict your local congregation?

6 In v. 13, when Paul speaks of the judgement of fire, is this about a general judgement of Christians? If not, explain.

Bible study

7 Read Amos 5.18–20; Malachi 4.1–3; Romans 2.5–11; 13.11–14; Philippians 1.6; and 1 Thessalonians 5.1–11.

 (a) According to these passages, what are some elements that characterize the 'Day of the Lord'?

 (b) How might Paul's reference to the 'Day of the Lord' impact the Corinthians' lives and speak to their current conflicts? How might Paul speaking about the judgement of Christian workers prompt the Corinthians to 'grow up' so to speak in regards to their divisiveness, quarrelling and the like?

Discussion and application

8 The Corinthians acted as spiritual babies. Are there areas in our lives where we have refused to grow and mature? How might such immaturity impair our judgement or discernment concerning what is most suitable for our lives in community?

9 In light of Paul's rebuke of the Corinthian congregation, what does this say about the often heard expression, 'I am just human', which is used many times to justify spiritual immaturity or sin among people in the Church?

10 Paul refers to the Corinthian congregation as the 'temple of God'.

(a) How have you heard this passage preached? Is it normally geared towards the individual as being the temple of God or towards the community of faith as being the temple of God? What are the implications of each?

(b) What does this say concerning our view of the physical edifices in which we meet as being sacred ground over against the people of God who occupy such buildings?

4.1–21: The nature of Christian leadership Part 2

 Summary

4.1–5: Leaders and criticism

4.6–13: Leaders as models

4.14–21: Correction: its basis and aims

 Introduction

In the previous chapters, particularly in the last three verses of 1 Corinthians 3, Paul has been refuting an exaggerated estimate of himself and

33

his fellow evangelists. Now he anticipates the questions, 'How then are we to think of you? What exactly is your role in the purpose of God?' The answers are provided in the text that follows. Paul is about to draw out some implications for the ways the Corinthians should respond to him as an apostle and to his fellow workers as stewards and servants. In carefully chosen words, Paul will show the Corinthians how to have a proper regard, one that is neither too exalted, nor too low, of himself and other Christian leaders.

Interpretation and notes

4.1. Servants of Christ and stewards of God's mysteries: Paul has explained what preachers are not, in order to show that people should not make themselves dependent on them. The apostle now declares what they are, so that church members do not judge them rashly. He speaks of himself and Apollos (**us**; cf. 6.6). They are to be regarded as Christ's subordinates and as stewards of the mysteries of God. The Greek word for 'steward' literally means a person who acts as rower under the orders of someone. It evokes the image of a slave-in-charge, a person labouring in the service of others. 'Steward' could be used for anyone entrusted with responsibility and therefore accountable to others (cf. Luke 12.42). Paul and his fellow workers are custodians and administrators of a truth (mystery) which is not theirs, but God's.

4.2. It is required of stewards that they should be found trustworthy: Paul turns to examine the character of those who are handling God's truth. They must show themselves trustworthy. Trustworthiness is a requirement, not an option. It is the benchmark for evaluation of leaders. Those who are called must take time to reflect upon the great task that is ahead of them as well as the integrity that is needed to characterize their lives as they fulfil those tasks. Servants and stewards must be trustworthy because their task is greater than anything in this world. The question is, 'Are we worthy of the trust of God? Is he able to trust us with his message and his mysteries?'

4.3–4. It is a very small thing that I should be judged by you . . . I do not even judge myself . . . It is the Lord who judges me: Paul reaffirms the truth that since he is the Lord's servant and steward, it is to the Lord that he owes responsibility. It is the Lord who judges him for the quality of his service. Human judgement has little value. Even self-evaluation is unreliable, Paul says. Christ is the Lord of the conscience and is the one who can evaluate it properly. John Calvin's comments on this passage are quite helpful. He writes:

> It is the part of a good pastor to submit both his doctrine and his life for examination to the judgement of the Church, and it is the sign of a good conscience not to shun the light of careful inspection . . . But

when a faithful pastor sees that he is borne down by unreasonable and perverse affections, and that justice and truth have no place, he ought to appeal to God, and betake himself to His judgement seat, regardless of human opinion.   (John Calvin, *Corinthians*)

4.5. Do not pronounce judgement before the time: The Corinthians are already judging. Therefore Paul tells them to wait until the proper time, that is, the time of the Lord's return. God has the right to judge and he will do so. Paul is confident because he has been faithful. When a minister can focus on the judgement seat of Christ, where he or she is confident of giving account of his or her ministry before an all-knowing Lord, he or she can discount the tainted and biased criticisms of others.

4.6. I have applied all this to Apollos and myself for your benefit: Paul has shown to them, by using himself and Apollos as examples of ministers and their ministry (3.5–9), how to avoid rivalries. He now proceeds to tell them that they should do the same, that is, think of Paul and Apollos properly, and not beyond what is written. They had become occasions for pride, 'puffing up', among the Corinthians. Paul's teaching must have proved disturbing to the Corinthians, but everything that he has said has been for their benefit, with a view to their spiritual welfare, more precisely, that they might learn through Paul and Apollos the meaning of **'Nothing beyond what is written'**.

4.7. For who sees anything different in you . . . ?: Paul provides another reason for rejecting pride by asking a series of rhetorical questions. The abrupt questions of v. 7 lead to a sustained contrast between the way the Corinthians see themselves and Paul's own experience of what it means to be an apostle. As the Corinthians see themselves, they are already blessed with everything God has to give. They are spiritual millionaires. They have arrived, even without any help from Paul. The Corinthians evidently thought they had reached full maturity and were ruling rather than walking humbly with God.

4.8. Already you have all you want! Already you have become rich!: Paul continues with an irony. The irony is that the Corinthians were trying to 'reign', while their spiritual fathers and examples were far from 'reigning'. The Corinthian church felt it had reached the pinnacle of spiritual attainment. The church was self-satisfied; so it was not aware of any spiritual hunger. They even thought that they had surpassed their teachers. The word 'already' is placed foremost and repeated. It expresses well the movement of this whole passage: 'Now already!' Paul and the other apostles are still in a world of suffering; but at Corinth the local church already lives in full triumph. The Corinthians' fullness consisted of self-satisfaction and contempt. The expression 'rich' alludes to the spiritual gifts which distinguished this church above all others. Paul has recognized them from the outset (1.5, 7). The rebuke applies, not to the fact of their possession of gifts, but to the feeling of pride which accompanied it. No one should be 'puffed up' or look on others with contempt. Christians may indeed enjoy the gifts that are given to certain leaders and individuals, but they should never become attached to one leader to the point of disparaging another leader with lesser gifts.

4.9. God has exhibited us apostles as last of all . . . a spectacle to the world, to angels and to mortals: In contrast to the Corinthians, Paul goes on to explain that God has publicly displayed the apostles as humble, despised people – people worthy of death. He pictures himself and his fellow workers as condemned to death and led forth by a conqueror. By his use of 'spectacle', he alludes to the figure of condemned men tortured and exposed to the wild animals in the colosseum. They are also pictured as despised before the whole 'world' and the angelic hosts. Paul's point is that, unlike the Corinthians, through their sufferings and the way they handled those sufferings, the apostles demonstrated or 'showcased' the grace of God.

4.10. We are fools for the sake of Christ . . . We are weak, but you are strong. You are held in honour, but we in disrepute: The contrast between Paul and the Corinthians expressed in vv. 8 and 9 is expressed in v. 10 in three antitheses, which are like blows for the arrogant Corinthians. Paul again puts side by side the perception of the Christian life entertained by his readers and his own experience of apostolic ministry. We are reminded of 1.25 by Paul's use of words like 'fools', 'weak', 'disrepute'. There, Paul showed that God's wisdom of the cross is foolishness in the eyes of the world. God's power, the power of the cross, is also weakness in the eyes of the world. So, although Paul may be a fool, he is a fool for Christ's sake. Though he may be weak, he is weak with Christ. But the Corinthians are dangerously close to being on the side of the world.

4.11–13: Paul describes in detail the hardships he and his fellow Christian workers have suffered throughout their ministry. He does not want to boast about his sufferings. But he intends to highlight the misery of his outward circumstances in contrast to the self-sufficiency of the Corinthians. Paul's experience of apostolic ministry stands in the sharpest contrast to the Corinthians' perception of the Christian life. The story is told of the Bishop of Singapore who during the Second World War was repeatedly beaten by his guards, whom he consciously forgave. Years later the bishop baptized and confirmed one of his torturers, who had been greatly moved by the forgiveness shown to him. Paul and his fellow workers embody the wisdom of the cross. Had the Corinthians embodied that wisdom, they would have begun to live peaceably among themselves, though they might have been subject to the ridicule of outsiders.

4.14–15: Paul now senses that this may well be the effect of what he has just said, and so he checks himself; he is not writing to make them ashamed but to admonish them as his beloved children. In anticipation of the correction that follows, Paul is writing to the Corinthians not as their tutor but as their spiritual father. Here the word 'guardian' should be seen as standing in contrast not only to 'father' but also to the word 'teacher'. The underlying Greek word, *paidagogos*, was used to denote the person, usually a slave, whose duty it was to conduct a boy of good family to and from school and generally superintend his conduct. The word is also used in a somewhat pejorative sense in Galatians 3.24. But Paul is not the tutor of the Corinthians nor merely the teacher but their father. As their father he has a unique right to address them as his own dear children. However many tutors, say, **ten thousand guardians in Christ**, they may have, he and he alone can claim to have 'fathered' their life in Christ, for it was he who first brought them the gospel of Christ, and initiated them into the new life in him.

4.16–21. Be imitators of me: On the strength of Paul's unique relationship with the Corinthians, he now appeals to them: it was he who first led them to Christ; let them continue to look to him as their example of how to live in Christ. Paul's Christ-likeness and selfless service are evident to the Corinthians. So he tells the Corinthians to imitate him. Paul's desire is not for the Corinthians to be engaged in hero worship directed at him but rather to emulate the spiritual qualities that they have observed in his life as their spiritual father. As a proof of his concern Paul has sent Timothy, a fellow worker and Paul's son in the faith, to Corinth to assist and remind them of their relationship with Paul and instruct them in God's truth. There are some in Corinth who think that Paul is either shy or afraid to visit Corinth. But Paul's purpose is to come to them as God has willed. He could come to them with either a rod for discipline or in love with meekness. The Corinthians must decide what they want.

 STUDY SUGGESTIONS

Word study

1 What does the Greek word translated 'stewards' in the NRSV literally mean?

2 What does the Greek word *paidagogos* mean? How does Paul utilize this word to show his relationship to the Corinthians?

Review of content

3 According to 1 Corinthians 4, what does Paul give as the benchmark of evaluating leaders?

4 Paul uses this section to show some marked differences between him and the Corinthian congregation. Compare and contrast Paul and the Corinthians.

Bible study

5   Read 1 Timothy 3.1–13; Titus 1.5–9.

   (a) How does Paul's description of the qualifications for leaders in the above passages relate to Paul's view of leaders in 1 Corinthians 4?

   (b) How significant are the issues of faithfulness and accountability in ministry?

Discussion and application

6   We often hear proclaimed that we can trust God because he is faithful, but can God trust you? What does it mean for God to be able to trust us?

7   The Corinthian Christians had an 'already' attitude. They felt they had already arrived at full spiritual maturity and had already received all God had for them. Do we see this attitude in the Church today? Explain. How does this attitude detrimentally impact the witness and mission of the local church?

8   Do you know Christians who are suffering in the way Paul described? Do we view them as less spiritual? What place does suffering have in the Christian community, and how should we respond to such suffering? Might this influence how we explain the Christian journey to others?

9   How would you measure your commitment to the gospel in light of Paul's sufferings and all that he willingly endured for the gospel?

10 Is it good practice for Christians to evaluate their service for the Lord? If so, by what standards? What dangers are involved in self-evaluation and how can they be avoided?

1 Corinthians 5.1—6.20

Moral problems in the Church

5.1–13: Discipline and purity

 Summary

5.1–5: The problem of sexual immorality and discipline

5.6–8: Christ, our Passover

5.11–13: Keeping the Church pure

 Introduction

In 1 Corinthians 5 and 6, Paul points out three instances of Corinthian conduct, which fall far short of what he believes should be expected of a Christian community (5.1–13; 6.1–11 and 6.12–20). The Corinthians should take appropriate action. In urging the Corinthians to put things right, he strongly asserts his apostolic authority. The two chapters are linked to the preceding two by the issue of authority.

 Interpretation and notes

5.1a. It is actually reported: Paul has heard a report about the problems in the Corinthian church. The report probably came either from the delegation named in 16.17 or from Chloe's people (1.11).

5.1b. Sexual immorality . . . with his father's wife: The Greek word, *porneia*, translated as 'sexual immorality' (NRSV), refers to general sexual acts outside of legal marriage. Paul does not use the word, *moicheia*, 'adultery', which makes it likely that the offender's father either was not living or else had divorced his wife. The offender must have married the father's widow, that is, his stepmother. This view is confirmed by the phrase 'living with', which literally translated is, 'have', pointing to a lasting state of marriage. It is a forbidden practice both in the Old Testament (Leviticus 18.8; 20.11) and in Graeco-Roman law. Hence Paul considers it repugnant.

Until recently, a similar situation to that described above would not have been considered 'sin' or 'taboo' in some places in Africa, particularly in polygamous settings. Eldest sons (if they so wished) could inherit their stepmothers and live with them as wives after their father's death. This, of course, raises the larger question of the relationship between culture and Scripture. The answer is not always simple. Whenever there appears to be a conflict between any particular cultural practice and one's faith beliefs, one must look at the issue in detail, look at the overall teaching of the Scriptures, consider its implications for oneself and the believing community, and the larger community, and make decisions as considered appropriate.

5.2. And you are arrogant!: As Paul would say, more serious than the problem was the attitude of the Corinthians. They should have mourned. But they were proud and did not take appropriate disciplinary action to prevent the problem from destroying the testimony of the church.

5.3–4. Absent in body . . . present in spirit . . . already pronounced judgement in the name of the Lord Jesus: Paul is intent on protecting the purity and preserving the testimony of the Church. He will not allow the problem of sin to remain unresolved (5.3–5). Physically absent but present with them in spirit, Paul has already reached his judgement on how the offender is to be dealt with. When they are all assembled in the name of the Lord Jesus, they are to pass judgement on the offender and carry out the sentence.

5.5: The Corinthian church, as a community, is to take this disciplinary action even though it has been recommended and commanded by Paul. There are three main views concerning 'handing over to Satan' and the destruction of the flesh. The first understands the text as a reference to death as in the case of Ananias and Sapphira (Acts 5.1–6). The second view takes the 'destruction of the flesh' as referring to the eradication of the offender's sinful orientation. The third view, which is adopted in this commentary, is that the offender is to be excluded from the community of faith, thus being handed over to the sphere where Satan rules. This view is in line with Paul's primary concern for the purity of the community and not the individual. But it does not exclude the possibility that Paul also hoped that the offender would be penitent and, consequently, Paul's action would be redemptive for the individual. The important principle here is that the Church must not shy away from discipline when it is necessary. Yet, the goal must be clear: redemption and restoration of the offender (see 2 Corinthians 2.5–10).

5.6–8. Your boasting is not a good thing . . . Clean out the old yeast . . . Let us celebrate the festival . . . with unleavened bread of sincerity and truth: Paul moves to a more general exhortation prompted by the attitude which the Corinthians have taken in the case of the offender. The Corinthians remained insensitive to the sin in their midst. Their pride was misplaced. Using the illustration of the yeast of the Passover feast, Paul argues that any sin can permeate the ranks of the Church and affect its entire life and usefulness. It was an image that was commonly used to describe something apparently insignificant but capable of permeating and affecting a much larger entity of which it was part. As the Hebrews searched out yeast in the Passover season and purged their houses of all of it, so the Corinthians must purge out sin from their midst. The Corinthians' inaction is a sign of a moral blind spot that is capable of corrupting the life of the whole community. Therefore, Paul commands that the Corinthians **clean out the old yeast** of sin. This action is here regarded as a symbol of purging one's life of evil ways. The primary reference in the context is to the removal of the immoral man, but the image is to be given a broader application in v. 8.

The Corinthians must remove the corrupting influence in their midst so that they become a new lump of dough before it is touched by yeast. They are to bring their conduct up to their confession, **as you really are unleavened**. Paul presents the feasts of Passover and unleavened bread as types pointing to Christ and fulfilled in him. Thus, Paul can say that Christ has been sacrificed as our Passover lamb. Paul draws a conclusion from what he said in v. 7, depicting the Christian life as one which must be of celebration in Christ. It is a life of constant festival that demands constant purity. Believers must continuously keep 'leaven' out of their lives and fellowship.

5.9–10: Paul had written earlier that the Corinthians must not keep company with sexually immoral persons. The basic thought here is that there should be no friendly mixing between the Corinthians and those who violate sexual norms. The purity of the community must be maintained.

5.11: Paul is concerned with a possible misinterpretation of his instruction. So he issues a clarification. Its intention was not to shut off Christians from the world but to clarify their standing in the world. It would be impossible to avoid all contact with all unbelievers. To avoid all contact with such people, the Christians of Corinth would have had to withdraw from society altogether, but that is not what Paul meant. Paul enlarges on what he has previously stated in v. 9 to include the covetous, those greedy of gain and quick to take advantage of others; idolaters; drunkards; those who slander others, and those who extort money. Paul admonishes the Corinthians to have nothing to do with any so-called Christian who lives in such a fashion. To hold fellowship with so-called believers living in sin would be to confirm their waywardness and become a party to it.

5.12: Paul clarifies the area of the Church's disciplinary responsibility. It does not extend beyond the Christian community, and he himself disclaims any desire to pass any judgement on those outside it. God is their judge. The Christian's authority for judging does not extend to those outside the Church, but it does include those within it. God has granted to believers in the Church some responsibility of judgement toward those who are within the Church.

5.13. Drive out: Echoing the language of Deuteronomy 17.7, Paul urges them to root out the wrongdoer from their community (v. 13). The responsible exercise of this discipline sometimes calls for the exclusion of an errant member from the fellowship, and it is precisely that sort of situation that the Corinthians are facing now.

In recent years, when prominent priests and ministers have been found guilty of sexual misconduct and financial impropriety, the reaction of church authorities has all too often been to cover up the matter, counsel the priests or ministers concerned to be more careful in the future and transfer them elsewhere. At other times, the offender may be treated as a sick person in need of some form of therapy rather than as a sinner who needs to repent. Certainly anyone who advocates firmer action, closer to that advocated by Paul in this passage, is likely to be accused of vindictiveness and witch-hunting. Paul's point in 1 Corinthians 5 is to show how important the Church is and, particularly, how its purity should be guarded. God values the Church to the extent that he commands us to put out those who endanger its purity. Therefore, we ought to love, respect and develop a greater appreciation for the safety it provides us from Satan.

 STUDY SUGGESTIONS

Word study

1   How is the Greek word *porneia* translated in 1 Corinthians 5.1 in the NRSV? What may be a more fitting translation?

2   What does the Greek word *moicheia* mean? What does this term reveal about the situation in 1 Corinthians 5?

Review of content

3   What are the three main views concerning 'handing over to Satan' found in v. 5? Which of the three seems most probable? Explain.

4   Considering the pervasiveness of sin, even a so-called minuscule sin has the potential to permeate one's entire life.

   (a) What metaphor does Paul use to talk about sin in the midst of the Corinthians?

   (b) Applying this metaphor to one's life, what must a person do if he or she knows of sin present in his or her life?

(c) Applying this metaphor to your local congregation, what is the importance of not allowing sin to pervade your life as it relates to the well-being of the church as a whole?

Bible study

5 Read the account of Ananias and Sapphira in Acts 5.1–11.

(a) What does the judgement of Ananias and Sapphira say about the importance of honest life-in-community?

(b) Why would it have been wrong for Peter not to confront Ananias and (later) Sapphira?

(c) Are there other biblical accounts in which persons are confronted for their sinful behaviour because of its impact not only personally but also on the community of faith (e.g. Achan in Joshua 5)?

6 How would you feel if your pastor or best friend were to be caught carrying on sexual immorality? Shocked, disgusted, grieved or open-minded? How should such situations be handled by the Church?

7 What is the significance of Paul requiring the Corinthian congregation to perform the act of church discipline rather than waiting to handle the situation when he arrived? What should be the ultimate goal of discipline? Does your church have a process of restoration of erring believers? If so, discuss the process.

8 When there are seeming conflicts between cultural issues and Scripture, what should guide the Christian in making decisions?

6.1–20: Pagan courts and Christian purity

 Summary

6.1–8: Conflicts among the saints. Believers must settle disputes among themselves.

6.9–11: Inheriting the kingdom of God. No unrighteous person shall inherit the kingdom of God.

6.12–20: Sexual purity, freedom and the body

Introduction

David Ben-Gurion, former Prime Minister of Israel, was reported to have said to a missionary, 'The New Testament teaching standards are wonderful, but where are those who live up to them? Are there any folk in the world who do? Are there any living the Christian life? Can this book really produce that which it sets forth?' Ben-Gurion's questions continue to echo in the minds of many people. Perhaps nowhere are those questions as pertinent as in Corinth. The Corinthians' spiritual deficiency revealed itself in various forms. At first it was seen in schisms within the church, followed by indifference to evil in their midst. Then they began to engage in legal controversies before unbelievers (6.1–11). Next, Paul addresses the issue of freedom and how it relates to sexual purity and how believers use their bodies. The Corinthians have failed to exercise sexual purity (6.12–20). Since they have been bought at great cost and since their bodies are the temple of the Holy Spirit, they ought not to go beyond the bounds of true grace.

 Interpretation and notes

6.1. Grievance against another: Paul expresses dismay at the thought that a believer who has a grievance, literally, 'matter' or 'lawsuit', against another should go to law, instead of having the matter resolved within the Christian community. Paul's shock is expressed in his statement, 'Does he dare?'; that is, 'How dare he?' or 'How in the world could that be?' Paul is troubled for obvious reasons. It was contrary to the spirit of Christianity for believers to haul their brothers and sisters before heathen magistrates for the adjudication of their differences. For Paul, such an attitude is an admission of Christian failure as well as a demonstration of a lack of understanding of the nature of the body of Christ.

6.2–4. Saints will judge the world . . . We are to judge angels: Paul is especially aggravated by the fact that the Corinthians have so little understanding of who they are in Christ. Believers will judge the world and angels. Therefore, they must not feel incompetent to judge themselves. It is part of their vocation. If believers are to judge angels then they should be able to handle the 'trivial' matters and disputes that confront them on a daily basis. By directing his questions to the whole congregation, Paul shows the implication of one person's sin for the entire community. The action of the 'one' affects the 'all', that is, the community should not have allowed the incident.

6.5–6. It is difficult for two believers to engage in a legal suit with one another without bringing damage to the Church before the community. As a Yoruba proverb goes, 'Friendship is never enhanced by litigation.' Paul's sharp rebuke shows that the action was incompatible with Christianity. The settling of inter-Christian differences by going to court was contrary to the best interests of the individual family and church. Paul contends that it is wrong for two Christians to become so involved in acute misunderstanding that they want to go to a heathen court to decide who was right. The failure of the people involved is primarily a failure of the Church to live up to its calling. It is an irony that the Corinthian church, which boasted of its wisdom, had no one among its members wise enough to decide matters between them.

6.7–8: The Corinthians' situation was that of spiritual deficiency. Paul questions them, asking why, since settlement is so difficult and perhaps sometimes impossible, they do not relinquish their rights and even allow themselves to be defrauded, rather than rush into heathen courts. If the very community which claims to be the object and instrument of the reconciliation of God is itself unreconciled, its credibility is called into question. Although Paul now addresses the initiator of the legal action, his use of the plural form of verbs shows that he still is concerned about the community as a whole. He asks whether it would not be much better to submit to wrong and let oneself be defrauded than to take such action.

The story is told of a pastor who unintentionally made a statement that angered one of his deacons. The deacon led him to the door, pushed him out of the house, and slammed the door in his face. As the pastor walked to his car, he became very angry and resentful. However, he had a change of attitude, humbled himself, returned immediately to the deacon's door, and asked for forgiveness. The result was unity and forgiveness instead of bitterness and division.

Is there ever a situation where a Christian or Christian church can legitimately take another to court? Although Paul would that we would rather be cheated, the application of this passage must be a matter of intense prayer and consultation with the body of Christ.

6.9–10: Paul backs up his rebuke with a warning. The conduct of the Corinthians was so deplorable that Paul considered it necessary and wise to remind them that unrighteous persons do not inherit God's kingdom. He goes on to list some of the sins from which the Corinthians have been cleansed. Paul's point is that the transforming experience that the Corinthians have experienced is belied by the problem of litigation that has gone on. They are now a new creation (cf. 2 Corinthians 5.17).

6.11. Washed . . . sanctified . . . justified: Paul's demand for a different style of life among the Corinthian congregation is to be predicated on the church's awareness of its own character as a washed, sanctified and justified people. The Corinthians have changed from a life of idolatry to the worship of Christ; from immorality to a life governed by the principles of Christ and his Spirit. A transformed moral life ought to be a result of a transforming experience. Those who, having experienced God's grace, engage in the kind of action condemned earlier in 1 Corinthians 6 can only be blind to what God has done for them.

A believer who was formerly a heavy smoker and drunkard was telling his neighbours at their annual community party what the Lord had done for him in saving him from the power of sin. He spoke with humility, hoping to win some of his former drinking partners for Christ. A former drinking partner scoffed, telling him that the new believer was dreaming, would wake up and would be back with them in a few days. The believer's son quietly whispered to his dad, 'I sure hope you don't wake up then, because our family likes what the Lord has done for you.'

6.12. All things are lawful: Paul sets the stage for his argument in the section by twice quoting a Corinthian slogan, *all things are lawful,* a phrase that suggests the carefree attitude of the Corinthians. The Corinthians thought that their freedom in Christ meant licence to sin. Paul quickly adds that all things are not necessarily beneficial nor do good. Thus, Paul insists that freedom is shown in doing what is beneficial to others. Yet it must be said that Christian freedom goes beyond the concern for others. It must be exercised responsibly and not lead to enslavement by anything.

6.13. The body . . . for the Lord, and the Lord for the body: Paul affirms that the body is not meant for immorality. As he moves from the question of food to that of sexuality, Paul introduces the term, 'body', so that the Corinthians know that the physical body and its activities such as sex are not immaterial to the life of freedom in the kingdom of God. The body is more than physical organs; it is a whole person capable of relationship. As such, bodily existence as Paul understands it connotes existence for others – existence in relationship. The body has a purpose. It is for the Lord; that is, it is the instrument in which we serve God.

6.14: Paul endeavours to put right not only the understanding of freedom held by the Corinthians but also their attitude to the body. Because of the body's relation to the Lord, it must not be given to immorality. Moreover, the body is destined for resurrection. Freedom consists of what demonstrates the resurrection power in the life of the individual.

6.15–16. Members of Christ: True freedom is what expresses being part of Christ's body and what shows the believer's new identity as a temple or dwelling place of the Holy Spirit. A believer should always ask questions such as, 'How does my action affect my brother or sister? Is my action edifying, that is, does it build up the body of Christ?' That which belongs to Christ cannot be surrendered for fornication. Paul hints at the concept of the

Church as the body of Christ, which is to be developed in 10.16f.; 11.27–34; and 12.12–31. Paul heightens the argument by referring to Genesis 2.24.

6.17: The nature of the relationship between the believer's body and Christ, and the consequent incompatibility between that relationship and union with a prostitute is further detailed. Paul reinterprets the freedom of the individual by setting it firmly in the wider context of significance and obligation. The union of the believer with a prostitute is wrong and disorderly because it violates and contradicts the most important union of all: with the Lord and the Lord's people. To join with a harlot is to become one with him or her. It is totally unacceptable.

6.18. Flee immorality: Paul commands the Corinthians to take flight from immorality. The word translated 'shun' (NRSV) is the Greek root word from which we get the word 'fugitive'. As such it is better translated as 'keep on fleeing'.

6.19. Paul's statement is particularly striking in that the word *body* is singular, but the word *your* is plural. Paul says that **your body is a temple of the Holy Spirit**. He has earlier told the Corinthians as a whole that 'you yourselves are God's temple' (3.16). The point is this: Paul is probably giving a double meaning to his words. The person who sins sexually sins against his or her body – both his or her individual body and the body of Christ.

6.20. Temple of the Holy Spirit . . . bought with a price: Paul's argument comes to a climax. Believers constitute the temple of God both personally and corporately. Paul has earlier used the same imagery in 1 Corinthians 3.16 (see discussion in that place). Therefore for the presence of God to remain with them, there is the need for purity. Believers are to glorify God in their bodies. This is a timely reminder to Christians in the twenty-first century that our bodies are to be holy and engaged in the pursuits of only such things as glorify God.

The Corinthians knew Greek philosophy, which separated body and spirit. They thought that if they were Christians it did not matter what they did with their bodies. Paul says that action with our bodies affects our spiritual life. The two cannot be separated. Fornication and prostitution must not exist among God's people. Today believers are surrounded with unsolicited pornographic advertisements on the television and bill boards, sexually explicit plays and movies on television, trash talk on radio waves. The Corinthians were to flee the things that confronted them. So must we. They were also to stand with lives of purity in a pagan community for Jesus Christ in such a way as to bring praise to him (cf. 1 Peter 2.10–11). So do we. The question is, shall we follow the world, or follow the Lord? We need to ensure that we do not adjust our lives to the shifting standards of the world. Instead, we must remain true to God at all costs and adorn the gospel of our Saviour and Lord, Jesus Christ.

STUDY SUGGESTIONS

Word study

1 In v. 18, Paul uses the word 'shun'.

   (a) What other word is derived from the root of the word translated 'shun'?

   (b) How is the word translated 'shun' better translated?

Review of content

2 According to Paul, why is it wrong or shameful for Christians to settle a legal dispute in court? How does this reflect poorly on the Church?

3 Paul quotes a Corinthian slogan, 'All things are lawful.' What does this reveal about the Corinthians' attitude? In light of Paul's discussion, what is true freedom?

Bible study

4 Read 1 Corinthians 3.16–17 and 1 Peter 2.9–12.

   (a) What is the significance of Paul using the temple of God as a metaphor for the Church?

   (b) Why would Paul advocate fleeing sexual immorality instead of simply resisting it?

   (c) What is the purpose, according to Peter, of Christians living honourable, holy lives among a world that does not?

Discussion and application

5 Have you ever been involved in a dispute with another Christian? How did you handle the dispute? Who mediated between you? Having now read what Paul says about disputes among Christians in 1 Corinthians 6, is there anything you would do differently?

6 Paul suggests that, instead of pursuing legal action, Christians should be willing to be defrauded. Why is this a foreign concept in the Church during our time? How might such an action impact the witness of the Church to unbelievers in the surrounding community?

7 What is the responsibility of the Church in matters involving disputes among its members?

8   Is everything permissible for believers? What are the implications of Paul's statement that 'all things are lawful but not all things are beneficial' for Christian living, particularly among people of other faiths?

9   How might Paul's warning to the Corinthians concerning unrighteous persons not inheriting God's kingdom inform our understanding of salvation, especially given the fact that the Corinthians had been 'washed, sanctified and justified'?

10 How do we flee sin without abandoning the world? How do we understand this admonition in light of building relationships with unbelievers with the goal of leading them to Christ?

1 Corinthians 7.1–40

Purity, sexual relations, divorce and marriage

 Summary

7.1–6: Problem one: sex and spirituality. How about sex and spirituality?

7.7–9: Problem two: questions about celibacy. Which type of lifestyle is best for being a follower of Jesus Christ? Is it better to be married or to be single?

7.10–11: Problem three: what about divorce? Is it better to stay married to unbelievers or divorce them?

7.12–16: Problem four: old relationships and post-conversion problems

7.17–24: A general principle: remain as you are!

7.25–40: Problem five: virgins, marriage, sex and widows

 Introduction

Chapter 7 of 1 Corinthians begins a new section in the Letter. Up to this point Paul has been dealing with issues he has heard about from others, but now he begins answering some specific questions the Corinthian church sent him in their letter. Here Paul deals with several issues related to marriage. The discussion in 1 Corinthians 7 is neither comprehensive teaching by Paul on marriage nor a systematic guide to marriage and the family. There are, nevertheless, some instructions and guidelines that could help believers today. Paul's argument in 1 Corinthians 7 contains his specific advice for the Corinthians on proper marital relations, with an inserted argument that devalues earthly status (e.g. slavery, circumcision) in general.

 Interpretation and notes

7.1b. It is well for a man not to touch a woman: There were some in Corinth who probably thought they would be more spiritual if they were to abstain from having sexual relations with their wives.

7.2. Because of cases of sexual immorality, each man should have his own wife: Paul gives them a clear answer. It is not 'more spiritual' to live as married people but abstain from sexual relations. In fact it will most likely lead to sinful behaviour. Notice that Paul uses the singular word 'wife'. Taken together with a passage such as Mark 10.7, it is clear that monogamy is the standard of marriage that best fulfils God's purpose.

7.3–4. The husband should give to his wife her conjugal rights: Rather than agreeing that they should stop sexual relations, Paul presents quite a radical sexual ethic for the day. Paul insists that each partner in marriage has an equal right.

7.5. Do not deprive one another except . . . by agreement: Paul exhorts husbands and wives willingly to give themselves to their spouses. God designed sex, and he meant married people to enjoy it as a tool for increased intimacy between them. His advice to married people was this: enjoy the sexual benefits of marriage and serve God where you are!

7.6. This I say . . . not of command: This refers to what Paul has just said in v. 5, that is abstinence from sexual relations should be only for a limited time and under the given conditions. What he says does not represent the ideal. It is just a concession. He does not want the Corinthians to think that sexual activity between husband and wife is wrong.

7.7. I wish that all were as I myself am. But each has a particular gift from God: Paul turns to the question of the unmarried (celibates and widows). As Paul looks at the matter of celibacy, he simply says that it is good. It has its advantages and is profitable. He agrees that it is good, but not for all people and not at all times. Paul states that certain individuals are given the gift of singleness and are able to control their sexual desires. For these people, Paul says it is better for them to stay unmarried (just as he himself is). Throughout history there have been people known as 'ascetics' who believe that the way to spiritual maturity is through the denial of anything the physical body finds pleasurable. They advocate eating simple food and dressing in plain clothes and they believe that denying sex enables them to focus upon their spiritual life.

7.8–9. To the unmarried and the widows . . . if they are not practising self-control, they should marry. For it is better to marry than to be aflame with passion: Paul does not suggest that marriage is a fallback arrangement or an antidote for lack of self-control. He is concerned with unmarried people who might be tempted to use their sexual desires in an illegitimate manner. Paul's advice is for them to get married. These verses hint that Paul did not consider pre-marital or extra-marital sex appropriate for Christians.

7.10–11: Some married Corinthians probably felt that they would be able to serve the Lord better if they were not married, so they probably thought of divorce. Paul reminds them that it is not God's will for Christians to separate from each other in order to be freed to serve him more effectively. In our time some may think that they are called to be missionaries in a foreign country or have a particular ministry, but their spouses disagree. Questions such as, 'Should I not pursue this calling for the sake of the kingdom, even though it means divorcing my spouse?' may come to mind at such a time. Paul's answer is a categorical *no*. It is never God's will that one divorces a spouse in order to free oneself to serve him. What Christians ought to do is serve the Lord in the situation they find themselves. The situation may be less than ideal or desired.

7.12–14: Paul now turns to those who were married before their conversion and who probably thought that their newfound faith and status in Christ demanded or required them to divorce their unbelieving spouses. They probably felt that living with an unbelieving spouse was detrimental to their Christian development or was limiting them in their service. Paul's answer is, stay together if the non-Christian is willing. The couple should remain married, since **the unbelieving husband is made holy through his wife** (v. 14). Paul adds that the children are holy as well. This does not mean the Christian spouses make the unbelievers in the family morally pure or that their salvation is guaranteed. They are, nonetheless, in a privileged position – they are living with a Christian in the sphere of the influence of the gospel – and that is a hopeful sign that, perhaps, they might one day come to know the Lord themselves. In that sense, and only in that sense, they are 'holy'.

7.15a. But if the unbelieving partner separates, let it be so: Nimota and Ibrahim were both Muslims before they got married. Nimota was converted about five years after their marriage. A full-time mother and teacher, Nimota became an active member of the women's ministry at church. Between caring for her husband and children, attending Bible studies, and her teaching job, life is quite busy – but she loves it and is very good at maintaining the balance. Sadly, her husband is not so keen on Nimota's commitment to Christ and the church. Ibrahim has attended church a few times, but found the gospel too hard to swallow. Now he is tired of her 'religion'. He does not want to remain married to a woman who is as much committed to Christ as she is, and who tries to 'convert' him. So, one Sunday evening after church, Nimota comes home to a dark, empty house and a note, 'Nimota, I am leaving you. I cannot live with a Christian anymore. I am sorry.' Paul offers advice for this type of situation in the next clause.

7.15b. In such a case the brother or sister is not bound: Paul seems to suggest that clinging to a marriage like that above, which the unbelieving partner is determined to end, will not lead to peace. It will lead to nothing but frustration and constant tension. It will only produce a strain that is not justified by the uncertain result of whether Ibrahim will be converted or not. Of course, this text does not mean that Christians should not pray to God and plead with their non-Christian spouses to stay married. There is nothing here, for example, to prevent Nimota from contacting Ibrahim, entreating him to reconsider, and praying that he will put his family first and return to the marriage. But if he persists, Nimota is no longer bound to the marriage.

7.15c. It is to peace that God has called you: Paul has advised Christians to let their unbelieving partners go if they so wish. Yet, as much as possible God wants his children to live in peace with their unbelieving spouses. The thrust of Paul's argument in this section is clear: conversion to Christianity is not to be used as a pretext for divorce or as an excuse to upset a marital harmony that previously existed.

7.16. Wife . . . you might save your husband. Husband . . . you might save your wife: Believers have been given an important role of bringing holiness to their marriages and families. As the only Christians in the family, believers have the privilege and obligation to show the love, acceptance and forgiveness of Christ to their spouses, and may even get the opportunity to lead them to receiving Christ as their Saviour! Therefore the believer is not to leave the non-Christian spouse in order to be a better Christian.

7.17–24. Let each of you lead the life that the Lord has assigned, to which God called you . . . In whatever condition you were called, brothers and sisters, there remain with God: Paul provides the theological basis for his argument in the entire chapter, which is, 'remain as you are'. He argues that the call of God transcends all relationships and one's situation or social location in life. For Paul, it makes no difference whether or not a person is single, married, poor or rich. One must live as a Christian, regardless of one's life situation. This is what Paul states in v. 17 and restates in vv. 22–23. The general call referred to by Paul is their salvation. Hence, Paul declares circumcision or lack of it is not what commends one to God (Romans 2.25f.; 18.8f.; Galatians 5.6; 6.15). The important thing is to keep God's commands right where you are, in the situation you find yourself. We sometimes think the grass would be greener if we were in some different situation, or we would be able to serve God more effectively if somehow our life situation changed. Although Paul makes a qualified exception in v. 21, it still is clear that being either slave or free is inconsequential in terms of one's relationship with the Lord.

7.25a. Concerning virgins: Although sometimes translated 'unmarried', the Greek word used here specifically refers to virgin women.

7.25b. I have no command of the Lord, but I give my opinion: Some have suggested that Paul's instruction here does not carry the same weight as elsewhere because he says that he has no direct command from the Lord. This is not necessarily so. Although he claims not to have a direct word from the Lord on the subject he is about to address, he believes his thinking is faithful and guided by the Spirit because of the Lord's mercy (v. 40).

7.26b. In view of the impending crisis . . . remain as you are: Paul exhorts the virgins to remain as they are. The phrase 'impending crisis' is better translated as 'present necessity' for three reasons, namely:

1 The word translated 'impending' is the same word translated 'present' in 3.22;

2 The ordinary meaning of the word translated 'crisis' is 'necessity' or 'urgency'. It is the same word that Paul uses in 1 Corinthians 9.16, and rightly translated as 'necessity' in the King James Version; and

3 It fits better with the context.

What then is the 'present necessity' that Paul refers to? There are two main views. First, it is a reference to some eschatological sufferings that Paul expects to come upon the Church. This interpretation is what informs the translation, 'impending crisis'. The second view, which is taken in this commentary, understands 'present necessity' as an urgent imperative of proclaiming the gospel. Virgins in particular, and the unmarried in general, are spared from the distractions and earthly cares that accompany marriage and children (v. 28b). Christian history is replete with examples of those who have served in this manner. Yet, Paul concludes that if the virgins marry, they do not sin.

7.29–35. The appointed time has grown short . . . Let even those who have wives be as though they had none: Because of the shortness of time, and in order to avoid distractions that attend marriage, virgins should devote their energy to the proclamation of the gospel.

7.36–38. If anyone thinks that he is not behaving properly toward his fiancée . . . Let them marry: Paul qualifies his previous statements on celibacy by making it clear that marriage is not to be despised. The word translated 'fiancée' (NRSV) is the word 'virgin'. So who is 'anyone' or 'he' in vv. 36–38? There are two major interpretations. Some consider it to mean the father of the virgin. Others see it as referring to the man who is engaged to her. Neither of these two interpretations is without difficulty. However, this commentary adopts the first view. Paul wrote these words in a patriarchal society where marriages were frequently arranged and fathers decided whom their daughter would marry. Such practices still continue among many tribes in Nigeria, where parental consent is of great importance. In some instances, parents have sometimes told their children to renounce their Christian faith in order to secure their blessing in marriage. Paul's point is that a girl of marriageable age should not be prevented from doing so.

7.39–40. A wife is bound as long as her husband lives . . . If the husband dies, she is free to marry . . . She is more blessed if she remains as she is: Paul answers the question of remarriage by widows. Paul, in closing, once again expresses his preference for the single state by urging the

Corinthians to remain as they are. Paul's opinion is that the widow will be more blessed, or better off (literally, 'happier') as she is.

 STUDY SUGGESTIONS

Word study

1 In 1 Corinthians 7.26, how is the phrase 'impending crisis' in the NRSV better translated? What are three reasons for this alternative translation?

2 The word translated 'fiancée' in v. 36 literally means what? With this in mind, what are the two views about the person to whom Paul is speaking in this verse (i.e. the person(s) referred to as 'anyone')?

Review of content

3 In what way does 1 Corinthians 7 differ from what has preceded it thus far in the Letter?

(a) What five questions does Paul address in this chapter?

(b) Can one properly conclude that Paul offers comprehensive responses to such questions? Explain.

4 How does Paul address the issue of whether present marital relationships should continue after conversion? What does Paul mean when he refers to the unbelieving spouse being made holy by the believing spouse?

5 In v. 26, Paul refers to an 'impending crisis'. To what is this phrase referring? What does this have to do with his admonition to virgins to remain unmarried?

Bible study

6 Read Philemon. Recalling 1 Corinthians 7.21–24, why would Paul appeal to Philemon to release Onesimus as a slave and receive him as a brother in Christ?

Discussion and application

7 Have you ever thought about celibacy as a gift? What are the implications of celibacy being a gift from God?

    (a) How does Paul's view of sexuality contrast with the 'ascetics' of church history? Is it more spiritual to be celibate?

    (b) Do you think Christian ministers would make better pastors if they were unmarried? Explain.

8 How should one address the subject of remarriage in the light of 1 Corinthians 7.8–9?

9 What are some implications of the general principle, 'remain as you are', in your life setting?

    (a) Can you name some instances in church history where this general principle had a positive impact for the kingdom of God?

    (b) Are there examples in which this general principle has been abused?

10 Given that the time is short according to Paul, how should believers live?

1 Corinthians 8.1—11.1

Food sacrificed to idols

8.1–13: Christian freedom and the common good

 Summary

8.1–3: Knowledge and love

8.4–6: There is only one God.

8.7–13: Love before liberty

 Introduction

Decisions are a normal part of living. Every day we are confronted with what to do in any number of ways. Some decisions are inconsequential, and some important. Will your decision detract from your Christian testimony? Will your action be unworthy of the name of Christ? Will it be a stumbling-block to others? History records that Greeks and Romans had integrated the worship of their pagan gods into the entire fabric of their national and domestic life. Small altars were erected in homes, and statues were placed in gardens. The temple ceremonies, state occasions, festival events and even family gatherings involved sacrifices to the pagan gods (idols) of the day. Virtually all of the food available for purchase had been offered on the altars of pagan gods. Should Christians eat or not? What would be the consequences, if any? These things posed serious problems for the Christians in Corinth as they do for believers, particularly new converts of various religious backgrounds, for example, Islam, Buddhism, Hinduism. The Corinthians had to make decisions. So do believers today. Therefore the Corinthians asked Paul for his counsel regarding these issues and it is to these that he speaks in 1 Corinthians 8—10.

 Interpretation and notes

8.1a. Now concerning: The opening phrase, with its similarity to 1 Corinthians 7.1, suggests that Paul is again drawing attention to a question that the Corinthians have asked him in their letter. It pertains to food which had been sacrificed to idols in pagan temples and now was ready to be eaten. Considering Paul's tone and answer, it would appear that some Corinthians felt that they were at liberty to eat such food, based on their 'knowledge' that idols were nothing.

8.1b. All of us possess knowledge: Paul begins by affirming what was common to him and the Corinthians, that they both had knowledge. 'Knowledge' is the keyword in the chapter – five of the ten occurrences of the word in the Letter appear here. Paul often uses the phrase, 'we know', in various Letters in passages where he is stating what he knows to be common ground between himself and his readers (cf. Romans 2.2; 3.19; 8.28; 1 Corinthians 7.14; 8.22; 2 Corinthians 5.1). However, Paul immediately proceeds to show that while knowledge is important, it is insufficient to determine our relation to God and fellow human beings, particularly Christians. Instead, the opposite is actually true, 'knowledge puffs up'. The word here translated 'puffs up', or literally 'inflates', has already been used four times in this Letter (see 4.6, 18, 19; 5.2) and it summarily expresses a major cause of the community's malaise. But, Paul says, 'Love builds up.'

8.2–3: Furthermore, Paul goes on to argue that real 'knowledge' is not just to know God but to be known by God. It is the person who loves God who truly knows God. But Paul speaks not only of knowing God but also of being known by God. Paul's assertions must have surprised the readers in two ways. First, Paul makes clear that knowing the truth about a particular issue is not enough. Rather, love is needed. Second, for Paul, true knowledge is based on relationship. Whatever knowledge we have of God is due to his loving initiative. Thus it can be said both that we love God only because God first loved us, and that we know God only because God first knew us.

8.4–5: Paul returns to the problem of 'food sacrificed to idols' in these verses. Still using the theme of knowledge, Paul now talks of what we know about God and the gods. His first assertion is that an idol has no real existence (v. 4). In other words, the gods that the idols represent are actually non-existent. An idol is nothing but a piece of carved stone or wood. Certainly it cannot contaminate food. Paul seems to contradict himself in v. 5 as he asserts that there are many gods and lords. His point in the verse is that although the gods specifically represented by the idols are really non-existent, there are unseen beings behind the idols, a point that Paul later expands on in 1 Corinthians 10.

8.6. For us: Paul clarifies his position with the short phrase, 'for us'. For Christians, there are no other beings in heaven or earth that may rightly be called God or Lord, apart from God the Father and the Lord Jesus Christ, but for others such beings do exist. To have the true God, one must be in Christ. Creation owes its existence to God. As believers in Christ we owe both our physical and spiritual existence to him. Paul next speaks of the Lord Jesus Christ as coequal with the Father. Before he has said 'from whom'. Now Paul says, 'through whom are all things'. Christ is the agent of all existence. Paul's point in this passage is clear. In Corinth, there are many gods and lords who command loyalty, obedience and service. Not so for the Christian. There is only one God who can demand total service and commitment, and only one Lord had made such service and commitment possible.

8.7–9: Paul has just admitted the truth of the position maintained by some 'knowledgeable' ones in Corinth that a false god has no real existence. But there remained some who thought that sacrificial food had been polluted by the gods represented by the idols. As such, if they ate of food sacrificed to idols, they thought that the mere act of consuming it amounted to participation in an idolatrous ritual. They could not eat such food without violating their conscience. However, Paul contends, eating is no proof that one is a good Christian; a refusal to eat is no proof that a Christian is spiritually deficient. For Paul, there was nothing either inherently good or evil in food itself. He knew the meaning of genuine Christian liberty. Just because we are free to eat does not mean we need to. There's no idea that freedom carries with it an imperative to act. Some people think that because you're free to do something then you should do it. The result of that kind of thinking is that freedom itself becomes slavery.

The strong Christians who possess the right knowledge about idols ought to be aware of others' feelings. People's sense of self-awareness is not sufficient to decide the course of action to take. Rather, Christians must be conscious of the effects of their actions on others. Those who are motivated by love for God and their fellow Christians will certainly not be indifferent to the harm their actions will cause others, including unbelievers. Unbelievers who have eaten idol food with impunity all their lives might consider the believer's participation a legitimization of eating such food. In such case, the exercise of Christian liberty without Christian love can become a stumbling-block to others.

8.10–11: Here is the power of example. We are easily influenced by the decisions and actions of those around us. So Paul describes how the thoughtless exercise of one's own liberty may lead to the downfall of a fellow Christian. If believers with weak consciences see those 'with knowledge' sitting down to a meal in a heathen temple they might be encouraged to eat food consecrated to the heathen deity even though they are unsure of the appropriateness of such a course. The result is tragic indeed. They now have a sense of having been disobedient to God. Having violated their consciences in one area of living, there is a breakdown of spiritual defences and they are exposed to violate their consciences in another area. Thus, they may suffer spiritual defeat and become useless to God (v. 11). That Paul is talking about eternal ruin is without doubt. This is the import of the word translated as 'destroyed'.

8.12: This is a very serious verse and one that believers need to consider afresh. An injury done to a child of God is an injury done to the Lord (cf. Acts 9.4).

It is grievous for people to exercise their personal liberty in a way that might cause fellow Christians spiritual harm. Christians are so closely identified with Christ that to hurt one hurts the Saviour. Hence, it is our responsibility to show an attitude of selfless concern for our brothers and sisters in Christ.

8.13: There are many areas of Christian life that cannot be classified as either absolute right or absolute wrong. Verse 13 speaks to such areas. However legitimate a thing may be, if under certain circumstances it becomes harmful to the members of the Christian family and to the cause of Christ, it must be avoided. The Christian must always ask, 'Will my behaviour build others up? Is love the controlling factor in my behaviour or is it a desire to exert my personal rights? Am I willing to waive my rights for the sake of another?' Our conduct must not be determined solely on the basis of knowledge. It must be based on love. The question may now be asked, 'What should the believer described in the situation in our introduction above do?' Paul's answer would be, 'Eat as long as no one is scandalized.'

 ## STUDY SUGGESTIONS

Word study

1   What is the key word in 1 Corinthians 8.1–13? How many times does this word appear in 1 Corinthians? How many of those occur in this chapter?

Review of content

2   Paul makes an assertion that real knowledge is not just to know God but to be known by God. In what two ways might this have surprised the Corinthian congregation?

3   Paul is answering a question posed by the Corinthian believers in this chapter.

  (a) What is that question?

  (b) Summarize Paul's response in five words or fewer.

4   In v. 5, Paul asserts that there are many gods and lords.

  (a) Does Paul contradict what he says in v. 4 that 'an idol has no real existence'? Explain.

  (b) What is Paul's ultimate point here?

5   What three questions must a Christian ask himself or herself when deciding upon certain courses of action which cannot be classified as either absolute right or absolute wrong?

Bible study

6 Read the conversion account of Paul in Acts 9. How might Paul's conversion have influenced his discussion in 1 Corinthians 8 (especially v. 12)?

Discussion and application

7 In responding to the Corinthians' questions, Paul underscores that the decisions we make should take into account the impact of those decisions upon others.

(a) Why is it important to consider the impact our decisions have upon other Christians?

(b) Are we willing to sacrifice our desires or relinquish our rights in order not to become a stumbling-block to the weak? Or have we adopted an autonomous view that our actions have no consequences for the well-being of others?

(c) How far should we go in giving up our rights for the sake of others, particularly for those of weaker consciences?

8 If there is not a particular Scripture addressing certain issues (e.g. smoking), how might Christian love be integral in exercising Christian liberty?

9 What are the implications of this chapter for cross-cultural ministry? How might Christian liberty devoid of love hinder missionary efforts? In light of v. 12, why is allowing oneself to be a stumbling-block to others such a serious offence?

9.1–27: Use and abuse of Christian freedom

 Summary

9.1–12a: Paul's apostolic rights

9.12b–18: Paul waives his rights

9.19–23: All things to all people

9.24–27: The need for discipline

Introduction

'The running horse at the back takes its cue from the one in front', so goes an African proverb that underscores the power of example. In his discussion of food sacrificed to idols in 1 Corinthians 8, Paul has clearly articulated the need for selflessness among the Corinthians. However, his teaching about freedom and self-denial does not end there. In 1 Corinthians 9 Paul provides himself as an example of disciplined freedom – freedom that was neither unrestricted nor uncontrolled. It was freedom that was tempered with love. He has freely surrendered his 'rights' for the sake of others. Therefore, he urges the Corinthians to consider his own example. He gives the Corinthians a model of how to and how not to use their Christian freedom and rights. Paul asks them to give up their 'right' to eat food sacrificed to idols, even as he gave up his own rights as an apostle. However, Paul will also use the occasion to defend his apostolic position before the doubting Corinthian Christians.

 Interpretation and notes

9.1. Am I not free . . .?: Paul begins with a series of questions that demand positive answers. On the one hand, the first two questions appear to affirm Paul's freedom to accept or renounce material support from the Corinthians. On the other hand, they speak to Paul's freedom to eat or reject any kind of food. Paul had every right to claim such freedom, by virtue of his calling to be an apostle. The evidence of Paul's true status as an apostle is further shown in the question: **Have I not seen Jesus our Lord?** Paul insists that he saw an authentic appearance of the post-resurrection Jesus.

9.2a. If I am not an apostle to others, at least I am to you: Although some among the Corinthian Christians doubted Paul's standing as an apostle, they should not have done so. The Corinthian Christians more than others ought to know Paul was a genuine apostle, because they had seen his work closely. This makes the doubt among the Corinthian Christians all the more ironic; something Paul is trying to let the Corinthians know!

9.2b. For you are the seal of my apostleship in the Lord: As the old saying goes, 'The proof of the pudding is in the eating'. The work of God among the Corinthian Christians was evidence enough of Paul's apostolic credentials. They were the seal of his apostleship. Paul was the one who planted the church in Corinth. Their conversion was a sufficient proof of the effectiveness of Paul's ministry.

9 3–6. My defence: As if he were a lawyer arguing a case, Paul now asserts his rights as an apostle. The words 'defence' (*apologia*) and 'examine' (*anakrino*) are both legal words, taken from the Roman law court. Paul feels as though he is on trial by the Corinthians who seem to have condemned him already. Paul then turns to his rights as an apostle.

1   He had the right to support from the Corinthians. The Corinthians did not question Paul's right to eat, but Paul means that he has the right to eat and drink at the expense of the churches that he serves. Paul has the right to be given food and drink for his labour.

2   He had the right to take a wife with him. Paul suggests that the other apostles had taken their wives with them on journeys. Therefore, he would have been free to travel around with his wife, and be supported by the church if he had one. This verse is especially interesting concerning Peter (Cephas), who was obviously married.

3   Paul had the right to be free from manual labour. Barnabas and Paul had the right to expect the churches to relieve them of the necessity to labour with their hands by accepting responsibility for their material support. If this was their right, then it was also their right to forgo that support. We might think this would give Paul and Barnabas greater respect in the sight of the Corinthian Christians. But curiously, it gave them less respect. It was almost as if the Corinthian Christians were saying, 'If Paul and Barnabas were real apostles, we would support them, but since they are not supported, we suppose they are not real apostles.'

9.7: Paul presses his point with more questions that require negative answers. In an army, the soldiers are supported; farmers feed on the field in which they work; and shepherds are supported by the sheep for which they care. Therefore, it should not seem strange to the Corinthian Christians that Paul has the right to be supported by the people to whom he ministers. Christian workers who serve the spiritual interest of their members should not be denied material support or compensation.

9.8–10: Paul substantiates his right to support by citing the Scriptures (cf. Deuteronomy 25.4). If God was concerned about the care of oxen, do you think God is less concerned about ministers? Again, if the Corinthians have given material support to other servants of God, Paul is entitled to support since he planted the church. If an ox gets to eat some of the grain it is helping to grind, Christians should support the leaders who minister to and among them. As one preacher rightly puts it, 'Since oxen cannot read, this verse was not written for them.' Paul is establishing the principle that a minister has the right to be supported by the people to whom he is ministering.

9.11. If we have sown spiritual good among you: Paul here makes it plain that it is right for the spiritual work of God's ministers to be repaid with the material support of the people to whom they minister.

9.12a. If others share this rightful claim on you: The Corinthian Christians supported others in ministry. The problem with them was they

63

refused to support Paul, and thought less of him because he did not receive it.

9.12b. We have not made use of this right . . . rather than put an obstacle in the way of the gospel of Christ: Paul affirms his right to be supported by the people to whom he ministers. He also affirms his right to not use that right – if using it will constitute an obstacle to the proclamation of the gospel of Christ. What matters is the work of the gospel. Paul is prepared to go without his rights, because he does not want to let money get in the way of the gospel.

9.14. Those who proclaim the gospel should get their living by the gospel: Paul's summary statement is conclusive. This command from the Lord (Matthew 10.10; Luke 10.8) means that those who preach the gospel have the right to be supported by those to whom they preach.

9.15. I have made no use of any of these rights: Although Paul would insist on financial or material support for others, he did not do so for himself. He would rather support himself with his business as a tentmaker than ask the Corinthians for money and muddy the waters about his motivation. In the Greek culture in which Paul ministered, people looked down upon all manual labour. So the Corinthian Christians seemed to think less of Paul because he worked to support himself. This does not embarrass Paul at all. He will boast about it!

9.16. An obligation is laid on me, and woe betide me if I do not proclaim the gospel!: Paul understands his ministry as not just a matter of choice or personal ambition. It is something he has been called to do, something he has to do. He was called to preach and feels compelled to fulfil the call. Paul's boasting is not that he preaches the gospel but that he is able to do it without asking his hearers for support.

9.17–18. For if I do this of my own will: In Paul's day, there were many religious entrepreneurs, who were out to preach in order to get money. Paul is happy to distance himself from such people by never taking an offering, so no one will think he might abuse his authority in the gospel. This is Paul's reward. However, for some ministers it has nothing to do with choice. It is just because of their circumstances. But if some do not receive support willingly, then they have a reward.

9.19f. I have made myself a slave to all: Have you ever been accused of being inconsistent? Some Corinthians probably accused Paul of inconsistency and contradictory behaviour. But Paul goes to great lengths to show that the apparent inconsistency of his conduct is solely due to his one overruling aim, to be the most effective witness to the gospel that he can possibly be. He sees an opportunity to show how other apparent inconsistencies in the pattern of his life have the same explanation. As he is to explain in the following chapter (10.23–33), it is his practice to eat or not eat marketplace food, depending on the situation. This is seemingly contradictory to his previous injunction in 1 Corinthians 8. Paul's defence is simple: people cannot be evangelized at arm's length. To bring the gospel home to men and women and win them to allegiance to Christ, the preacher must get alongside them. Paul is willing to shed every vestige of his inherited Jewish lifestyle and adopt the lifestyle of anyone at all or, on the other hand, to resume Jewish manners and customs, in order to reach out to others. Such is Paul's passion for the gospel.

9.22–23. I have become all things to all people, so that I might by any means save some. I do it for the sake of the gospel: Paul's passion is to see people be saved, not to stand proudly on his rights. He will gladly give up his rights if it helps others to believe. As noted by Gordon Fee, 'This passage has often been looked to for the idea of "accommodation" in evangelism, that is, of adapting the message to the language and perspective of the recipients.' But as Fee goes further to say, 'Despite the need for that discussion to be carried on, this passage does not speak directly to it.' This has to do with how one lives or behaves among those whom one wishes to evangelize. We should not think Paul changed his message to appeal to different groups (cf. 1 Corinthians 1.22–23); but he would change his behaviour and manner of approach. If he lived today, would Paul eat pork in the presence of a Muslim while trying to win him to Christ, or in his own time would he have eaten non-kosher food (e.g. a bacon burger) in front of a Jew while he told him that Jesus loves him? Probably not. He will not eat meat from the pagan temples with those who are still in awe of idols as gods. Paul's primary allegiance is to Christ and his identity is wrapped up with being in Christ. His particular actions with any one group will not betray Jesus. But he will act in ways that make it easier, not harder for others to come to faith in Jesus.

9.24. Run in such a way that you may win it: Paul uses an athletic metaphor to press home his point. He reminds the Corinthians that in a race only one of the contestants wins the prize. He then goes on to urge the Corinthians to run in such a way that they will win. Using himself as an example, he warns the Corinthians against presumption. Paul tells the Corinthians to train and compete as athletes who really want to win. Without effort, nothing can be won in a sporting event. To compete as athletes, people must be temperate, a term that refers to the manner in which Roman athletes had to train for ten months before being allowed in the games.

9.25–27. Athletes exercise self-control in all things: Continuing with the athletic imagery, Paul refers to the rigorous training that every athlete undergoes. The athletes subject themselves to rigorous discipline to win a fading wreath. Paul knew that Christians were to practise self-denial that they might win a garland that never fades, a crown of life. In other words, the Christian life calls for total commitment. The garland that never fades is eternal life. A runner who stops to enjoy the view will not win the race. Paul wanted nothing to happen that would disqualify him from receiving the ultimate prize.

STUDY SUGGESTIONS

Word study

1   What do the terms *apologia* and *anakrino* mean? How were these terms commonly used in Paul's day? What does Paul's choice of these words tell us about his situation?

Review of content

2   In this chapter, Paul provides himself as an example of disciplined freedom. Explain the significance of this in light of the current Corinthian situation.

3   Why did Paul insist on doing manual labour when the Corinthian culture disdained those who did such work?

4   What was Paul's one overriding aim? How did this impact his dealings with different people groups (i.e. Jews or Gentiles)?

Bible study

5   Read Matthew 10.5–15 and Luke 10.1–12.
   (a) What instructions did Jesus give those he sent to minister concerning their daily provisions?
   (b) From reading these passages, what (if any) responsibilities lie with the people of the Church in providing for ministers, missionaries, etc.?
   (c) What were the consequences for the towns that did not accept those whom Jesus sent? What are the implications of this for us today?

Discussion and application

6   In your local church context, what are some possible benefits relating to the pastor receiving financial support from the church? Is this support in any way detrimental? Explain. How might the refusal of material support or compensation today serve to further the gospel, especially considering the consumerist mindset prevalent in many churches?

7   In what ways might money hinder the gospel message?
   (a) Could a lavish lifestyle in the name of 'ministerial compensation' do harm to the promulgation of the gospel?
   (b) Given the viable option of pastors receiving monetary support, in what ways does your church decide the amount of the monetary compensation?

8 Why is disciplined freedom in one's life so important in the Christian journey?

   (a) What is the relationship of the call for unity of the Corinthian church to the disciplined freedom in which each believer is to live?

   (b) In what ways is your own life characterized by such disciplined freedom?

9 Paul's decisions pertaining to his lifestyle are always made in relation to others. What are the implications of this for our own missionary efforts today? How should this impact the way we 'do' church in our particular context?

10 What are the implications of Paul's statement, 'I have made myself a slave to all, so that I might win more of them', for Christian leaders? As ministers, are we to be served or to serve? Is such servant leadership modelled in your congregation? In what ways?

10.1—11.1: Flee from idolatry

 Summary

10.1–13: Danger of idolatry and warning against overconfidence

10.14–22: Incompatibility of idols with Christian communion

10.23—11.1: Use of Christian freedom for the sake of others

 Introduction

Chapter 10 of 1 Corinthians continues the discussion introduced in chapter 8 and picked up again in chapter 9 with regard to what the Corinthian Christians should do concerning food which has been sacrificed to idols. In chapter 8, Paul argues that the Corinthians' right to eat food sacrificed to idols, based on their 'knowledge', is to be set aside for the sake of their 'weaker' brothers and sisters. Love must trump knowledge. In chapter 9, Paul provides himself as an example of the type of sacrifice that he demanded from the Corinthians. Although he has 'rights' such as marriage and material support, he forgoes them so that his ministry of the gospel will be enhanced. In this chapter Paul goes on to cast his discussion in a wider historical and scriptural context – the exodus story. For Paul, the problem of the Corinthians simply mirrored the problem of the ancient Israelites when they left Egypt for the promised land of Canaan. They were plagued with the problems of self-indulgence and instant self-gratification. The consequences were dire. So Paul warns the Corinthians to avoid the mistakes of the Israelites, lest they suffer the same fate.

 ## Interpretation and notes

10.1a. I do not want you to be unaware: Paul continues with the theme he has introduced in 1 Corinthians 9.24–27, in which he emphasizes the danger of disqualification. In doing so, he points to the example of the ancient Israelites who, although they experienced many miracles and enjoyed many blessings and special privileges, failed to enter the promised land of Canaan. Instead, many of them perished in the wilderness. Paul goes on to enumerate the blessings of the Israelites.

10.1b. Our ancestors were all under the cloud, and all passed through the sea: In the exodus story, Israel was not only miraculously delivered, but also was guided by God in its journey through the wilderness by means of the pillar of cloud by day and the pillar of fire by night. Israel's experience in the exodus from Egypt prefigures that of the Corinthians becoming Christians.

10.2. All were baptized into Moses: The point of Paul's comparison is to show that the Israelites were baptized into Moses in the same manner as the Corinthians have been baptized into Christ. Hence, Paul compares the situation of the Corinthians with that of the Israelites in which baptism conveys identification with someone. The Israelites were identified with Moses just as the Corinthians were identified with Christ.

10.3–4. All ate the same spiritual food, and all drank the same spiritual drink: In referring to the manna (Exodus 16.12–35) and the water from the rock (Exodus 17.6; Numbers 20.11) as spiritual, Paul suggests that, although the food and drink were physical and ordinary, they nevertheless have spiritual significance. Paul emphatically declares that 'the rock was Christ'. Thus, he symbolically connects Christ with the water-giving rock in the wilderness.

10.5. Nevertheless, God was not pleased with most of them: Here is Paul's point of comparison. God supernaturally met all the needs of all the Israelites during their wanderings in the wilderness. However, in spite of all the divine provision, the Israelites failed to enter into the land. It is important to notice the use of 'all' five times in vv. 1–4. Many Israelites left Egypt; all shared divine blessings and privileges; only two (Joshua and Caleb) entered the promised land. The lesson is clear: divine blessings and privileges are not guarantees against disqualification if one chooses to live contrary to God's word. No one can ever say that they failed to finish the race because they were not adequately provided for. Those who failed to enter into the promised land were those who lacked self-discipline, and who fell due to their self-indulgence.

10.6. These things occurred as examples for us: In vv. 6–10, Paul identifies the specific sins that plagued the ancient Israelites, resulting in their failure to please God and to possess the land of Canaan. Each of these failures is a sin of self-indulgence, and each points to a sin that is prominent in the Corinthian church of Paul's day, as well as in our Church today. In allowing these things to happen, God had in mind not only that generation but our own. What were their problems? The answer lies in Paul's exhortations to the Corinthians.

10.7. Do not become idolaters: Paul alludes to the story of the golden calf in Exodus 32.6. This is a command that directly relates to the problem addressed by Paul in 1 Corinthians 8—10. The ancient Israelites ate in the presence of the golden calf. With this, Paul shows a direct parallel between the misconduct of the Corinthians and the eating of cultic meals in the idol's presence in Corinth. The verb underlying 'play' quite possibly carries overtones of sexual play.

10.8. We must not indulge in sexual immorality: The Corinthians are to abstain from sexual immorality, a grievous sin that led to the destruction of 23,000 Israelites in one day. This command dovetails with Paul's earlier discussion in 1 Corinthians 5.1–13 and 6.12–20 concerning sexual immorality among the Corinthians. The story in Numbers 25.1–9 to which Paul alludes is particularly relevant to the Corinthians. In that instance the plague that God sent on Israel was due to sexual immorality that was associated with idolatry.

10.9. We must not put Christ to the test: Paul warns the Corinthians against putting the Lord to the test as the Israelites did, whereupon they were bitten to death by fiery serpents. Paul alludes to the story in Numbers 21.4–9 so as to show the self-indulgence of the Corinthians. Like the Israelites of old, they had cravings that could not be easily satisfied. They rejected the manna due to their lack of satisfaction with God's provision. They wanted 'something else', thus tempting God.

10.10–11. Do not complain as some of them did: Finally, Paul warns the Corinthians against their constant complaints and grumbles, something that also characterized the Israelites. The Israelites seized every opportunity to grumble against God and Moses. As a result they were killed in the wilderness. The Corinthians, like the Israelites, grumbled against Paul about his leadership, teachings and corrections. Paul concludes his warnings by repeating what he said in v. 6, that the experience of the Israelites in the wilderness happened for 'our benefit'. It was, in a sense, symbolic and recorded as a warning for Paul's day and ours.

10.12. Watch out that you do not fall: The Corinthians must learn from the example of the Israelites lest they suffer the same fate. They must avoid self-confidence, self-reliance and complacency. Presuming upon God's grace is a great danger that believers must avoid.

10.13. No testing has overtaken you that is not common to everyone. God is faithful . . . but with the testing he will also provide the way out so that you may be able to endure it: Paul goes on to show that God's power is available to keep the Corinthians standing. Paul seeks to build up a proper confidence, not in themselves but in God, who will not allow them to be overwhelmed by trial. God keeps faith and will not let you be tested beyond your powers, but when the test comes he will at the same time provide a way out and so enable you to endure.

10.14. My dear friends, flee from the worship of idols: Paul appeals to the Corinthians as dear friends, and the exhortation is an urgent one: that the Corinthians flee from the worship of idols. He has just demonstrated the consequences of idolatry as seen in the story of Israel.

10.16. The cup of blessing . . . is it not a sharing in the body of Christ?: Participation in the Lord's Supper brings about a particular bond with Christ. When partaking of the Lord's Supper, believers enter into a communal relationship with others in their fellowship and with the Lord. Just as the Lord's Supper speaks of unity and fellowship with Jesus, so these pagan banquets, given in the honour of idols, speak of unity with demons who take advantage of misdirected worship.

In Africa today, as it was in the ancient world, meals are significant. To eat at the same table with someone indicates friendship and fellowship with that person. So to eat at the table of a pagan temple was not as innocent as it seemed. To eat at a pagan temple banquet was to have fellowship at the altar of idols. Paul's point may seem unclear to us, but it was plain to the Corinthians. The pagan sacrifices to idols in Corinth were a tough issue for the Church. Does a believer eat the meat used in such sacrifices when it is resold in the market? Does one go to dinner in a person's house when they might use such meat? Could one participate in the ceremonies themselves? Idolatry was not merely a theoretical issue in Corinth. It was a real-life, everyday problem.

10.18. Consider the people of Israel: Paul develops the warning first sounded in v. 14. He has stressed the reality of the participation brought about in the Lord's Supper, a participation in the body and blood of Christ with others. Now he is to argue that participation in any cultic meal is not a harmless act but one that relates the worshippers, to their detriment, to some reality behind the rite.

10.19f.: The Corinthians were justifying their participation in pagan cultic meals on the grounds that an idol has no real existence, so that any food offered to an idol is no more than mere food (v. 19). Paul insists that any food offered on a pagan altar is not offered to any being worthy of the name of God, but this does not mean that the worshippers are not in touch with anything at all. He echoes a belief expressed in a number of Old Testament passages that pagan sacrifices, as well as the sacrifices offered to pagan gods, are in fact offered to demons (see especially Deuteronomy 32.17). It follows that the two forms of sacred meals, the Lord's Supper and the pagan cultic meal, are incompatible.

10.21–22. You cannot drink the cup of the Lord and the cup of demons: Paul has already acknowledged an idol is nothing in the world (8.4). As such, he is not saying idols are actually demons. Instead he is saying demonic spirits take advantage of idol worship to deceive and enslave people. Without knowing it, idol worshippers are glorifying demons in their sacrifice. The unwitting fellowship of some of the Corinthian Christians with demons, by participating in the dinners at the pagan temples, will provoke the Lord to jealousy. He has a right over all our worship, and has a right to be offended if we give our fellowship to demons.

10.23. 'All things are lawful', but not all things are beneficial . . . but not all things build up: The Corinthian Christians, with their focus on their own 'rights' and their own 'knowledge', were asking the wrong question. They should have shown less concern for what harm the eating of food sacrificed to idols could cause to them and more concern about how beneficial or edifying it was to others. So Paul argues that because something is permitted does not mean it is beneficial. The Corinthians wanted to know how much they could get away with and still be Christians. For Paul, that's the wrong approach.

10.24. Do not seek your own advantage, but that of others: Just because something is harmless in itself does not mean it should be done. Individual or personal 'rights' or what people know to be permissible for them are not the standards by which they judge their actions or behaviour. Paul urges the Corinthians to look after the interests of others, not their own, and in this way build up the community. This is, in fact, the dominant emphasis of the whole passage, that the Christian's conduct must always be determined by consideration for the neighbour's spiritual welfare, the neighbour's conscience, so that the Church may be built up (cf. vv. 28, 32).

10.25–27. Eat whatever is sold in the meat market without raising any question: Paul has previously said that the Corinthians are not to eat of things sacrificed to idols because they have been offered to demons. He now tells them they may eat food sold in the marketplace. The sacrifices lose their religious character when sold in the market, so Paul permits the Corinthians to eat whatever food is provided for them at a private meal without asking any questions. Paul does not prohibit socializing with non-Christians; only the meal of fellowship at the pagan temples.

**10.28–29. But if someone says to you, 'This has been offered in sacrifice',
then do not eat it:** Here, Paul has in mind the setting where Christians
are warned about the food by their unbelieving hosts, or Christian hosts
with sensitive conscience. In that case, believers must not eat for the sake
of the conscience of others. Christians are not to act in a way that would
make it difficult for another person either to hear the gospel or to remain
a believer.

10.30. If I partake with thankfulness: Paul allows the believers who
desire to eat food offered to idols to do so, as long as they neither injure
their consciences nor offend the conscience of others. To drive home his
point, Paul says that the believer who eats the food should do so with
thanksgiving since the food itself is not the problem. This policy opens
Paul to the criticism of being inconsistent. Although it may appear so,
he is very consistent according to one principle: liberty is to be exercised
within the limits of love and the welfare of others.

10.31. Do everything for the glory of God: The purpose of our lives is
not to see how much we can get away with and still be Christians; rather,
it is to glorify God.

10.32–33. Give no offence: Giving offence means something more serious
than hurting people's feelings. An offence is an occasion to stumble,
causing an injury, or leading someone else into sin. Paul is saying none of
our actions or behaviours should encourage another to sin. His concern
was not seeking his own advantage but that all might be saved. It should
be ours too.

11.1: Paul concludes his discussion with an exhortation that the Corinthians are to imitate him. The verse is a fitting conclusion to Paul's
emphasis on selflessness. While it is true that Christians must all
ultimately look to Jesus, ministers should be examples for those who are
looking to Jesus. Paul is quick to add that he is to be followed as he in turn
follows Christ, setting a limit and direction on the way Christians imitate
others.

 Special note B

Case studies

1   Chinua Achebe's *Things Fall Apart* was first published in 1959. The
    book was written against the backdrop of Nigeria's struggle for
    independence and as a response to novels, such as Joseph Conrad's
    Heart of Darkness, that treat Africa as a primordial and cultureless
    foil for Europe. Fed up with reading white men's accounts of how
    primitive, socially backward and, most importantly, how naïve
    Africans were without language, Achebe sought to convey a fuller

understanding of one African culture and, in so doing, give voice to an under-represented and exploited colonial subject. The book portrays the clash between Nigeria's white colonial government and the traditional culture of the indigenous Igbo people. One of the cultural traditions of the Igbo is the breaking of kola nut, which is accompanied by prayer to ancestors. In the book, when Unoka presented Okoye with kola nut, he prayed to their ancestors for life, health and protection from their enemies. That is the practice in the community. Given what Paul has just said in this section, the question then is, 'What would Okoye have done if he were a Christian?'

2 Deji is a Christian and has a sister who is married to a Muslim. He happened to visit his sister during one of the religious festivals. He witnessed the slaughtering of the ram that was accompanied with some recitations. It was time to eat and he suddenly found himself in an awkward situation. If he did not eat, he risked offending his sister and brother-in-law. More importantly, he thought he might shut the door on every opportunity to present the gospel to them. On the other hand, he thought that his participation would amount to a validation of their practice. What should he do?

 ## STUDY SUGGESTIONS

Word study

1 In 1 Corinthians 10.7, Paul alludes to the story of the golden calf as found in Exodus 32.6. The verb meaning 'play' may have what connotation? How might this be significant concerning Paul's admonishment of the Corinthians?

Review of content

2 While considering Paul's exhortations to the Corinthians in 1 Corinthians 10, discuss some of the sins that Israel committed. What relation do such sins have to the present situation of the Corinthians?

3 Based on the content of this chapter, give a definition of 'offence'. In light of Paul's admonitions, which is primary when considering our relationships with others, liberty or love? What is the relationship between the two?

4 In view of the Lord's Supper, why was participating in a pagan celebratory meal not acceptable? The Lord's Supper speaks of unity and fellowship with Jesus. Of what do these pagan banquets speak?

Bible study

5 Read Exodus 16.1—17.7; Numbers 20.1–13 and Deuteronomy 1.34–40.

 (a) In what ways did God supernaturally provide for the needs of the Israelites while they were in the Desert?

 (b) Who of the Israelites did God allow to enter into the promised land?

 (c) Why did the remaining Israelites not enter into the promised land? Does this reflect poorly on God's provision for the Israelites? Justify your answer.

Discussion and application

6 In reference to 1 Corinthians 10.5, the lesson emerged that 'divine blessings and privileges are not guarantees against disqualification if one chooses to live contrary to God's words'. How might this impact our understanding of salvation specifically regarding individual and communal responsibility?

7 What is the promise of God available to the Christian in times of temptation? In what ways do you think that this promise may be abused?

8 In 10.31 Paul says, 'So, whether you eat or drink, or whatever you do, do everything for the glory of God.' What might this look like in your home, in your job, in your relationships, etc.? Are there things that cannot be done to the glory of God? If so, name some of them and give reasons why.

9 How important is consideration for the spiritual welfare of others in determining a specific course of action? Does not this make us liable to lose our liberty as individuals?

10 In 10.13, what do you think Paul means by, 'No testing has overtaken you that is not common to everyone'? Is this comforting or offensive to you? Why? How might this affect our understanding of suffering?

1 Corinthians 11.2—14.40
Christian worship

11.2–34: Head covering and the Lord's Supper

 Summary

11.2–16: Head covering: let men be men, and women be women

11.17–34: The Lord's Supper

 Introduction

In 1 Corinthians 11—14, Paul focuses on various issues related to Christian worship. But Paul addresses two specific problems in 11.2–34. First is the problem of head covering (vv. 2–16). Some Corinthians seemed to be violating the prevalent cultural norm regarding head covering. While some Corinthian women were praying and prophesying without head covering, some men prayed and prophesied with their hair long. So Paul repudiates the abandonment of the prevalent custom of the day – head covering for women and short hair for men. Second, Paul addresses the problem that surrounded the practice of the Lord's Supper (vv. 17–34). He reminds the Corinthians that when they gather together to share in a communal meal at the Lord's holy table, it is not the table of any particular patron. Behaviour or practices that exclude members of the congregation from partaking in the Lord's Supper because of their social status are a serious hindrance to establishing authentic Christian community. So Paul tells the Corinthians that their attitude and actions at the table not only betray its purpose but also contradict the nature of the Church, that is, the body of Christ.

 Interpretation and notes

11.2. I commend you: Paul starts by commending the Corinthians for always remembering and keeping the traditions he has taught them. However, he proceeds at once to give specific instructions on the appropriate manner in which women and men are to dress for worship, perhaps as a result of reports that he has received about a problem concerning attire.

11.3. Christ is the head of every man, and the husband is the head of his wife, and God is the head of Christ: Paul makes an important statement about the mutual relationships of God, Christ, man and woman, from which he issues further directives. But the main question remains. What does Paul mean by the word 'head' and how is it to be understood, particularly in terms of the relationship between husband and wife? There are three possibilities, all of which have interpretative difficulties.

1 The word 'head' can be used either in a literal (vv. 4a, 5a and 7a) or metaphorical (v. 3) sense. Most commentators translate the word *kephale* to mean 'authority' or 'ruler'.

2 A common idiomatic use of *kephale* in Greek is to denote a source. Understood in this way, Paul is thinking not of hierarchies of rulers and ruled but of a series of relationships of derived being.

3 Recent interpreters suggest that 'head' simply denotes something or someone who is pre-eminent or 'topmost'. Thus, the head of the household is the public face or the one who represents the family. Although this is close to option 1 above, and as such may denote authority or rulership, that is not its basic denotation.

What is important to Paul in this passage is 'honour'. Each head should be honoured. Paul does not suggest that man is the lord of woman. In the following verses Paul is concerned that men and women in practical ways show their respect to God in matters of worship, particularly in praying and prophesying.

11.4: Paul states his main argument, that men who pray or prophesy with their heads covered bring shame on their head; but women bring shame on their head if they pray or prophesy without covering their heads. Why does Paul say this? A variety of possible reasons have been given.

1 It is the cultural practice of that day.

2 It blurs the proper male/female relationship. The Corinthian women, it appears, were acting as if distinctions between the sexes no longer existed. Such behaviour would be entirely consistent with the eschatological view of the Corinthians. The Corinthians would probably have argued that if the age to come had been consummated already and was here now, it would follow that distinctions between men and women would have been eliminated.

3 Some interpreters suggest that well-to-do women in the Corinthian church, especially those who came from the areas of the Mediterranean where head coverings were not considered necessary, considered the requirement or restriction of wearing a veil in public unnecessary.

Head veiled and unveiled: An important question in this passage is what 'veil' or, literally, 'covering' means. There are two main views. The first understands the passage as primarily referring to women having long or short hair. The second is the interpretation that understands the passage to be primarily about a literal covering or veil. In keeping with the former understanding, not too long ago, many in the Wesleyan tradition as well as Pentecostals understood the passage to be about women having long hair as a covering. A woman with short hair was considered a 'liberal' or even thought to have backslidden. The Apostolic Faith in Nigeria fits into this category. Even today, many Mennonite women wear 'prayer bonnets' in order to conform to their understanding of the passage. Head covering remains an important practice in many African churches. In its entire context, and particularly in light of v. 16, the second interpretation appears to be in keeping with Paul's thought. However, it must be understood that Paul was addressing a specific, cultural problem in the Corinthian congregation.

11.5. Any woman who prays or prophesies: The passage is important because it shows that Paul clearly accepted the right of women to pray and prophesy aloud and in public although some argue that he must be talking about praying and prophesying in private. It is true that prayer may be a private matter, but prophecy is public by its very nature. Although Paul was a Jew, and was brought up in a patriarchal Jewish tradition, it is clear that he expected women to take an active and significant role in the ministry and worship of the Church. He refers elsewhere to women as his co-labourers in the gospel (cf. Philippians 4.2, 3) and mentions the ministry of Priscilla and Aquila without making a distinction between the kind of ministry and work the men were engaged in and that of the women.

11.7–9. A man . . . is the image and reflection of God; but the woman is the reflection of man: Paul provides further theological justification for his arguments in preceding verses. His argument is based on the creation account of Genesis 2. Paul explains his assertion that the woman reflects the glory of man because she is formed from him. Man and woman are equal in Christ but Paul does not suggest that in Christ all distinctions between male and female have disappeared. Equality is not to lead to the abandonment of social norms or the abolition of gender differences. Instead these verses suggest a divine order of sexes that affirms the family headship of man, headship that must exclude dominance, injustice, maltreatment, humiliation or harshness.

11.10. A woman ought to have a symbol of authority on her head, because of the angels: Although Paul's statement in v. 10 is enigmatic, it is interesting to note that, in many parts of Africa, whether Christians or not, during prayer women cover their heads with a scarf or hat. They usually do so because of the sense of a divine presence, not necessarily that of angels. It is also not unusual to hear people say when there is a sudden, unexplainable interruption of silence during a conversation or prayer that 'an angel is passing by'.

11.11–12: Lest Paul's words be misunderstood as a call for the absolute subordination of women, he affirms male/female equality and mutual interdependence in vv. 11 and 12. Paul must have invoked the issues of hierarchy only in order to address the situation in Corinth.

11.13–15: Paul's next argument for head covering refers to nature. He begins with a call to the Corinthians to judge for themselves and an appeal to their sense of what is fitting. Paul says that whereas long hair disgraces a man, it is a woman's glory. This argument simply reinforces the conclusion that it is appropriate for women to pray and prophesy with heads covered but for men with heads uncovered.

11.16: Finally, Paul appeals to the custom among the congregations of God's people (literally, 'the churches of God'). Paul seeks to check the enthusiasm of the Corinthians, not by asserting the subordination of women to men even in Christ, but rather by maintaining that when women and men exercise their God-given gifts in worship they should do so in a way that does not obscure the continuing differences between men and women. Though in Christ, they are still living in the present age, which is characterized by sexual differentiation.

11.17–18: Paul now addresses another aspect of the worship life of the Corinthians that has been reported to him. Although the exact order is not known, it would appear that the Lord's Supper is held in conjunction with a communal meal. Paul is not concerned with the sequence of events during the celebration. Instead he criticizes the manner in which it is celebrated. He mentions the first disturbing news: the Corinthians are divided, a problem that echoes the situation addressed in 1 Corinthians 1. However, it appears that the division here was not over personalities but between the 'haves' and 'have-nots'. In Graeco-Roman society, people were usually seated according to socio-economic status at meal tables. The rich had contempt for the poor and despised them even though they were in the same community. Paul condemns such behaviour. The Lord's Supper is an event that should be accessible to all social levels. By shaming those less fortunate in the community, the Corinthian church in fact shames itself. Rather than honouring the body of Christ, the Corinthians have brought reproach to the Church.

11.20–22: Paul's condemnation is more pointed in this verse than in v. 17. The Corinthians were celebrating the Lord's Supper in a manner that denied its very nature. Paul now gives further evidence of the unworthiness of their celebration of the Lord's Supper. What ought to be a visible expression of their oneness and equality in Christ has become an occasion at which the less privileged members of the community are degraded and humiliated. It is the slighting of the less privileged members of the community and that alone that evokes Paul's rebuke in the present paragraph.

11.23. For I received from the Lord what I also handed on to you. Here, as later in 15.1 and 15.3, Paul uses words that are regularly used in the New Testament of the reception and transmission of tradition. Paul's point in the context is that the tradition that he passed on to the Corinthians came from the Lord, in the sense that Jesus himself was its ultimate source. The celebration of the Lord's Supper is grounded in Jesus' final meal with his disciples. It is a tradition that has come straight from the Lord. Thus, Paul is reminding the Corinthians that the supper that they are abusing is rooted in the words and actions of Christ on the night of his betrayal, something that demands that they take time to reflect the intense pathos of that event. For Paul the supper is not only rooted in Christ's words but also his actions.

11.24f. Do this in remembrance of me: Paul impresses upon the Corinthians that every time they eat this meal it is to be for the remembrance of Christ. As such we must be careful not to minimize the significance of the Lord's Supper by reducing it to a mere symbol. Paul puts the emphasis on remembering Jesus, on what he said about the meaning of his own death for us. They are powerful pictures to partake of, to enter into, as we see the Lord's table as the new Passover. Christ's death, which is celebrated in the Lord's Supper, established the new covenant between God and his people – a covenant that promises forgiveness for every sinner that repents. Because of what Jesus did on the cross, we can have a new covenant relationship with God.

11.26. You proclaim the Lord's death until he comes: The Lord's Supper is of crucial importance because of its confessional nature. It proclaims the Lord's death until he comes. Participation in the Lord's Supper becomes a visible proclamation of the message of the Church: Christ's death and resurrection.

11.27. Answerable for the body and blood of the Lord: Paul's warning against offending against the body and blood of the Lord is best understood as a reference to Christ who died for these brothers and sisters. The thought of the presence of the risen Christ is not prominent, as we have seen. On the other hand, an allusion to the Church is ruled out by the reference to the blood.

11.28. Examine yourselves: Paul's exhortation to the Corinthians to examine themselves is not just a call to self-examination or moral introspection but a concern for the believing community to ensure that their attitudes and activity are worthy of the spiritual tradition that the Lord Jesus left for believers.

11.29. Discerning the body: This verse has sometimes been understood to refer to disregard for the sacrament or failure to discern the body of Christ in the elements as distinct from common meals. This is highly unlikely. Such an interpretation fits neither the Letter as a whole nor the passage. In the light of v. 27, 'not discerning the body' may imply that the Corinthians did not discern the body given for them (cf. v. 24). It amounts to closing their eyes to the meaning of the death of the Lord for them and for everyone. But as Paul has shown in the Letter, failure to recognize fellow Christians for what they are, brothers and sisters for whom Christ died, is in itself a failure to discern the meaning of the cross. Hence, it seems better to understand the 'body' in this verse as referring to the Church. The Corinthian believers are failing to appreciate that what makes this meal different from any other is the fact that here they constitute one body, the body of Christ. The Corinthians are failing to discern that body as represented by the members of the church, particularly the least and lowliest.

11.30–32. For this reason many of you are weak and ill, and some have died: Their abuse of the Eucharist (a potential fellowship with the Risen Christ and remembrance of the earthly Jesus) was serious and had grave negative consequences. Because the Corinthians have failed to discern the body, they have fallen under the judgement of God. It has brought upon many of them sickness and even death. Yet as Paul argues, the aim of this judgement is salvation. Judgement has been inflicted upon them precisely in order to save them from being condemned with the rest of the world.

11.33–34. My brothers and sisters, when you come together to eat, wait for one another: Paul concludes the passage with specific and practical directives: when you meet for this meal, wait for one another. And if you are so hungry that you cannot wait for latecomers, eat before you leave home, so that in meeting together you may not fall under judgement.

 STUDY SUGGESTIONS

Word study

1   In the first part of 1 Corinthians 11, what Greek word is used for 'head'?

   (a) In what two metaphorical ways can this word be used?

   (b) How often is its Hebrew equivalent found in the Old Testament?

   (c) What was a common idiomatic use of the Greek term meaning 'head', and how does this affect the meaning of Paul's discussion in vv. 3–7?

2   What is the Greek word in v. 10 meaning 'authority'? What two interpretations of this verse are mentioned in this chapter?

Review of content

3   Why did Paul give specific instructions on how men and women were supposed to pray? What was happening socially at that time

to prompt these instructions, and how did the Corinthians' view of eschatology affect this situation?

4 What are the four arguments Paul gives for the use of head coverings? Did Paul support the public prayer and prophecy of women?

5 Paul speaks of a division in the Corinthian church in conjunction with the Lord's Supper. To what division is he referring?

Bible study

6 Read Matthew 26.14–56. This is the account of the institution of the Lord's Supper and the betrayal and arrest of Jesus.

(a) Compare and contrast the institution of the Lord's Supper by Jesus and the observance of the Lord's Supper by the Corinthians in vv. 17–23 in light of the events surrounding Jesus' institution of the sacred meal.

(b) What do you think Jesus would have done differently in Corinth?

Discussion and application

7 When Paul speaks in 11.8–9 of the relationship between men and women, how do these verses relate to v. 3 pertaining to the definition of 'head'? How can the interpretations of these verses affect the life of the Church?

8 The Lord's Supper is to be a time of intense reflection – it is to proclaim the Lord's death until he comes. Based on the manner in which the Lord's Supper is practised in your local church, is there priority upon such reflection and/or proclamation? What are some creative ways in which your local church could observe the Lord's Supper in a manner which encourages such reflection and/or proclamation?

9 What should be the focus of the Lord's Supper? Personal introspection and confession, or the unity and loving fellowship of the community? What are the possible consequences of participating in the Lord's Supper without having the right attitudes?

10 Paul states in v. 29 that 'all who eat and drink without discerning the body, eat and drink judgement against themselves'. To what does the word 'body' refer here? Are we guilty of this same thing? How must we respond?

12.1–31: Many members, one body

 Summary

12.1–3: Concerning spiritual gifts

12.4–6: Same Spirit, same Lord, same God who gives the gifts

12.7–11: Differing gifts are given for the common good.

12.12–13: One Spirit, one body

12.14–20: One body, many members

12.21–27: Many members, one purpose

12.28–31: God's gifts

 Introduction

It was the year 1985 in the Philippines. A popular American Bible teacher was broadcasting a series of Bible studies on 1 Corinthians 12 and 14 on a Christian radio station. He argued forcefully that the manifestation of the spiritual gifts has ceased. The nightly broadcast was immediately followed by a rebuttal by an influential Filipino Pentecostal pastor. This went on until the series was completed. It was a matter of one Bible, and the same text, but two Christian preachers and two different interpretations. One wonders if some of the listeners would not have been confused. This story underscores the importance of 1 Corinthians 12—14 today. The importance and proper manifestation of spiritual gifts have been, and continue to be a divisive issue among believers. As such, believers are divided along the lines of those who believe in the practice of the gifts and those who reject it. In chapter 11, Paul has dealt with two issues that relate to Christian worship: head coverings and the Lord's Supper. Beginning from chapter 12, Paul addresses another important issue about which the Corinthians wrote to him: the exercise of spiritual gifts in the Church. The chapter begins Paul's long and detailed discussion about spiritual gifts (chapters 12—14).

 Interpretation and notes

12.1. Concerning spiritual gifts . . . I do not want you to be uninformed: The introduction demonstrates the importance that Paul attached to the topic. He does not want the Corinthians to be uninformed. This is one of three important truths of which Paul, in his Letters, specifically would not

want his readers to be uninformed. They were not to be ignorant of God's plan for Israel (Romans 11.25), of spiritual gifts (1 Corinthians 12.1), and about the second coming of Jesus (1 Thessalonians 4.13).

12.2–3. When you were pagans, you were enticed and led astray to idols that could not speak . . . and no one can say 'Jesus is Lord' except by the Holy Spirit: Because of their idolatrous background, the Corinthians were prone to a misunderstanding of the gifts. So, at the start, Paul lays down a broad principle for discerning matters regarding spiritual gifts: the Corinthians are to judge things by how they relate to Jesus Christ. This is an important principle that is applicable in all contexts.

Among the Aladura churches in the western part of Nigeria, specifically, in the Cherubim and Seraphim denomination (the writer attended the church and school from age six to 12), one is not hard pressed to see practices that are not scriptural. Yet there are 'prophecies', 'tongues' and 'miracles'. There are instances of spirit possession among African traditional religionists. In the Philippines, traditional healers known as *abularios*, often derided as 'fake healers', sometimes claim to have and exercise 'spiritual gifts'. One must ask important questions such as, 'Does a supposed spiritual gift glorify Jesus or is it for self-promotion? Does it promote the true Jesus, or a false one?'

12.4–6. There are varieties of gifts, but the same Spirit . . . there are varieties of services, but the same Lord . . . there are varieties of activities, but it is the same God who activates all of them in everyone: Paul's description of the gifts begins with both their nature and source. Paul uses three important words: 'gifts' (v. 4, Gk. *charismata*); 'services' (v. 5, Gk. *diakonia*), and 'workings' (v. 6, *energemata*). Paul's choice of words is not merely stylistic. While the gifts (*charismata*) emphasize the truth of the spiritual manifestations as an expression of God's grace, the administration or services (*diakonia*) suggest that the purpose of the gifts is not for self-enjoyment or edification. Rather the gifts are for loving ministry within the body of Christ. No one can boast of his or her spirituality or greatness. The operations or workings (*energemata*) suggest that in all these manifestations, God is powerfully at work through the Spirit.

The source of the gifts is the Triune God – the Spirit, the Lord, and God. It is not the Spirit alone who distributes the gifts. Paul accentuates the coherence of the gifts that God distributes as a unity-in-diversity, thus leaving no room for rivalry and competition within the body of Christ. Paul will develop this theme later in vv. 12–30. One particular gift must not and cannot be viewed as superior to the others; all come from the same God. His emphasis on unity-in-diversity in vv. 4–6 is rooted in the nature of the one, holy and triune God.

12.7. To each is given the manifestation of the Spirit for the common good: Paul indicates that the gifts are given to all the people of God for the benefit of all or the common good. God gives these gifts for the edification of the body. The gifts are not to bring personal benefit, advantage or status to the individual but advantage to the whole community. This advantage consists of building up the body of Christ into his image.

12.8–10. To one is given through the Spirit the utterance of wisdom, and to another the utterance of knowledge according to the same Spirit: After speaking in general terms, Paul mentions different manifestations of the Spirit in vv. 8–10. He begins by mentioning the word of wisdom. This is the unique ability to speak forth the wisdom of God, especially in an important or difficult situation, as shown in Solomon (1 Kings 3.16–18), Jesus (Luke 20.20–26), Stephen (Acts 7) and Paul (Acts 23).

This is followed by the word of knowledge. A Pentecostal preacher once defined it as 'a divinely granted flash of revelation concerning things which were hopelessly hidden from the senses', citing the examples of God's judgement for Eli, given as a voice in the night to Samuel (1 Samuel 3.13) and God's word to Peter regarding the arrival of messengers from Cornelius (Acts 10.19).

Next on the list is the gift of faith. Faith is an essential part of every Christian's life. Paul is not referring to the initial faith that is necessary for salvation. The gift of faith is the unique ability to trust God in all circumstances, as Peter did when he walked out of the boat onto the water (Matthew 14.22–33).

Next are the **gifts of healing**. The plural form of gifts may suggest that the manifestation of these gifts takes different forms at different times, depending on the particular needs. Moreover it is to be observed that these gifts are for the benefit of the community.

Next is the **working of miracles**, which seems to be a general term, encompassing supernatural activity including healing. In most cases the Holy Spirit overrides the power of nature.

The gift of prophecy refers both to the foretelling of the future and to the forthtelling of the mind of God for a particular situation. Some Christians have defined prophecy as 'preaching' but there are different words for preaching and for prophecy. Whereas preaching basically deals with proclamation, prophecy involves a supernatural revelation and words that are spoken under direct inspiration from God.

'Distinguishing between spirits' or 'discerning of spirits' (AV) describes the God-given ability to determine whether a supernatural manifestation has its source in God or not. An example is that of Paul in Acts (16.16–18).

The list continues with 'speaking in different kinds of tongues'. This refers to a supernatural utterance in a language that was not learnt by the speaker and which may or may not be a language known to others.

Lastly, Paul mentions the **interpretation of tongues**. Essentially, this refers to an intelligible presentation of the content of what was spoken in an unknown tongue.

12.11. All these are activated by one and the same Spirit: Paul reiterates the one source of the gifts – the Spirit. He goes on to proffer another reason for unity and a reason against any sense of superiority regarding the gifts. They are distributed not according to human will, but as the Spirit of God wills.

12.12–13. The body is one and has many members . . . For in the one Spirit we were all baptized into one body: Paul explains further what he summarily stated in v. 7: that the gifts are given for the advantage of all. Paul is concerned that the Corinthians' distorted view of the gifts has led to a lack of social cohesion among them. So Paul employs the analogy of the human body to drive home the points that he has been making in vv. 4–11. To correct the problem, Paul insists that the Corinthians have all been immersed (baptized) in one Spirit into the body of Christ. Believers in the Wesleyan tradition have sometimes emphasized the role of the Spirit in entire sanctification so that the emphasis of Paul on the role of the Spirit at salvation and baptism is sometimes neglected. Paul links baptism with receiving the Spirit in 12.13. He is not speaking of sanctification here or any other experience beyond salvation or conversion. Paul is speaking of a common ground to all Christians.

12.14–20: Paul starts and ends the paragraph with the same point: **the body does not consist of one member but of many.** How are we to think of the gathering together of believers? Paul introduces the metaphor of the human body. Just as it is totally absurd to think that the body is made up of only the most noticeable parts, so it is to think that the body could function without its less prominent parts. As such there is no room for either an inferiority complex or superiority complex within the body. Each part of the body needs the others in order to function well. One part must not be taken for the whole. So it is in the body of Christ. We need each other to function as God intends. By application, no one of the gifts is by itself sufficient.

12.21–27. The eye cannot say to the hand, 'I have no need of you': Paul's message in vv. 21–27 is quite clear. In the body every part is important. No member can do away with another. Some parts of the body that we regard as lacking honour are absolutely essential for our survival. Every member of the body, no matter how weak, is necessary. Take for example the small glands and the hidden parts of the human body such as kidneys and lungs that are not seen. Are they less important than the visible parts? No. While they may be considered less honourable because their functions are hidden, they are no less vital to the body than the visible members. The body is an example of mutual dependences. What happens to one part of the body affects the rest. In the context of Paul's discussion of the spiritual gifts we are to understand that all are to rejoice in the gifts of others. While a member who has no gift must not be despised, the one who seems to have an abundance of gifts is neither to boast nor to be envied. The application to Corinth and to congregational life today is clear. Those who appear to flaunt more spectacular gifts may actually turn out to be less indispensable than the quiet, faithful, prayerful, devoted, humble members whose values and contributions are often overlooked by the power seekers. Paul's overriding concern is with the unity of the social body of the Church, which he expresses in terms of a concern for the wholeness of the physical body.

12.28–31: Paul ends 1 Corinthians 12 with a list of some of the gifts that God gives to the community. In v. 28 Paul lists five gifts, starting with the apostle. He does not grade the gifts or create a hierarchical structure. He is simply enumerating the gifts. Apostles included not only the twelve, but also those like Paul and others. The climax of Paul's argument comes in vv. 29–30. He does not think that everyone will have every gift. The diversity of the gifts within the body of Christ is not only acceptable or expected; it is God's plan for how the body of Christ is to function. Thus, Paul's argument comes in a full circle. There are some important observations.

First, God distributes gifts and callings according to his pleasure. In the same manner that the Church does not bestow the gifts of healings, tongues and interpretation of tongues, etc., upon individuals, the Church does not create apostles, prophets, teachers and other ministry gifts. In recent years, there has grown renewed interest among some in the charismatic movement to restore 'apostolic-prophetic ministries' in the Church. Many ministers, particularly in the United States, and mostly African Americans, now take on the title 'apostle'. Three things are to be noted in contrast to Paul's use of the term.

1 Paul understood his commissioning as an apostle from the onset of his ministry, and not after the fact.

2 Paul and other apostles were so commissioned by God and did not require an ecclesiastical validation.

3 Paul's understanding of apostleship shows it to be more of a function than an office to be held.

The second observation is that the list does not exactly match the earlier list in 12.8–10, something that suggests that neither list is exhaustive. Paul discusses the ministry functions in dialogue with the existing situation at Corinth as well as in the light of the forms of leadership that suit his own cultural context. Paul does not suggest that these offices are the only or exact forms of leadership that are both timeless and universally normative.

Third, these verses, in context, press home Paul's argument in the entire chapter by way of summary. If these gifts are given generously as God wills (vv. 4–6), and if they are for the common good of the whole Church (v. 4), it is right to say that the gifts do not serve the purpose of comparison and competition among ministers for the sake of enhancing one's status. The members of Christ's body ought not to be in competition with one another to gain prestige, position or power. Rather they should work together for the well-being of the whole assembly. Paul does not suggest that there is any particular individual who functions in all these capacities. The gifts transcend the capacity of any individual to possess them. Significantly, these gifts are complementary. They function together within the community – the local church.

 STUDY SUGGESTIONS

Word study

1 In 1 Corinthians 12.4–6, Paul uses three important Greek words: *charismata*, *diakonia* and *energemata*. Say what each of these words mean and describe the importance of each word in Paul's discussion.

Review of content

2 What are the three important truths of which Paul, in his Letters, did not want his readers to be uninformed?

3 At the beginning of this chapter, Paul gives a principle for judging spiritual gifts.

(a) What is that principle?

(b) Why was it important that Paul give the Corinthians this principle?

(c) What are the gifts of the Spirit that Paul lists? Is his list exhaustive?

Bible study

4 Read Acts 16.16–24.

(a) What spiritual gift used by Paul can we see in this passage?

(b) Did Paul receive personal benefit by using this gift (see v. 24)?

(c) What was the benefit of Paul utilizing this gift in this situation?

5 Read Acts 7.

(a) What spiritual gift used by Stephen can we see in this passage?

(b) Did Stephen receive personal benefit by using this gift (see Acts 7.60)?

(c) What was the benefit of Stephen utilizing this gift in this situation?

Discussion and application

6 What is a reason Paul offers for the preference of unity over superiority when speaking of the gifts of the Spirit? What metaphor does

Paul use in illustrating this point? How should this affect the way in which we view the Church coming together? Is the attitude that Paul prescribes visibly seen in our churches today?

7   What is the source of the 'spiritual gifts' and what is their purpose? What are the results of the proper use of spiritual gifts?

8   How might Paul's teaching of the coherence of the gifts of the Spirit as unity-in-diversity critique the gravitation of many churches today toward uniformity (e.g. concerning class, colour, socio-economic standing, etc.)? What place have we given members such as the disabled as being viable instruments of the gifts of the Spirit in building up the local assembly?

9   Do you think we have a tendency to view any of the gifts mentioned in 1 Corinthians 12 as superior to the others? Why, and what is the danger in this?

10   How can I be sure that the gifts of the Spirit are operative in my life? In what ways might such gifts edify the local church of which I am part? How might I celebrate the gifts which operate through other sisters and brothers in ways that are congenial to the 'common good' as opposed to focusing too much upon a select few?

Applied theology essay 1
The Holy Spirit and spirituality

KIRSTEEN KIM

Pentecostals and charismatic Christians around the world have always been fascinated with Paul's first letter to the Corinthians, especially chapters 12 and 14 where the spiritual gifts are discussed. The exercise of the gifts, or *charismata* in Greek, is one of the defining features of the Pentecostal and charismatic movements. Paul lists the gifts here as: 'the utterance of wisdom', 'the utterance of knowledge', 'faith', 'gifts of healing', 'the working of miracles', 'prophecy', 'the discernment of spirits', 'various kinds of tongues' and 'the interpretation of tongues' (1 Corinthians 12.8–10). The nature and evidence of these gifts has been much discussed, especially the gift of tongues, which is held by some to be the definitive sign of receiving the Holy Spirit. What is particularly significant in the biblical text is that gifts are given by the one Spirit to different people impartially. At the outset of his Letter Paul thanks God that the Corinthians are 'not lacking in any spiritual gift' (1 Corinthians 1.7). However, it later becomes clear that he does not regard their conduct of worship and exercise of the gifts as befitting those he addresses as 'saints', 'sanctified in Christ Jesus' (1 Corinthians 1.2). The Letters therefore become a discussion of what is true spirituality, what it is to be holy and to be partakers of the 'the one Spirit', the Spirit of Jesus Christ (1 Corinthians 6.17).

In aiming at a higher order of spiritual blessing, Pentecostal and charismatic movements implicitly (and sometimes explicitly) suggest that some other churches may not be 'spiritual' enough. They therefore raise questions about what true spirituality is, as Paul does in 1 Corinthians. This is an important question in these days when all kinds of spirituality are on offer in the religious marketplace. The spirituality of the traditional churches is criticized not only by Pentecostals and charismatics but also by those who leave the churches for other religions, or for movements of holistic spirituality such as New Age and neo-paganism. A recent study in the UK led by Paul Heelas and Linda Woodhead explained the decline in church-going by suggesting that 'religion' in the sense of organized, corporate, public worship was giving way to 'spirituality', referring to a private, subjective experience of the sacred. Given that there are similar forms of spirituality practised across religious boundaries, it is necessary to ask what is distinctive about Christian spirituality.

At the turn of this century 'Pentecostal-charismatic' Christianity was identified by David B. Barrett and his colleagues as one of the largest and the fastest growing movements in world Christianity. Allan Anderson and others have studied Pentecostalism as a global movement with many and complex manifestations, including classical Pentecostalism, African Initiated Churches (AICs), the charismatic movement, and neo-Pentecostalism.

Classical Pentecostalism arose in the USA in the first decade of the twentieth century and resulted in denominations of churches which identify themselves as Pentecostal. They are in some way connected with a revival at Azusa Street in Los Angeles in 1906 led by an African-American preacher in the holiness tradition, William Seymour. This event was remarkable not only for the ecstatic behaviour and reports of miracles, which were said to result from the 'baptism of the Spirit', but also because those who participated were from different races and social classes, which shocked the 'respectable' society of the time. Such was the witness to the impartial blessing and indiscriminate power of the Holy Spirit that the revival had worldwide repercussions. In the revival the experience of the gifts of the Spirit, especially the gift of tongues, was interpreted theologically as baptism in, or filling with, the Holy Spirit, which was distinct from the water baptism administered by the churches. This teaching was not new, nor was the emphasis on tongues as the sign that this spiritual baptism had taken place. In particular it was taught by Charles Parham, a white man, at his Bible school in Topeka, Kansas. Seymour had tried to enrol in Parham's classes but in the racially segregated society of the time, he was allowed only to listen from outside the room. The white Pentecostal churches which resulted from Parham's ministry were finally reconciled with the other churches – white and black – that emerged from

Azusa Street only in 1994. That year, in the 'miracle of Memphis' the all-white Pentecostal Fellowship of North America was dissolved to form the Pentecostal/Charismatic Churches of North America.

Although highly significant for the theology of Pentecostalism, neither Azusa Street nor Topeka was the first twentieth-century revival in which the gifts of the Spirit were experienced. Many of the features of the revival at Azusa Street occurred in other revivals around the world in the years before and after 1906. Most of these were linked in some way through missionary networks and the earlier holiness spirituality arising from the US awakenings. However, they were not the direct result of the events in the USA, nor were the churches formed as a result dependent on the emerging Pentecostal churches in North America. Revivals occurred in Wales in 1904; Pune and the Khasi Hills in India in 1905; Korea in 1907; Oslo and Sunderland in 1907; Valparaiso, Chile, in 1909; Lagos, Nigeria, in 1918; and other places. In Wales the Methodist chapels in mining communities were revived. In India, Welsh Methodist mission work sparked the revival in the Khasi Hills; the Pune revival was among widows and orphaned girls at Pandita Ramabai's Mukti Mission. The Korean revival encouraged indigenous leadership and growth of Presbyterian and Methodist churches. The revivals in Oslo and Sunderland were linked through Thomas Ball Barratt, a Norwegian Methodist who met missionaries from Azusa Street. The events in Valparaiso began in a large Methodist congregation. In Nigeria, an Anglican prayer group eventually grew into the independent Christ Apostolic Church, part of the Aladura movement of churches.

AICs are another very diverse grouping. The movement includes any church founded and led by Africans independently of the mission churches – such as the Aladura churches mentioned above. Many of these practise gifts of the Spirit in a similar way to the classical Pentecostals, although their emphasis is on gifts of healing and prophecy rather than on tongues. Many were started by people who believed themselves to be prophets of God, such as William Wadé Harris and Simon Kimbangu in West and Central Africa. They styled themselves on the Old Testament prophets who are described as empowered by the Spirit of God and represented an alternative source of power from the practitioners of African Traditional Religion.

The charismatic movement refers to the emergence in Roman Catholic, Protestant and even Orthodox churches of the exercise of *charismata* in ways similar to Pentecostal Christians. This crossover has been happening since about 1960 around the world. Some church leaders resisted the teaching of baptism or fullness of the Holy Spirit and the practice of speaking in tongues and other of the more 'supernatural' gifts. They argued that the sacraments of baptism (and confirmation) were synonymous with receiving the Holy Spirit. Many church leaders rejected miracles as confined to the period of the apostles, and some pointed out that Paul himself strongly criticizes the Corinthians for emphasizing gifts at the expense of loving conduct (1 Corinthians 12.31). However, the growth of the charismatic movement within, and the rapid growth of Pentecostalism without, has encouraged a charismaticization of worship across most churches around the world. Many traditional denominations now incorporate into their services of worship lively choruses from charismatic revivals, clapping and dancing, simultaneous prayer and prayer for healing. They also encourage lay participation and exercise of different gifts among their congregation. Although the Second Vatican Council (1962–5) was not a charismatic event in the Pentecostal sense, the Catholic theologian Yves Congar regarded it as a movement of the Holy Spirit because the bishops redefined the Church as 'the people of God' rather than the hierarchy of priests and bishops, and thus empowered the laity. New denominations have resulted from charismatic revivals which were not accommodated within existing churches. Some of these, such as the Vineyard, meet informally as part of networks in what has been called the 'third wave' of the charismatic movement.

The latest generation of Pentecostal churches, known as neo-Pentecostal, are found worldwide, especially in urban centres. They emphasize God's blessing particularly in terms of church growth, wealth and success – so-called prosperity teaching. They take seriously another aspect of Paul's message to the Corinthians. In 2 Corinthians 8—9 Paul introduces his project to take up a collection from the churches to help the Christians in Judaea who are suffering due to famine. Since the Corinthians excel in giftedness, Paul reasons, they should also excel in giving. God rewards generosity, he writes (2 Corinthians 9.6–11), and Jesus became poor so that 'you might become rich' (2 Corinthians 8.9). Prosperity preachers, some primarily televangelists and others who are pastors of large local churches, sometimes persuade their congregations to give generously of their wealth by crudely equating the riches of Christian faith with material wealth and worldly success. However, others, like Mensa Otabil in Nigeria, preach a message of spiritual blessing and power over evil but encourage the development of gifts by education and self-improvement. They urge generous giving as a grateful response to God's love, rather than reducing Christian faith to a financial investment policy. In this way they contribute to the development of society and help people to cope in the modern world. Their understanding of spiritual gifts and the blessing of the Holy Spirit is not limited to the supernatural or miraculous, because spiritual life is not separate from but encompasses the life of this world. In other churches to which Paul writes, the gifts are understood to include more mundane activities as teaching, encouraging, giving, leading, showing compassion (Romans 12.7–8; Ephesians 4.11). So the gifts of the Spirit may be seen as a form of personal and social empowerment.

The Nigerian Methodist Mercy Amba Oduyoye has stressed that, although some proud people may need to be reminded of their sinfulness, the message of the gospel for the poor is of encouragement to realize and celebrate their giftedness by the Spirit, and their riches in Christ. 'The Spirit gives life' (2 Corinthians 3.6), and the Circle of Concerned African Women Theologians, which Oduyoye initiated, has sought to develop and direct the spiritual gifts of African women towards the good of their families and the wider society. Liberation theologians – such as José Comblin in Brazil, Samuel Rayan in India and Suh Nam-dong in Korea – have developed liberation theologies of the Holy Spirit. They see the gifts of the Holy Spirit, especially the 'discernment of spirits' (1 Corinthians 12.10), as given to empower Christians in the struggle not so much against supernatural forces as against the economic and social forces of oppression. They regard true spirituality as evidenced by liberation from oppression. The anointing of the Spirit should be good news to the poor (Luke 4.18). Much of Paul's teaching to the Corinthians is about sharing with the poor – in the Holy Communion and through the collection (1 Corinthians 11.17–34; 2 Corinthians 8—9).

Contemporary Pentecostal and charismatic Christianity is not the first reappearance in history of a pneumatic kind of spirituality such as was practised in Corinth, in which supernatural spiritual gifts and ecstatic behaviour were to the fore. Other examples include the Montanists in Asia Minor (modern Turkey) in the third century. Some of the mystics of the Orthodox churches, such as Symeon the New Theologian (949–1022), spoke in tongues. Various movements since the Reformation, such as the Quakers and Methodists, have included outbursts of ecstatic behaviour in their beginnings. The widespread nature of the Pentecostal and charismatic revivals, and the recurrences of such events in history, implies to commentators such as Harvey Cox that Pentecostalism is not one movement. Rather it is the re-emergence in a Christian form of a 'primal spirituality' common to all humanity and also found in East Asian shamanism, African Traditional Religion, and other indigenous spiritualities and popular religiosity which existed before, and often run alongside, the major world religions. It was a form of spirituality that the Corinthians would have also inherited from the paganism they practised before turning to Christ (1 Corinthians 12.2).

Pentecostal leaders naturally resist any suggestion by theologians or sociologists that their Christianity is merely a disguised form of paganism. David Yonggi Cho, for example, senior pastor of the largest single congregation in the world, Yoido Full Gospel Church in South Korea, has robustly defended himself against accusations of Shamanism. He points out that he and his congregation are converts who have turned away from the spirit-world of shamanism. Unlike the shaman, who tries to appease them, Cho and his followers reject the spirits and exorcize them by the power of the Holy Spirit. The difference between Cho and his critics is that he retains a sense of the reality of the spirit-world and recognizes the need to deal with its continuing power over the lives of some of his congregation. This awareness of a spirit-world accounts for the continuity which others see between Pentecostal or charismatic Christianity and 'primal spirituality' but does not imply capitulation to it.

A very different form of Christian spirituality is found in the 'kenotic' traditions associated with monasticism in which the emphasis is not on receiving gifts from God but on self-denial, cross-bearing and self-emptying after the example of Jesus in his incarnation (Philippians 2.6–11; 1 Corinthians 11.23–26). This is an example Paul himself has followed and he recounts to the Corinthians the suffering he has experienced in fulfilling God's mission (1 Corinthians 4.9–13; 2 Corinthians 11.16–33). But Paul does not criticize the Corinthians for being gifted by God – he recognizes that the grace of God in Jesus Christ is enriching for humanity (1 Corinthians 1.4–7; 2 Corinthians 8.9) – but for the way they exercise the gifts. Paul identifies some serious problems with Corinthian spirituality, such as factionalism, jealousy, selfishness, quarrelling, disorderly behaviour and vanity. In his discussion of spiritual gifts he tries to correct this by urging the Corinthians not to get fixated on tongues, and possessing all the gifts, but to desire a 'more excellent way', the gift of love, which he extols in the famous hymn in 1 Corinthians 13. For Paul, the chief characteristic of the Holy Spirit is not power but Christ-likeness – he himself comes to them in weakness but as an ambassador of Christ (2 Corinthians 4—5). Spiritual gifts are accompanied by the power of the Spirit only if they are exercised in love because their purpose is not self-aggrandisement but the building up of the body of Christ (1 Corinthians 14). In his teaching about the gifts Paul therefore stresses that they are given by the one Spirit and intended for the common good.

In the twentieth century many European Christians became distressed at the disunity of the Christian churches, especially as this seemed to be partly responsible for the terrible wars between European nations, and also hindered Christian witness in many countries. The disunity of the Corinthian church was a biblical example of the same sort of problems, and any contemporary group which practised spiritual gifts was feared to be divisive. In its early stages the ecumenical movement tried to demonstrate that the one body of Christ cannot be divided (1 Corinthians 1.13) by negotiating toward structural unity of the churches. Some notable progress was made in this direction, for example in the formation of the Church of South India in 1947, but those who sought to unite churches were exasperated by the emergence of more and more new denominations in the twentieth century. Eventually toward the end of the century ecumenical movements, particularly the World Council of Churches, came to the conclusion that the visible unity of the churches might not necessarily entail structural and organizational unity. It was clear, looking round at world Christianity, that the work of the one Spirit was manifest in many different forms and that differences between churches were not only doctrinal and structural. The different spiritualities of the churches are not necessarily signs of heresy from one norm but different cultural and contextual expressions of Christian faith. Ecumenism does not mean uniformity but unity-in-diversity, a common vision inspired by the Spirit of Jesus Christ but worked out in different ways in different parts of the world.

Pentecostal theologians Walter Hollenweger and, more recently, Amos Yong have argued that it is of the essence of Pentecostal experience to be ecumenical in outlook. This is not a perspective emphasized in all

Pentecostal accounts but Hollenweger and Yong see a radical pluralism in the Pentecost account which both links and differentiates many nations and languages (Acts 2). They also point out that, historically, Azusa Street and other Pentecostal movements have crossed denominational, racial, class and gender boundaries, led to forgiveness and reconciliation, and inspired global missionary movements. Recently Pentecostal leaders have been among those supporting the Global Christian Forum initiative to bring together the widest possible gathering of representatives of the world's Christians. The Holy Spirit and spiritual gifts are given to each, and each contribution is to be honoured (1 Corinthians 12.7, 24–25). The Holy Spirit is not a spirit of division – these are 'human inclinations', writes Paul (1 Corinthians 3.1–4). According to the apostle, the ministry of the Spirit is the ministry of reconciliation (2 Corinthians 3—5). Through Jesus Christ, God has dealt with sin and reconciled the world to himself (2 Corinthians 5.18–21). So in true spirituality, the *charismata* are a means to overcome evil and work toward peace.

13.1–13: The way of love

 ## Summary

13.1–3: The pre-eminence of love

13.4–7: What love is

13.8–13: An everlasting love

 ## Introduction

Jonathan Swift in his famous book, *Gulliver's Travels*, wrote: 'We have just enough religion to make us hate one another, but not enough religion to cause us to love one another.' Swift's observation is an apt description of the Corinthians and a good summation of Paul's point in this chapter. The Corinthians had failed in the practice of love. There were factions and immaturity; they engaged in lawsuits against one another; Christian liberty was misconstrued as unbridled freedom; the Lord's Supper was abused in its intent and practice. Moreover, because of their self-seeking worldly attitude, they abused the use of the spiritual gifts. It is therefore no coincidence that 1 Corinthians 13 is located at this particular point in the argument of the Letter. It focuses on love, a subject that is found throughout Paul's discussion of worship and emphasizes the importance of the edification of others. The chapter not only provides an answer to the Corinthians' attitude to the exercise of spiritual gifts but also proffers a solution to the divisiveness that was at the root of almost all their problems. Paul shows them a more excellent way – a way that stands in sharp contrast to theirs. The gifts were to operate in an atmosphere of love. So Paul tells the Corinthians to 'strive for the greater gifts. And I will show you a still more excellent way.' The more excellent way is what is described in 1 Corinthians 13; it is the way of love.

 ## Interpretation and notes

13.1–3. If I speak in the tongues of mortals and of angels . . . if I have prophetic powers, and understand all mysteries and all knowledge . . . and if I hand over my body so that I may boast, but do not have love, I gain nothing: The Corinthians were fascinated with spiritual gifts, particularly the gift of tongues. Paul reminds them that even the gift of tongues is meaningless without love. Without love, the gift of tongues, as well as others, is valueless. Although the Greek word (*glossais*) translated 'tongues' has the simple idea of 'languages' in some places (Acts 2.11, Revelation 5.9), its usage here, with particular mention of the 'tongues of angels' can be understood only as referring to a supernatural language. Therefore, 'tongues of mortals' refers to previously unlearned languages by which believers communicate with God.

Paul says that prophecy, knowledge and faith to do miracles are likewise irrelevant apart from love. Giving one's body to be burnt (NRSV margin) is a barren gesture unless it is inspired by love. Paul's point is clear: the Corinthians were missing the motive and the goal of the gifts, making the means their own end. So Paul draws their attention back to the preeminence of love. Love trumps all. For Paul it is not an issue of love versus the gifts. Christians are not required to choose between love and gifts of the Holy Spirit. Paul is stressing the focus and end of the gifts: love, not the gifts for their own sake. The motivation and purpose of the spiritual gifts are ineffectual unless they are guided by love.

What is love? (vv. 4–7) The Greek word used by Paul in this chapter is *agape*, which is the usual word for love in the Septuagint (Greek translation of the Old Testament). It is often used of God's love, not ordinary human love. It is rooted in the notion of regard, respect and care for the well-being of others who may not be like us in their culture, gender, race or concerns but who, nevertheless, are fellow believers or human beings whom God loves. This is in contrast to the word *eros*, a word that often denotes a passionate but also sensual, erotic and emotive force.

Agape love is a matter of an other-directed behaviour and not a feeling. It is not an abstract, airy concept. It is described with action words. Paul is not writing either about how he feels or how he expects the Corinthians to feel. Rather, he is writing about what they should be as Christians. True love is always demonstrated by action.

What love does not do

1 **Love is not envious:** Whereas jealousy says that 'I would like to have what you have', envy says, 'I wish you did not have what you have.' Envy is one of the least productive and most damaging of all sins to those who allow it. It accomplishes nothing, except to hurt the one who harbours it. But love keeps its distance from envy and does not resent it when someone else is promoted or blessed.

2 **Love is not boastful or does not parade itself:** Love in action can work anonymously. It does not have to have the limelight or the attention to do a good job, or to be satisfied with the result. Love gives because it loves to give. It does not seek praise by showing off.

3 **Love is not arrogant:** To be arrogant is to be puffed up and self-focused. It speaks of someone who has a 'big head'. Love does not get its head swelled; it focuses on the needs of others.

4 **Love is not rude:** that is, is not ill-mannered or brash. Where there is love, there will be kindness and good manners. A person who loves does not just speak his or her mind but minds his or her speech.

5 **Love does not seek its own:** an idea that Paul expresses in a slightly different manner in Romans 12.10 and Philippians 2.4. This is being like Jesus in a most basic way, being an others-centred person instead of a self-centred person.

6 **Love is not irritable:** This is perhaps the most difficult to understand among the characteristics of love. In plain language, love is neither touchy nor irritable.

7 **Love is not resentful:** It does not store up the memory or keep an account of any wrong it has received. It puts away the hurts of the past instead of clinging to them. After all, nobody is more hurt by bitterness than the person who keeps it.

8 **Love does not rejoice in wrongdoing:** 'I told you so' and 'It serves you right' are familiar statements but they are not the language of love. Love desires the best for others and does not derive personal satisfaction from the failure of others. Instead love rejoices in the truth.

What love does

1 **Love suffers long:** It is the type of love that characterizes Jesus, of whom the Scripture says that 'the Lord is not slow about his promise . . . but is patient with you, not wanting any to perish, but all to come to repentance' (2 Peter 3.9). If God's love is in us, we will be longsuffering to those who annoy us and hurt us. William Tyndale, the great Bible translator, was an eloquent man. He was seriously persecuted. It is said that every time something was done against him,

he returned persecution with a tender love. He is said to have told his persecutors that, although they might take his possessions and try to destroy his reputation, as long as Christ lived in his heart he would continue to love them.

2 **Love is kind:** Kindness is demonstrated in simple acts such as giving a cup of cold water to the thirsty (Matthew 25.35). It is possible to be religious without being kind. Christ-like believers are kind, even to those who are unkind to them.

3 **Love rejoices in the truth:** Love wants the truth to prevail.

4 **Love bears, believes and endures all things:** The word *panta* translated 'all' can also be translated as 'always'. Paul's point is that love never tires of support, never loses faith, never gives up hope and never gives up. Most of us can bear all things, and believe all things, and hope all things, but only for a while! The greatness of agape love is it keeps on bearing, believing and hoping. It does not give up.

In his book, *Run Baby Run*, Nicky Cruz tells of his encounter with David Wilkerson, while Cruz was a gang member in Brooklyn, New York. When he took out a knife and threatened to kill David, David told Nicky that if he were to cut him into a thousand pieces, every part would say, 'I love you.' Love does not focus on the negative. Paul demonstrates these qualities. He bears with the Corinthians, hoping that they will change and overcome the problems in their midst.

13.8. Love never ends. But as for prophecies, they will come to an end; as for tongues, they will cease: Paul attests to the permanence of love as he continues to put the spiritual gifts and virtues in perspective. Love never ends. Paul is addressing the overemphasis the Corinthian Christians gave to the other gifts of the Holy Spirit. He shows they should emphasize love more than the gifts, because the gifts are temporary 'containers' of God's work; love is the work itself. The spiritual gifts remain until the end, but are imperfect and will eventually come to an end. However, nothing in the verse suggests that the miraculous gifts ended with the apostles, a view held by some Christians. Obviously, knowledge did not pass away with Paul. Some Christians do not appreciate tongues and prophecy as legitimate gifts but their opinion does not invalidate these gifts nor justify their being wished away.

13.9–12. For we know only in part, and we prophesy only in part: Paul gives the reason why other gifts apart from love will cease. Those gifts, such as prophecy or knowledge, are specifically meant to equip the believer to endure in this age. In due course, they will be brought to nothing. The milieu in which they operate will one day come to an end and will be superseded by a situation in which they become totally unnecessary or inappropriate. Paul likens the situation to that of growing up. There is a life appropriate to a child, which is manifested in thought, speech and reasoning power. But when adulthood arrives, these characteristics are no longer viable and, as such, must be left behind. Tongues will cease when the Lord returns and completes his plan for Christians. Partial knowledge such as the Corinthians and Christians now have will be brought to nothing. Not so with love. Therefore, all gifts except love can be characterized as partial. In mistaking the part for the whole and the partial for the final, the Corinthians, unlike Paul, are childish.

13.13. And the greatest of these is love: For Paul the three great pursuits of the Christian life are not 'miracles, power and gifts'. They are faith, hope and love. Though the gifts are precious, and are given by the Holy Spirit today, they were never meant to be the focus or goal of our Christian lives. Instead, we must pursue faith, hope and love. Paul wants the Corinthian Christians to remember that giftedness is not the measure of maturity, the display of love is. Each Christian must ask: 'Am I exercising God's gift out of love, in order to glorify him and bless others, or do I have a secret motive or desire to enhance myself, to receive human praise, to cover up some deep personal problem or to appear more spiritual than others?' We must allow the Holy Spirit to purify our motives. We must do all things and respond to all situations out of love. To love, we must desire to love. Love is a choice! Paul's discussion of love is not meant to persuade the Corinthians to abandon their prized spiritual gifts. Rather, it is intended to convince them to exercise their gifts with love. If otherwise exercised, they are spiritually unfruitful or barren.

 STUDY SUGGESTIONS

Word study

1   The Greek word *glossais* is translated 'tongues' in places such as Acts 2.11 and Revelation 5.9. How is the meaning of this word in 1 Corinthians 13.1 different from the previous references, and why?

2   Compare and contrast the meanings of the two Greek words *agape* and *eros*. Which does Paul use in this chapter? Why?

3   How is the Greek word *panta* translated in v. 7? What is an alternate translation? How is this word important to the overall theme of this chapter?

Review of content

4   What is the significance of this chapter's location in relation to the Letter as a whole?

5   According to Paul, what are eight things love does not do?

6   According to Paul, what are four things love does?

Bible study

7 Read Matthew 25.31–46.

   (a) Which aspect of love does this passage demonstrate?

   (b) Are our churches showing this aspect of love to those around us? Why or why not?

   (c) How could your church further demonstrate this aspect of love?

8 Read Matthew 6.9–15.

   (a) What is the importance of forgiving others?

   (b) What aspect(s) of love as found in 1 Corinthians 13 does forgiveness complement?

Discussion and application

9 What is the relationship between 'love' and 'gifts'? Can one function without the other? If so, what are the consequences of such a functioning?

10 Is there anyone in your life whom you find difficult to love? Does this chapter encourage or discourage you in that respect? What has this chapter taught you about situations in which it is hard to love?

11 Paul mentions that the greatest of any gift is love. What are some of the things he specifically says love is greater than in this chapter? Does your life and that of your local church reflect the truth that all of these things you listed are incomplete without love?

14.1–40: Spiritual gifts and edification

 Summary

14.1: An urgent exhortation: pursue love

14.2–6: Prophecy versus tongues in the edification of the Church

14.7–12: Sounds and signification

14.13–19: The mind and the Spirit

14.20–24: Reorder your thinking

14.25–40: Order in public worship

 Introduction

Paul has spoken in 1 Corinthians 13 regarding love as the context in which the spiritual gifts should operate. He now resumes his teachings concerning the gifts that began in chapter 12, focusing on the issue of intelligibility and order during the worship service. The somewhat disorderly situation in Corinth required that Paul pay more attention to the gifts of speaking in tongues and prophecy. Perhaps some Corinthians were misusing speaking in tongues with the result that others were against its use and would want it stopped. For Paul, whatever is done in the local church should be for God's glory, the edification of other believers, and the sake of a witness to the unsaved. We must not gather simply to entertain one another.

Interpretation and notes

14.1. Pursue love . . . and especially that you may prophesy: Paul has stressed the pre-eminence of love. Now he wants those in the Church to excel at edifying others with their spiritual gifts, as an application of that love. Paul begins the section by affirming the superiority of prophecy to tongues. The reason prophecy is superior to tongues is that it is understandable. Prophecy is to be preferred to uninterpreted tongues because, in the case of tongues, no one is edified unless the tongues are interpreted. The admonition 'pursue' speaks of intensity, perseverance and an attitude that always achieves its goal. It is a continuous and ongoing pursuit of love.

14.2. Those who speak in a tongue do not speak to other people but to God: The reason Paul commands the Corinthians to pursue love and seek to prophesy is given in vv. 2–4. Paul shows the contrast between prophecy and tongues. The two main issues here are intelligibility and the upbuilding or edification of the whole assembly. A person who speaks in tongues can speak mysteries in the Spirit but such speech has no beneficial result in the congregation if it cannot be understood.

14.3–4. Those who prophesy speak to other people for their building up and encouragement and consolation. Those who speak in a tongue build up themselves: In v. 3, Paul identifies content for prophecy. In prophecy the speaker speaks to other people and what he or she speaks to people is edification, exhortation (encouragement) and comfort. Paul first used the word 'edification' in its verb form in 1 Corinthians 8.1 when he wrote, 'Love builds up.' The same verb appears in 1 Corinthians 8.10;

10.23; twice in 14.4; and in 14.17. Thus 'edification' is one of the pivotal concepts for Paul in his problems with the church at Corinth. 'Edification' is a criterion that Paul uses to evaluate the appropriateness of behaviour. If an action builds up the Church it is beneficial. Paul thought of edification primarily in terms of the local Christian community. His ministry was to 'build up and not to destroy' (2 Corinthians 10.8; 13.10). For Paul, edification does not primarily refer to individuals whose goal is to mature into spiritual, individual personalities, but rather to the Church, which, for Paul, exists in local concrete communities. Paul directly states the issue in v. 4. Those who speak in a tongue edify or build up themselves. Those who prophesy edify or build up the church. It is the building up of the church that matters, not the building up of oneself.

14.5. One who prophesies is greater than one who speaks in tongues, unless someone interprets, so that the church may be built up: Paul attempts to soften the impact of the contrast in the previous verse. He states that he wishes that all the Corinthians spoke in tongues. However, he would rather they all prophesied. Prophesying is greater than speaking in tongues unless someone interprets the tongue. Interpretation allows the possibility for a 'message from God' to be conveyed to the congregation by the utterance spoken in tongues. That offers the opportunity for the 'obedience' (hearing) mentioned in v. 2. The verse concludes with Paul's main point, edification. Interpretation allows the congregation to be built up or edified.

14.7–12: Paul reinforces his point by the use of three analogies. In vv. 7–11 he illustrates what he means by uninterpreted tongues through the use of musical instruments and languages unknown to a speaker. Mere sound produces no real effect on the hearer, unless it has some meaning. In his first analogy Paul cites flutes and harps. If the players of these instruments make no clear distinction in their tones, no recognizable tune will be produced. Musical instruments must use a certain pitch and beat to communicate a song. If they do not, the music is not accessible to the listener. Sounds are coming forth, but they cannot be understood. The trumpet that makes an uncertain sound is of no profit for others. An indistinct trumpet call will rouse no soldier to battle. An example is what is known as the 'talking drum' in South-West Nigeria. It is used for both celebration and declaration of hostilities. Paul's third analogy is drawn from languages. There are many different languages in the world, but unless one understands the force, the intent, of what is being said by a foreign speaker, his words will be to the hearer mere gibberish.

Paul draws the argument to a conclusion in v. 12. Once again, he affirms his central argument that the Corinthians ought to seek to use their gifts for the edification of the Church. Speaking in tongues without conveying an intelligible message does not build up the Christian community. Since the Corinthians are eager for gifts of the Spirit, let them aspire above all to excel in those which build up the Church.

14.13–19: Here Paul stresses the need for the interpretation of tongues in prayer and worship so that the believer who does not have the gift of interpretation may benefit. He has made the point that speaking in tongues without interpretation fails to edify. Paul now urges anyone who speaks in tongues to pray for the further gift of being able to interpret what they say (v. 13). No one but the speaker is edified. Paul says, 'For if I pray in a tongue, my spirit prays but my mind is unproductive.' Paul says two things here about praying in tongues: it is the expression of a real relationship with God, yet it does not engage human reason. In v. 15, Paul mentions two distinct activities: on the one hand, praying and praising in tongues and, on the other hand, praying and praising in intelligible words. He intends to continue doing both. He then reverts in the next verses to the point already made that tongue-speaking, when not accompanied by interpretation, does nothing for the bystander. Lest his remarks be misconstrued as a denigration or total rejection of tongues, Paul gives thanks to God that he is more gifted in tongues than any of his readers (v. 18). The most natural way to understand this verse is that Paul claims to speak in tongues, first, privately; and second, without his mind. Paul seems to assume in v. 19 that the tongues are not 'with my mind'.

14.20–24: These verses constitute a practical application of the issue of intelligibility in worship, an issue that is connected with edification. The Corinthians need to reorder their thinking concerning their disproportionate emphasis on tongues. The childishness and lack of maturity (conveyed by Paul's use of *nepion*) of the Corinthians are both evidenced by their exaltation of the gift of tongues. These words would probably have raised the eyebrows of his readers, who clearly prided themselves on their maturity (2.6). What Paul basically does here is to invite his readers to consider the effect upon uninstructed persons, or unbelievers, first, of entering a service of worship where everyone is speaking in tongues and, second, a gathering where all are prophesying. In the former, a visitor could easily reach the conclusion that the worshippers were all mad. In the latter, however, the visitor would hear something that searched his or her conscience and brought conviction, revealing the secrets of his or her heart, and thus be forced to worship and acknowledge that God was indeed in their midst.

14.26–28: Paul's argument for the superior value of prophecy over tongues in gatherings of the community for worship has come full circle. Now he proceeds to apply the principles he has been expounding to the Corinthian situation and sets guidelines for the use of tongues and prophecy in worship. The Corinthian church must have been unstructured and participatory in worship (v. 26). It was a 'charismatic' styled church rather than one with ordered worship or sermon time. Paul is not suggesting that all the aspects of worship listed in v. 26 should take place at a particular given service but that whatever the Corinthians do in worship, it should build up the body. Whatever their individual gifts, all are to aim to edify the church (cf. 14.3–5, 12, 17, 26). Paul then moves to restore some order and gives precise instructions to regulate speaking in tongues. Paul does not prohibit the use of tongues in worship. Rather he seeks to limit it and give it order (v. 27). As in v. 2, Paul acknowledges that speaking in tongues is a true means of communication with God. But no spiritual self-indulgence is to be allowed in church. So, without interpretation, a tongue-speaker must keep silent (v. 28).

14.29–32: Paul gives instructions for the regulation of prophecy. Prophetic utterances are to be weighed. They are not to be accepted uncritically, without questioning and discussion. As such, no single prophet has the absolute say. In recent years, there are prophecies that have cast the Church in a bad light in many places around the world. For example, in Nigeria, a prominent preacher prophesied that the then Head of State would not only lose his re-election campaign, but would also, as a matter of fact, be assassinated. Neither of the prophecies were fulfilled. Moreover, Paul says that the spirits of prophets are subject to the prophets (v. 32).

14.34–35: Paul then addresses the issue of women speaking in the church. These verses have been subjected to various interpretations, the extreme of which is the prohibition of women from being ordained as ministers in various denominational circles. As such, some have labelled it as one of the several so-called Pauline 'terror texts'. What is the exact problem that Paul addresses here? Some say that women, especially wives, were interrupting the worship services by asking questions that not only demonstrated their ignorance but also disgraced their husbands. We must read these verses in relation to Paul's discussion of prophetic speech in the church. A contextual reading forces us not to take it as an absolute statement or as a rule without exception. Paul is responding to some specific issues that bother him. Can we imagine Paul excluding someone like Priscilla from speaking in church? The key for Paul is that worship be orderly so that God may be glorified by everything that takes place, and unbelievers will find Christianity attractive rather than repulsive. This should be our goal today and it is the responsibility of both male and female congregants. Since Paul assumes that women can prophesy in 1 Corinthians 11.2–16, these verses cannot and must not be used to prevent women from engaging in spiritual ministry. God values both men and women equally and speaks through both.

14.36–38: The Corinthians, like many present-day denominations, acted as if they were the only Christians in the universe. Paul lets them see that they are a part of something much bigger, and as such need to submit themselves to God's will for the Church as a whole (v. 36). Paul sees the importance of charismatic prophecies being tested and tried. He then moves on to claim the right to speak for God and to assert his authority over any prophet who might claim not to be subject to his rules (v. 37).

Not all who think of themselves as spiritual are truly spiritual. Anyone who supposes that he or she is a prophet or spiritual person should recognize Paul's authority (v. 38).

14.39–40: Paul concludes his argument in 1 Corinthians 14. He gently steers the Corinthians away from tongues in public worship toward prophecy. He does not forbid tongues, for he accepts it as a legitimate gift from God. Paul does not intend to 'quench the Spirit' (1 Thessalonians 5.19). He restates the underlying principle behind his entire exhortation in 1 Corinthians 14: 'But all things should be done decently and in order' (v. 40). Pentecostals have rightly maintained and emphasized that the Church is the place where the Holy Spirit moves and works. A worship service can be so rigidly structured that it not only stifles but enslaves the Spirit. There must be freedom for the Holy Spirit to move but the Holy Spirit is never the source of confusion and disorder. The concepts of order and peace manifest themselves differently in different cultures as well as in different denominations and groups. What is considered orderly among evangelicals is not necessarily so among Pentecostals and what is orderly among Africans is not necessarily so among Asians or Europeans. Therefore we must refrain from judging too quickly or condemning those whom we perceive not to be doing things in exactly the way that we would have done them.

 STUDY SUGGESTIONS

Word study

1 In 1 Corinthians 14.20, Paul uses the Greek word *nepion*.

   (a) What is the meaning of this word?

   (b) What idea does Paul convey by using this word?

Review of content

2 Why is prophecy superior to speaking in tongues? (Paul gives two main reasons in vv. 2–4). How does this relate to 1 Corinthians 13, where Paul spent an entire chapter speaking of love?

3 What does Paul use in this chapter as his primary means for evaluating behaviour?

4 What spiritual gift allows for the gift of tongues to edify the entire church body?

5 In vv. 34–36, is Paul setting a rule that women should never speak in church? What does a contextual reading of this verse reveal?

Bible study

6 Read 1 Thessalonians 5.12–22.

(a) Compare and contrast 1 Corinthians 14 with this passage.

(b) In 1 Thessalonians 5.19, Paul states, 'Do not quench the Spirit.' How is Paul's discussion in 1 Corinthians 14 not teaching the Corinthians to quench the Spirit?

(c) In 1 Thessalonians 5.21–22, Paul tells us to 'hold fast to what is good; abstain from every form of evil.' Discuss the dynamics of speaking in tongues in corporate worship in light of this admonition.

Discussion and application

7 Paul states that when people speak in tongues, 'nobody understands them'. Does this mean that we should forbid speaking in tongues in communal worship? If so, why? If not, what is the proper use of this spiritual gift?

8 Paul uses three analogies in vv. 7–11 to show how uninterpreted tongues do not edify the entire congregation. What are these analogies? Create an analogy of your own.

9 What does doing things 'decently and in order' mean? Have you experienced a situation that seemed disorderly to you but was orderly to those who are normally present in that context? If so, describe the situation. If not, can you think of a situation where that could easily occur?

10 What must be the overarching goal in our worship, regardless of different styles of worship? Why must consideration be given to how outsiders interpret our worship services? Do the services at your local church speak to outsiders that God is present?

Applied theology essay 2
Women in Corinthians

LISA MEO

What can we learn about Paul's attitude to women in 1 Corinthians? Can this Letter help the body of Christ today? These are the questions I want to explore by studying several passages in 1 Corinthians. The reflections stimulated by these passages will then be applied with reference to my own context, that of the experience of Pacific Islander women in the Church. I begin with a reflection on 1 Corinthians 12 which, after noting the various gifts of the Spirit that are poured out upon believers, goes on to affirm that as Christians we are all members of one body, the body of Christ, and that each member of the body is necessary, equally valued and to be accorded respect (vv. 12–27). But although all are of equal importance, 'God has so arranged the body, giving greater honour to the inferior member' (v. 24). We can only conclude that women are fully incorporated as members of the body of Christ, although Paul may have assumed that women were among the so-called 'inferior' members (who nonetheless merited special regard).

Disunity among members of the body of Christ was a critical issue in the church at Corinth that Paul was attempting to resolve. It seems that one element of the disunity in the church may have been the conflict between women's inferior status in society and their new found freedom in the church. This is implied by passages telling women to keep silent and to keep their heads covered in church. Against this backdrop of societal patriarchy, Paul's assertion in 1 Corinthians 12 about the equality of all members of the body must be viewed theologically as an affirmation that women's roles in the Church are equal to those of men. Paul is assuring the congregation at Corinth that each individual is a full-fledged and essential member of the body of Christ, with no exception. Paul also reverses conventional wisdom and says that those whom the world considers the most inferior are to be given the greatest honour in the Church.

Each member of the body needs respect because every believer has a special ministry role for building up the body of Christ. Paul lists these functions as the ministries of apostles, prophets, teachers, those with deeds of power, gifts of healing, forms of assistance, forms of leadership and various kinds of tongues. All these varieties of gifts, given to various members, are to be used for the benefit of the whole people of God (vv. 27–31). These 'ministers' exercise their different gifts, working in harmony with others, through their love for one another.

The Corinthian congregation confronted a variety of challenges. Members wanted Paul's wisdom and guidance. Paul addresses these issues by appealing to all members to embrace the Gifts of the Spirit. He points out that all God's gifts 'are activated by one and the same Spirit, who allots to each one individually just as the Spirit chooses' (v. 11). There are varieties of gifts, but it is the same Spirit who gives them; there are 'varieties of services, but the same Lord, and there are varieties of activities, but it is the same God who activates all of them in everyone' (vv. 4–6). Clearly those who receive these gifts are not chosen by virtue of their status, class, race or gender. Paul uses the words 'everyone', 'each' and 'individual' because any member of the faith community can receive them.

In vv. 24b–26, Paul reminds his readers that:

> God has so arranged the body, giving the greater honour to the inferior member, *that there may be no dissension within the body*, but the members may have the *same care for one another*. If one member

suffers, all suffer together with it; if one member is honoured, all rejoice with it.

The 'greater honour' is given to the so-called 'inferior' members precisely as a means of building greater *unity* in the body. By welcoming every member equally, especially those most rejected by the world, believers will learn how to practise empathy and compassion. This is a great message of hope for women who, in many societies, are not often treated as equals.

The question for us today is this: 'Who are we to devalue God's gifts given freely to all?' Or 'Why are so many members of the body of Christ still honouring some members and looking down on others?' Such discrimination directly contradicts the theological foundation of our life in the one body, as summarized by Paul in 1 Corinthians 13.1–13. Our gifts of ministry are useless if their motivation is not unconditional love. If we enact our various gifts out of our love for each other, we will build up a peaceful and loving community where each member will live for the betterment of every other member. 'Since God loved us so much, we also ought to love one another . . . if we love one another, God lives in us, and his love is perfected in us' (1 John 4.11–12).

This clear theological foundation for our practice of ministry makes the following 1 Corinthians passage appear exceedingly strange:

> Women should be silent in the churches. For they are not permitted to speak, but should be subordinate, as the law also says. If there is anything they desire to know, let them ask their husbands at home. For it is shameful for a woman to speak in church. (14.34–35)

This passage seems to indicate that female members of the Corinthian congregation must have been quite active, having a vocal role in worship and perhaps raising questions and participating in theological discussions – and that some have objected to this. Yet Paul's attempt to prevent women having their own voice flies in the face of the very theological foundation he has built for life in the one body.

This contradiction leads us to ask several questions:

- Why are women discriminated against in the Church?

- Why are women considered subordinate based on the law, rather than on the gifts that the Spirit bestows?

- Should women listen to what the Spirit nudges them to do, or should they be intimidated into silence by church authorities who may still, after all these centuries, seek to silence them?

- Why are married women expected to let their husbands speak on their behalf?

These questions are primarily sociological, both in Paul's time and still today. It seems that social norms regarding how women should be treated have a strong impact in church communities as well as in secular society. This is why Paul contradicts himself in Corinthians regarding the place of women in the Church. His call for women to be silent opposes his appeal to the one body, and his Galatians manifesto, 'There is no longer Jew or Greek, there is no longer slave or free, there is *no longer male and female*; for all of you are one in Christ Jesus' (Galatians 3.28). The Galatians passage supports the equal standing of all believers in relation to the gifts of the Spirit and membership in the one body expounded in 1 Corinthians.

How are we to understand Paul's contradictory statements today? Paul was influenced by Jewish and Hellenistic traditions. These traditions subordinated women and they were enforced by law. Paul was a product of a patriarchal world view. This social conditioning comes through clearly in 1 Corinthians 14.34, where his appeal to 'the law' does not refer to Old Testament law but to first-century Mediterranean customs and law.

This lapse of Paul's into a reliance on social convention, rather than on the radically new gospel theology, occurs more than once in Corinthians. For example, in 1 Corinthians 11.13–14, Paul appeals solely to social conventions when he says (as an argument for women covering their heads in worship), '*Judge for yourselves: is it proper* for a woman to pray to God with her head unveiled? Does not *nature itself teach you* . . .?' Since there is no theological justification for women covering their heads, Paul reverts to social conventions as the basis for his argument. It is especially contradictory that he uses 'the law' as the premise for his instruction to women to keep silent since, in Galatians 3.17–19, Paul said the law was temporary. It was no longer binding after Jesus Christ.

This social conditioning is seen in other parts of Corinthians as well. When Paul gives his supposedly complete list of all of Jesus' post-resurrection appearances in 1 Corinthians 15, he neglects to mention Jesus' appearances to Mary Magdalene (Mark 16.9; John 20.14) and the other women (Matthew 28.9). Why? Because, in a patriarchal culture, where the word of a man was taken more seriously than that of a woman, the testimony of women would be doubted.

Let us return to Paul's command that women be silent in church in 1 Corinthians 14.34–35. It even contradicts what Paul had said earlier in 11.2–16, concerning head covering, where he asserted that it was acceptable for a woman to pray or prophesy during worship as long as her head was covered. Now, in 14.34–35, this freedom for women to speak (as long as they observed social norms) has been forbidden altogether. Paul also singles out married women, saying that it is shameful for them to speak in church, and that if they desire to know anything they should ask their husbands.

Why should Christians be ashamed of women speaking? As we have seen previously, 1 Corinthians 12 pointed out that the gifts of the Spirit are given to each individual to be used for the good of all; if women's gifts are used for the good of the Church, why then are they considered shameful? Paul himself said, 'You were bought with a price; therefore glorify God in your body' (1 Corinthians 6.20). All human beings, including women, have been bought with a price, which is the precious blood of Jesus Christ that transcends every barrier that separates us. Paul also said that 'where the Spirit of the Lord is, there is freedom' for all who believe in Christ (2 Corinthians 3.17). If the Spirit of Christ is in the church community, there is freedom for all members. If those married women to whom Paul referred were bestowed with the gifts of the Spirit, then Paul is marginalizing women by second-guessing the power of the Spirit to empower them for ministry.

There were some active and influential women, including married women, who were engaged in ministry in the first-century church. Paul respected many of them. In Corinth, for example, there was Priscilla, the wife of Aquila, who was a leader in the Corinth faith community (1 Corinthians 16.19; Acts 18.2, 18, 26; 2 Timothy 4.19). Priscilla was a teacher and patron, and hosted believers in her home, both in Ephesus and in Rome. She was well known to the early Christian community because of how she used her spiritual gifts for the upbuilding of other believers. Another woman who had a leading role in Paul's ministry was Phoebe, a deacon (*diakonos*) with a ministry of service, who sometimes journeyed with Paul or conveyed Paul's greetings, and who shared her faith wherever she travelled (Romans 16.1–2). Lydia, a prominent businesswoman, had an important ministry of patronage, opening her home to believers and offering hospitality and financial support to Paul and his companions (Acts 16.14, 40). Junia was a woman who was explicitly named by Paul as a respected co-apostle (Romans 16.7). Paul also writes that she was imprisoned with him, implying a role similar to that of Paul. These and other women mentioned in the New Testament were not marginalized. They were free to speak and act as ministers of the gospel.

The social conditioning which caused Paul to occasionally contradict his egalitarian theology of the 'priesthood of all believers' by conforming to patriarchal social norms is still operative in many cultures today, including my own Pacific Islands culture. In my travels around the Pacific, I have discovered that at least one Bible translation does not even include the first creation story (Genesis 1.26–31). It was purposely omitted because it offers an alternative to the dominant patriarchal world view, by affirming that both women and men are created in God's image. More recently, church leaders in this particular island culture have decided they now want to include the first creation story in their Bibles, as they have become better educated and exposed to international norms of human rights.

Yet patriarchy still continues to dominate both Church and society in the Pacific Islands. There are numerous misuses of biblical texts that devalue women. Church, political and community leaders in the Pacific largely follow the dominant patriarchal culture. Church members naturally follow their leaders and victimize, silence and sideline women. Biblical passages that exhort women to be silent and to be submissive to their husbands are routinely used to keep women in a subservient state.

I observed a male church leader in the Pacific rebuke one of the few women preachers, saying to her scornfully, 'I heard your sermon last

Sunday; don't you know that the Bible says in Corinthians that women are not allowed to speak in church?' Such remarks discourage women. Women in ministry continue to experience such intimidation and ridicule. Those who are against women in church ministry use their church leaders' uncritical appropriation of texts, such as those we have explored in Corinthians, to validate their cultural conditioning that women should not speak in public, and should not be seen in leadership roles. In Church and society, therefore, women are subordinate. Segregation of men and women in community gatherings and church services continues.

For eight years I worked for the South Pacific Association of Theological Schools as an advocate for women in theological education throughout the churches and theological schools of the Pacific Islands. It was a challenge to communicate with the patriarchal leadership of the churches and to urge them to provide greater opportunities to women to be trained as theologians and ministers of the gospel. There was great resistance in some churches and cultures. Yet, during those eight years, I was heartened to witness that some theological colleges did begin to accept women students. It is easier to do this at a regional and ecumenical institution like the Pacific Theological College in Fiji. There, women students often excel in comparison with male students and increasing numbers of women graduate as masters of theology with distinctions. It is eye-opening to local theological colleges to see that their women can do as well as or better than their male counterparts. Once they graduate, however, another problem arises: to find placements for these women in church ministries, especially married women. Their ministry gifts are still woefully underutilized by the churches of the Pacific. This state of affairs is dictated by culture, not by gospel. Just as Paul at times fell into the trap of not following his own powerful theology of the oneness of the body of Christ and the priesthood of all believers, so today many church leaders in the Pacific, and in other parts of the world, fall into the same trap. They use Paul's patriarchal slip-ups to justify their continued marginalization of women in the church.

To summarize Paul's theology in 1 Corinthians: the Holy Spirit bestows gifts to all; there is no distinction based on race, gender or social status. It is therefore a sin to discriminate against women and to bar them from ministry in the Church. When the Church does not give women positions of leadership for which they are gifted by the Spirit, this is an affront to the Holy Spirit, who channels God's gifts to be used for the good of others.

Moreover, disunity in the Church is caused when some members wrongly assume that their gifts are superior to others. As Paul so beautifully puts it, the gifts of the Spirit can be compared to the parts of the body that work together in unity to enable the body to function. The parts of the body which society deems inferior are especially honoured as important builders of unity in the one body. This is a huge message of hope for women in the Church. The gifts with which they are blessed by the Spirit surpass all cultural barriers and world views that discriminate against women. Paul provides a prophetic word in his overarching theology in Corinthians that women are equal to men in every facet of life, and should therefore be respected and encouraged in their ministries. The fact that Paul sometimes strays from his own theology and succumbs to his own cultural conditioning is a reminder of our priorities to the Church today in every culture. Although we are all products of our cultures and we celebrate the fact that we are cultural beings, the culture of the Christ who embraces all, and calls us all into his royal priesthood, must be paramount in our lives and in the witness of the Church.

1 Corinthians 15.1–58

The resurrection

 Summary

15.1–20: The fact of the resurrection of Christ

15.21–22: Assurance of believers' resurrection

15.23–34: The order and importance of resurrection

15.35–58: The resurrection body

 Introduction

Corinth was a Greek city and, due to the prevalent philosophy of that day, many of its inhabitants did not believe in the bodily resurrection of the dead. The human body was considered a prison and, as such, death was actually welcomed as deliverance from bondage. Some of the scepticism in the Corinthian society had spilled over to the believing community. Some were now denying the resurrection (v. 12), because of their inability to conceive of how any kind of bodily existence could be possible after death (v. 35). Nevertheless, for Paul, the resurrection has important doctrinal and ethical implications for life that are too important to ignore. It stands at the heart of Christian belief, particularly New Testament Christian belief. Paul answers four basic questions: Are the dead raised? When are they raised? Why are they raised? and How are they raised? Paul answers these questions by moving through basic steps: a recall of the basic proclamation about Jesus' resurrection (vv. 1–11), an affirmation of the logical inconsistencies involved in denial of the resurrection (vv. 12–34), and an attempt to perceive theologically what the nature of the resurrected body must be (vv. 35–58). Paul shows that a denial of the resurrection is not only a contradiction of the Corinthian believers' own profession but also destroys the very foundations of their faith.

 Interpretation and notes

15.1–2. Now I should remind you . . . of the good news that I proclaimed . . . through which you also are being saved: Paul starts by reminding the Corinthians of the basic truth of the gospel, which he preached and affirmed as the very foundation on which the faith of the Corinthians was built. The Corinthians are saved by the gospel. They have not only responded to the gospel but also are standing in it.

15.3–5. I handed on to you . . . what I in turn had received: that Christ died for our sins in accordance with the scriptures . . . he was buried, and . . . was raised on the third day in accordance with the scriptures . . . he appeared to Cephas, then to the twelve: Paul's belief in the resurrection was not a figment of his own imagination. It was what he had 'received'. The Corinthians received (Gk. *parelabete*, v. 1) what Paul himself had also first received and then handed on to them (Gk. *paredoka*, v. 3). What do you think of the words 'tradition' or 'creeds'? Of what value is a confession such as the Apostles' Creed? The words 'received' and 'handed on' suggest that Paul's belief in the resurrection could have been part of early Christian tradition or confession of faith. What is the absolute core of what we must believe in order to be saved? What is the bare minimum of Christian belief? Paul identifies some basic beliefs in the tradition that he passed on.

1   Christ's death was for the sins of humanity and was according to the Scriptures, that is, according to God's plan.

2   Christ was buried.

3   Christ was raised from the dead on the third day according to the Scriptures, that is, according to God's plan.

4   He appeared to Peter and then to the twelve.

Paul specifically says that the first and third articles of his confession about the resurrection were according to the Scriptures. His point is that the Old Testament provides the lens through which the events of the life of Christ should be viewed (Isaiah 53; Psalm 16.10; Hosea 6.2; Jonah 1.17). Christ was raised from the dead. He did not raise himself. The resurrection was the vindication of Christ by God.

15.6–8: The empty tomb and Christ's subsequent appearances to his followers present irrefutable proof of his bodily resurrection. Some might argue that Paul and Peter were out of their minds. Paul would say that, if they were, they were not alone. He notes not only that Peter had seen the resurrected Christ, but also that the other disciples had as well: **he appeared to more than five hundred brothers and sisters . . . James . . . all the apostles . . . he appeared also to me.**

15.12–19: Paul begins with the question of resurrection in general – some of the Corinthians were saying that there is no resurrection of the dead (v. 12b). But Paul reasons that if there is no resurrection of the dead, then Christ has not been raised; and, if Christ has not been raised, three conclusions of devastating consequence for the Christian life must follow.

1　His message or proclamation is in vain, that is, of no power or consequence. In the same vein, the faith of the Corinthians is in vain since the foundation on which it is built is non-existent.

2　It stands to reason that if Christ has not been raised, every preacher, teacher, missionary in the world is – wilfully or ignorantly – perpetrating a hoax, perpetuating an error and misleading people to trust in a delusion, not simply with respect to the resurrection as a fact of history, but with regard to the gospel that depends on it. In this regard, Paul says that those who proclaim the gospel are then found to be false witnesses about God, for they testify about God that he raised Christ from the dead when in fact he did not (vv. 14, 15). Paul here uses the Greek word *kerygma*, a word which means 'proclamation, announcement, preaching'. It is the initial gospel proclamation designed to introduce a person to Christ and to appeal for conversion. For example, the *kerygma* includes the preaching of the cross as a central element. In this context it is synonymous with the word *euanggelion*, the gospel or good news.

3　Without the resurrection of Christ as an historical fact, Paul tells the Corinthians, their faith is futile and, as such, they are still in their sins (v. 17). If Christ has not been raised, then every person who has trusted in Christ for the forgiveness of sins and, on the basis of faith in Christ, has been assured that his or her sins are forgiven, is in fact miserably deluded.

4　If there is no resurrection, there is no hope beyond the grave – those also who have fallen asleep in Christ are lost (vv. 18, 19). The rigours, sufferings, self-denials, greatest hopes and aspirations of this life have been for nothing. What a pitiable state believers are in!

 ## Special note C

The *kerygma* of the early Church

It is easy to distort the Christian faith into something it is not by ignoring the most important aspects of its message. The proclamation of the early Church, particularly of Paul, not only contrasts with that of the twenty-first century but also provides a summary of what is considered important for the salvation of humankind.

1　God's promises in the Old Testament have now been fulfilled with the coming of Jesus the Messiah (Acts 2.30; 3.19, 24, 10.43; 26.6–7, 22; Romans 1.2–4; 1 Timothy 3.16; Hebrews 1.1–2; 1 Peter 1.10–12; 2 Peter 1.10–19).

2　Jesus was anointed by God at his baptism as Messiah (Acts 10.38).

3   He began his ministry in Galilee after his baptism (Acts 10.37).

4   Christ went about doing good and performing mighty works by the power of God (Mark 10.45; Acts 2.22; 10.38).

5   The Messiah was crucified according to the purpose of God (Mark 10.45; John 3.16; Acts 2.23; 3.13–15, 18; 4.11; 10.39; 26.23; Romans 8.34; 1 Corinthians 1.17–18; 15.3; Galatians 1.4; Hebrews 1.3; 1 Peter 1.2, 19; 3.18; 1 John 4.10).

6   He was raised from the dead and appeared to his disciples (Acts 2.24, 31–32; 3.15, 26; 10.40-41; 17.31; 26.23; Romans 8.34; 10.9; 1 Corinthians 15.4–7, 12f.; 1 Thessalonians 1.10; 1 Timothy 3.16; 1 Peter 1.2, 21; 3.18, 21).

7   Jesus was exalted by God and given the name 'Lord' (Acts 2.25–29, 33–36; 3.13; 10.36; Romans 8.34; 10.9; 1 Timothy 3.16; Hebrews 1.3; 1 Peter 3.22).

8   Christ gave the Holy Spirit to form the new community of God (Acts 1.8; 2.14–18, 33, 38–39; 10.44–47; 1 Peter 1.12).

9   Christ will come again for judgement and the restoration of all things (Acts 3.20–21; 10.42; 17.31; 1 Corinthians 15.20–28; 1 Thessalonians 1.10).

10 All who hear the message should repent and be baptized (Acts 2.21, 38; 3.19; 10.43, 47–48; 17.30; 26.20; Romans 1.17; 10.9; 1 Peter 3.21).

15.20. But in fact Christ has been raised from the dead: Paul presents an unqualified declaration of the resurrection of Christ, of which he has no doubt. Paul confidently declares Christ's resurrection. He saw him on the road to Damascus (v. 8). But the resurrection of Christ also assures the resurrection of all in him. Hence Paul elaborates this by the motif of the first fruits which comes from the Mosaic law (Exodus 23.16, 19). The first fruits were an offering that represented the entire harvest that was to come. They were also a testimony that there would be a harvest (Leviticus 23.10, 17). In other words, there was more to come. It is in this sense that Jesus is declaring by his resurrection that we will also be raised, those of us who have fallen asleep (or died) in the Lord.

15.21–22. For since death came through a human being . . . so all will be made alive in Christ: Paul states that Adam's sin brought death upon all humanity. Because of Adam's sin, all humans are destined to die. But the opposite is also true. Christ's resurrection brought life to all humanity. Does it follow that everybody will live eternally regardless of their faith in Christ Jesus? In other words, who are the 'all' that will be made alive? Is 'living' eternally the same as 'being saved' eternally? Paul does not teach universalism in this passage. His point is that those who have participated in Christ's death will participate in his resurrection (Romans 6.3–7).

15.23. Each in his own order: Christ the first fruits, then at his coming those who belong to Christ: What does it mean that Jesus is the first fruits of our resurrection? Does that mean he was the first one raised from the dead? What about the widow of Zarephath's son (1 Kings 17.17–24), Jairus' daughter (Mark 5.35–43), Lazarus (John 11.38–44) and Eutychus (Acts 20.7–12), among others? Each of these was raised from death in the same body he or she died in, and each eventually died again. Christ's resurrection is not the same. He rose in a new body that is suited for life in eternity, and he rose never to die again.

15.24–28. Then comes the end: In these verses, Paul shows that the ultimate goal of history is for everything to return to submission to God. The present state of affairs of humanity's rebellion against God will not continue forever. God will put everything under Christ's feet, an Old Testament expression that implies a total conquest or complete victory. As Gordon Fee states, 'In raising Christ from the dead God has set in motion a chain of events that must culminate in the final destruction of death and thus of God's being once again, as in eternity past, "all in all".'

15.29–34: In this paragraph Paul mentions a few problems that would follow if there were no resurrection. Paul refers to the practice of some people that are being baptized on behalf of those who have died. This practice, which is still continued by the Mormons, is known as 'baptism by proxy'. It usually involves the elaborate keeping of ancestry records on the part of the practitioners because they want all their deceased relatives to be saved. Paul does not endorse the practice. Nor is there any passage in the Scriptures that commends or commands it. Paul's purpose is to show the absurdity of the argument of those who deny the resurrection of the dead while they engage in baptism by proxy. His point is: 'If there is no resurrection, why are they doing this? What is the point if there is no life after death?' Paul returns to his own plight if there is no resurrection. If there were no resurrection, it would be absurd for Paul to live the way he lived and go through the sufferings and untold hardships that he did.

15.35–38. How are the dead raised?: One objection to belief in bodily resurrection might be the difficulty in understanding it. This is the point of the questions, 'How are the dead raised? With what kind of body will they come?' Paul considers such questions as foolish and appeals to nature to show why he does so. Even the questioners, had they thought about it very well, would have known that the seeds they sow in the garden do not come out or spring up in the exact form in which they were planted. As a plant which sprouts from a seed is directly linked to it but remarkably different from it, so too will be the relationship of a natural and a resurrected body. Even a seed planted in the ground must degenerate, or die, in order for the new and better life to come forth. It retains the same nature. A seed of corn does not become an oak tree, but it does not become simply a bigger seed either. Believers will have a new body. Hence, belief in the resurrection is like belief in seedtime and harvest. Neither can be completely understood but both are real. Furthermore, believers will be fitted for eternity. Not only will we have a new body, but also the new body will be fitted for eternity.

15.39–44. Not all flesh is alike . . . So it is with the resurrection of the dead: Unlike the body we currently have, our new resurrection bodies are going to be made for the new dimension of eternity. To make his point, Paul says that all flesh is not the same. And then he lists different kinds of living creatures: humans, animals, birds and fish. He mentions heavenly bodies and earthly bodies, the sun and the moon, and stars. He says that each star differs from other stars in splendour, going on to say that the resurrection will be like that. What does he mean? God created everything uniquely designed for its purpose. Fish swim in water, while birds fly in the air. Paul gives four contrasts between the believer's present body and the future resurrection body: corruptible against incorruptible, dishonour against glory, weakness against power, and natural against spiritual.

15.45–49: Paul takes up the last comparison between what is sown and what is raised. He does so by contrasting the first man, 'Adam', with the last Adam, 'Christ'. The first man was created and placed in the garden of Eden. The first man, Adam, gave humanity one kind of body; the second man will give those who trust in him another kind of body. He is a life-giving spirit. As all humanity have borne the image of the first Adam, so those who put their trust in the last Adam will also bear his resurrection image.

15.50–53. Flesh and blood cannot inherit the kingdom of God . . . and this mortal body must put on immortality: Paul states that a new resurrection body is absolutely necessary if anyone would participate in the kingdom of God. He goes on to tell the Corinthians how the transformation from flesh and blood will take place. It is a 'mystery' (see 2.1) that has been revealed to him by God and is to be signalled by the sound of a trumpet. It is immediate and will include both the living and those that are asleep in Christ. It is quite interesting that Paul could equate death with sleep. A common prayer among the Yoruba is that 'one should not pass from sleep to death', something that denotes the dreaded nature of death. Not so with Paul. Writing to the Thessalonians he refers to the 'dead in Christ' as those who are asleep. It does appear that the main question is, 'On which side of eternity will one wake up when one falls asleep in death?'

15.54–57: Paul shows that resurrection is the final defeat of death. Death is swallowed up in victory. A resurrected body is not a resuscitated corpse. It is a new order of life that will never die again. Death is defeated by resurrection. Sigmund Freud, the well-known psychologist, once said: 'And finally there is the painful riddle of death, for which no remedy at all has yet been found, nor probably ever will be.' But he was dead wrong. Paul declares triumphantly, 'Death has been swallowed up in victory!'

15.58. Your labour is not in vain: How do you feel when your labour is neither appreciated nor well compensated? Do you sometimes feel like giving up, thinking that your labour is not worth the price you are paying? The hope of resurrection means that your labour is not in vain in the Lord.

Special note D
Resurrection and reincarnation

Although many religions believe in reincarnation in some form or another, it must not be confused with the Christian teaching about the resurrection of the dead. Partial reincarnation is an essential tenet of many traditional African religious systems and philosophies. Belief in rebirth of the living-dead is noticeable among the Akamba (Kenya), Akan (Ghana), Lango (Uganda), Luo (Zambia), Yoruba (Nigeria), Nupe (Nigeria), Illa (Zambia) and many others. The belief in reincarnation includes the rebirth of an ancestor in the same family. For example, among the Yoruba, one hears such names as Babatunde (father has come again) or Yetunde (mother has come again). Such names are given to children who are born either before or after the death of parents or grandparents, especially if the family observes certain traits in common between the child and the living-dead person. Among other religions such as Hinduism reincarnation may involve an endless cycle of rebirths linked to a notion of cleansing and refinement of the inner nature. It is believed that the soul of a person can be reborn in an animal. But the believers' resurrection that Paul spoke of is not the same. It relates only to believers in Christ and it is by the power of God. It does not continue in endless cycles because the new body given by God is no longer subject to death.

 STUDY SUGGESTIONS

Word study

1 In 1 Corinthians 15.14, what Greek word does Paul use which means 'proclamation, announcement, preaching'?

(a) What does this word include as a central element?

(b) In the context of this scripture, with what other Greek word is this one synonymous? Give its definition.

2 The Greek word *parousia* can have more than one meaning.

(a) How is the word commonly used?

(b) When it is used of Jesus, it has special reference to what?

Review of content

3 What four core beliefs did Paul pass on to the Corinthian congregation pertaining to the resurrection?

4 What are four implications of assuming Christ has not been raised from the dead?

5 Explain the difference between reincarnation and resurrection.

Bible study

6 Read Acts 2, 3 and 10. (If possible, reading Acts in its entirety is preferred.) In 1 Corinthians 15, we studied 10 points of the *kerygma* of the early Church. In light of Acts 2, 3 and 10:

(a) Identify concrete examples of the *kerygma* in these chapters.

(b) List ways in which such elements impacted the actions of the early Church.

Discussion and application

7 What might be the importance of Christ not raising *himself* from the dead? What does this say about our understanding of God as trinity?

8 What are some key elements of preaching in the Church today? In your local assembly? On TV? On the Internet? Compare and contrast these with the *kerygma* of the early Church.

9 In vv. 24–28, Paul speaks of God being 'all in all'. How might these verses affect communities, families or persons who find themselves subject to oppressive powers, circumstances or people? How might a person's geopolitical milieu affect his or her reading of this text?

10 How might Jesus' assurance of his future resurrection from the dead by God be a driving force for the manner in which he lived and ministered? How does our understanding of resurrection correspondingly impact our willingness to live and minister like Jesus?

1 Corinthians 16.1–24

Finance and farewell

 Summary

16.1–4: The collection

16.5–12: Paul's travel plans

16.13–24: Exhortations and greetings

 Introduction

In his book, *Money Talks*, Tom Rees writes,

> Yes, money talks! Whether or not we talk about money – money talks about us, and it talks both loudly and eloquently. It talks about our character . . . The surest way of gauging a man's love for Christ is by the way he spends his money.

As Paul ends the Letter, he addresses one final question that the Corinthians have asked him. It is about money. Paul wanted the Corinthians to take an offering among themselves for the needs of the poor Christians of Jerusalem. They could not say, 'Money is unspiritual. We will just pray for them.' Having encouraged the Corinthians to participate in the collection project, Paul then goes on to lay down his travel plans (vv. 5–12), and end the Letter with exhortations and his customary greetings.

 Interpretation and notes

16.1. Now concerning the collection: Paul responds to a question in a letter that the Corinthians sent to him about the collection that he had organized on behalf of the poor saints in Jerusalem (Romans 15.26). There was a great need there, and Paul was pulling together money from other churches to help them. The offering could also have been Paul's gesture of reconciliation with the Jerusalem church where he had been viewed with much suspicion (Acts 21.20–24).

16.2. On the first day of every week: Paul lays down some important principles and practical guidelines for giving.

1   It must be regular. The Corinthians are to take a collection on the first day of every week because it is the day on which they gather for worship. Giving is to be part of their corporate worship.

2   The offering is a special offering with a specific purpose. Giving must be purposeful and deliberate. The Greek word *logeias* is always used for financial contributions, especially for a sacred purpose.

3   Paul asks the Corinthians to set aside in keeping with their income. Unlike the modern-day preachers and televangelists, Paul neither states a particular amount to be given, nor indicates a specific percentage. He only expects giving proportionate to their income. Fee's words on how to manage the collecting of the money are right on target: 'No pressure, no gimmicks, no emotion. A need had to be met and the Corinthians were capable of a role in it.'

4   Each one is to contribute. Paul expects every Christian in Corinth to give to the collection.

16.3. When I arrive, I will send any whom you approve with letters to take your gift to Jerusalem: Paul takes meticulous care in the handling of the collection. Paul talks about giving letters of introduction to the men the Corinthians approve, who will personally take the gift and present it to the church in Jerusalem. Why did Paul need to write letters of introduction? Perhaps he did not want to be confused with the increasing number of 'teachers' who were using the gospel as an opportunity to enrich themselves (1 Timothy 6.10) or like those whom he accused of 'peddling' the Word of God for profit (2 Corinthians 2.17).

16.5–9: Paul promises to visit the Corinthians, **if the Lord permits**. He plans to go through the region of Macedonia, visiting Corinth, but leaves all his plans up to the will of the Lord (cf. James 4.15; Acts 18.21; 1 Corinthians 4.19; Romans 1.10; 15.32; Hebrews 6.3). However, as we learn from 2 Corinthians, things happened differently from what Paul had planned. Instead, Paul soon made a painful visit to Corinth personally to confront them in some areas (2 Corinthians 2.1–4). Although believers must plan and do things in orderly fashion, they must leave room for God's interference. Paul knows that his schedule is not his alone to make. He knows he can do this only if the Lord permits. He is aware that he is serving God's purposes, not his own. So he needs to remain flexible to the leading of the Spirit as to the timing of what he is called to do. We need both vision and flexibility. Paul wisely relies not only on his own desires, but also on God's open doors. Paul knows the secret of directed service. He says that a great door for effective work has opened to him and so he has decided to stay at Ephesus in order to take advantage of that opportunity. Nevertheless, Paul also knows that opposition often accompanies opportunities. This is a great lesson for all believers, especially Christian ministers.

16.10–11: Paul mentions the impending visits of two of his trusted fellow workers, Timothy and Apollos. Timothy, whom Paul was mentoring, was the one carrying on the work of the Lord together with Paul, who vouches for his integrity, instructing the Corinthians to receive him well and then send him on his way in peace. Paul is expecting Timothy to return along with the brothers, obviously other co-workers.

16.12: Paul turns his attention to Apollos, whom they knew as one who had ministered among them. Even though Paul had strongly urged him to go to see them, apparently Apollos was quite unwilling to go at that time. Apollos appears to be independent of Paul. Is this a lack of respect for Paul or a disparaging of his authority? We must learn to defer to God's will in all matters, and leaders should avoid any form of coercion of their fellow workers and those whom God has placed under their authority.

16.13–14. Keep alert, stand firm in your faith, be courageous, be strong. Let all that you do be done in love: Paul gives various exhortations as he ends the Letter.

1   The Corinthians must keep alert, that is, be on their guard. They, as we, must never forget that there is a spiritual enemy. Satan relentlessly prowls about like a lion seeking whom he may devour (1 Peter 5.8). Think about the various influences and forces that are potentially detrimental to our faith. We must be on our guard against temptation, against Satan, against false teaching, against bad influence. The Greek word *gregoreite* (watch, keep alert) also has an eschatological connotation. As such, it suggests the idea of watchfulness in light of Christ's coming (Mark 13.34–35; Luke 12.37; 1 Thessalonians 5.6; Revelation 3.3).

2   Stand firm in the faith. The early Church, as did the Corinthians, faced many challenges that tested their faithfulness to Christ. So Paul encourages the Corinthians to stand firm in the faith. Standing firm involves spiritual discipline and resolve, and a strong sense of what the faith is. It indicates the constancy with which the Corinthians were to hold their commitments in the face of adversity, strife and divisions (Philippians 1.27). Christians must not let anything move them away from the truth of the gospel. How appropriate is the prayer of Thomas Aquinas: 'Give me, O Lord, a steadfast heart, which no unworthy affection may drag downwards; give me an unconquered heart, which no tribulation can wear out; give me an upright heart, which no unworthy purpose may tempt aside.'

3   Knowing that we are in a battle, we must be men and women of courage. Courage does not mean the absence of fear. It is doing what needs to be done in spite of fear. Paul is telling the Corinthians to forget the strong expectations from those around them to accept or acknowledge

the cultural pluralism of the society. To be people of courage spiritually would be unpopular, perhaps even unacceptable, behaviour in first-
century Corinth. It could mean loss of stature in society, perhaps loss of
jobs and economic opportunities, and loss of friends among the pagans.

4   The Corinthians are to be strong in the battle, putting on the armour
    of God and allowing the power of God to flow through them in
    conflict. The admonition to *be strong* literally is translated *be strength-
    ened*. It is in the passive voice, as opposed to the first three admoni-
    tions. When Paul tells his readers to be on guard, to stand firm, and to
    be people of courage, he is telling them things they are to do. When
    he tells them to be strong, however, he is referring to a willingness to
    allow God to strengthen them – something God does to them and for
    them, not something they can do for themselves. The instruction is to
    submit to the strengthening power and work of our Saviour.

5   Paul's final exhortation is to do everything in love. It sounds strange
    that Paul enjoins the Corinthians to fight in love. To fight in love is
    not to fight for oneself but for the Lord.

16.15–20: As Paul ends this Letter to the church in Corinth, he mentions
a number of individuals who are his co-workers and to whom he wants
to give recognition. This, of course, was his common practice in ending
all of his Letters. The list has practical teaching value for us. It makes the
profound statement that while Christians must make their own individual
commitments to Christ, they are then called to live out that commitment
in the context of Christian community and social relationships. Believers
are interdependent and are called to work together in the common cause
of proclaiming the gospel of Christ to the whole world. The passage
reminds us that it takes more than a few talented individuals to get the
job done, something we need to be reminded of often. It is so easy for us
to focus on the 'superstars' of Christianity, one of the very problems they
were experiencing in Corinth.

Paul also shows that those of longer standing in the Church deserve
respect. He first commends the members of **the household of Stephanas**.
They were among the earliest Christian converts in **Achaia** and had a good
record of faithful service: **they have devoted themselves to the service of
the saints**. For this reason Paul enjoins his readers to put themselves in
service of such people. Believers are to encourage their leaders by honouring them (Hebrews 13.7; 1 Peter 5.5). Paul goes on to mention several
people who have been of help to him as well as those who have sent their
greetings to the Corinthians. He concludes his greetings by encouraging
the Corinthians to greet one another with a holy kiss. The exchange of
kisses among family members and close friends was a common practice in
the Mediterranean world of Paul's day. It is probably equivalent to hand
clasping or other forms of greetings in various cultures today.

16.21–24: Paul ends the Letter with some wishes. He greets the Corinthians
himself by writing the closing lines with his own hand. For Paul, love for

the Lord is a mark of a true Christian. Such is his deep conviction that he pronounces a curse on whoever does not love the Lord. So, first, he says, 'let anyone be accursed who has no love for the Lord'. Second, he expresses a sentiment that was common to the early Church, 'Come, Lord!' which is the translation of the Aramaic phrase *Maranatha*. Paul's third wish is that the grace of our Lord Jesus be with the Corinthians.

 ## STUDY SUGGESTIONS

Word study

1 How is the Greek word *logeias* always used?

2 Define the word *gregoreite*. What is the significance of its eschatological connotation?

Review of content

3 List four important principles and practical guidelines that Paul lays out for the Corinthians.

4 What is the significance of the passive voice of the verb 'be strong' in v. 13?

Bible study

5 Read 1 Timothy 6.6–9, Mark 10.17–31 and Matthew 5.19–34.

(a) How does Paul view money according to the passage in 1 Timothy? Is it inherently evil?

(b) What are possible dangers in strongly desiring to be rich?

(c) How does Paul speak of those who are rich? What does he tell them to 'store up'?

(d) How should we understand Paul's admonition about finances in light of Jesus' teaching in Mark and Matthew?

Discussion and application

6 Why is it important for the Church to be involved in meeting the needs of others? How often should it be done? How much should Christians give for the needs of others?

7 Does your local church preach/teach about finances? What is discussed? Compare and contrast what is discussed with Paul's principles and guidelines for giving.

8   Should Christians be involved in relief work? Why or why not?

   (a) Does your church have regular programmes or funds to care and provide for the needy?

   (b) What is your Christian responsibility to believers and churches in other places where the members are suffering or facing persecution?

9   What do we learn about accountability from the way Paul managed the collection for the Jerusalem saints?

10 List people in your local community who have made an impact on your life in Christ. How could you honour or esteem them in a manner that does not fall prey to following such persons as if they were 'superstar' Christians? Why is it important to do so?

2 Corinthians

2 Corinthians 1.1—7.16

Paul's visit, tearful letter and apostolic ministry

1.1–24: Greeting, prayer, thanksgiving and travel plans

 Summary

1.1–2: The writer, addressees and greetings

1.3–7: Thanksgiving and comfort amidst afflictions

1.8–11: Paul's trouble in Asia

1.12–14: Paul's 'boast'

1.15–17: Paul's changes of plan

1.18–24: Yes in Christ

 Introduction

Many times in life we become entangled in a relationship of misunderstanding and distrust from which there is no easy way out. We impugn motives and refuse to give those with whom we have disagreements the benefit of the doubt. The atmosphere is permeated with distrust and suspicion. The misunderstanding could be in our families, at work or at church. This is the situation in which Paul finds himself as he writes 2 Corinthians. The Corinthians did not trust the apostle for many reasons ranging from the change in his travel plans to his refusal to accept financial support from them. What could Paul do to rectify the situation? He had only one choice, which was to explain himself to the Corinthians as best as he could and appeal to them for understanding and love.

 Interpretation and notes

1.1a. Paul, an apostle of Christ Jesus by the will of God: The opening of the Letter is short and to the point. As is customary with Paul's Letters, the introduction gives a hint of the issues that Paul will address later in the Letter. Paul's authority as an apostle is in question by some in Corinth, so he begins by stating that he is an apostle by the will of God, that is, not an apostle by human appointment. He did not choose this as a career. Moreover, he is not an intruder into the Corinthian church. Rather, he came into the church as an apostle of Jesus Christ. If the Corinthian Christians hold him in low regard, it does not diminish his standing as an apostle before God. In this book that focuses very much on Paul's integrity as an apostle, Paul's assertion of the origin of his apostleship is important.

1.1b. To the church of God that is in Corinth, including all the saints: Paul addresses the letter to the church of God. In its ordinary usage the word rendered as 'church' (Gk. *ekklesia*) refers to any assembly. But Paul transforms its usage here. The Church differs from all other assemblies because it is brought into existence by God through the redemptive work of Christ (2 Corinthians 1.21), and it is also a community where God is present. Because of its nature, then, on the one hand, leaders must beware of how they lead God's people. They must realize that they are accountable to God both for their conduct and service. On the other hand, members of the community must live in a manner that befits their new status. It is also remarkable that, considering their many problems, Paul calls the Corinthians saints (Gk. *hagiois*). Today the word 'saint' is primarily used in two ways. First, in its common usage, it refers to individuals in the Roman Catholic Church who, due to what is considered as extraordinary service and having met certain criteria, are declared by the church hierarchy as 'saints' after their death. Second, it remains to be used as a 'title' for the writers of the New Testament Scriptures. The word is hardly ever understood or used to refer to people who are alive. But how does Paul use the word? Of what importance is it to us?

1　The word 'saint' refers to all believers in Christ rather than a select few (Romans 1.7; 1 Corinthians 1.2; 2 Corinthians 2.1; Ephesians 1.1; Philippians 1.1; Colossians 1.2).

2　Believers are called saints because of their relationship with Christ. As such, 'sainthood' is not a status to be conferred on individuals due to some special work or after death.

3　The word 'saint', although primarily denoting relationship, implies the ethical manner of life that is expected of those who are so called.

'Including all the saints throughout Achaia' also shows us that Paul intended his Letter to be spread among churches. This was not just for the Christians in the city of Corinth but for all the Christians in the region who might read the Letter. The greeting that follows the addressees is Paul's normal greeting. He wishes his readers 'grace and peace' (1 Corinthians 1.3; Romans 1.7; Galatians 1.3; Philippians 1.2, 1 Thessalonians 1.1b; 2 Thessalonians 1.2).

1.3–5. Blessed be the God . . . the Father of mercies and the God of all consolation, who consoles us in all our affliction: Paul departs from his normal way of thanksgiving and prayer. Paul usually gives thanks for the church, but here Paul focuses on God. Paul opens the Letter by praising the God who has shown so much mercy and comfort to him. The word 'consolation' (better translated as 'comfort') in this passage is the Greek word *paraklesis*. The idea behind this word is always more than soothing sympathy. It has the idea of strengthening, of helping, of making strong. Paul praises God for divine encouragement in the midst of suffering. We are comforted so that we may be empowered to comfort others.

1.6–7. If we are being afflicted, it is for your consolation and salvation: Paul sees his sufferings in sacrificial terms. Paul never had a victim mentality. Paul uses this same language with Christ. A great purpose of God in comforting us is so that we can bring comfort to others. God's comfort can be given and received through others. Whatever spiritual comforts we have are not given us for our use alone. They are given to us so that they may be distributed or become instruments of help to others. Because Paul's sufferings were the sufferings of Christ, Jesus was not distant from Paul in his trials. He was right there, identifying with the apostle, and comforting Paul. God had a larger purpose in Paul's suffering than working on Paul himself. God was bringing consolation and salvation to others through Paul's sufferings. Paul's life is not focused on himself but on the Lord and on those whom the Lord has given him to serve. When Paul suffers, it is so God can do something good among the Corinthian Christians. His comfort is to be a means of blessing and encouragement to the Corinthians. Suffering or comforted, it is not all about Paul; it is all about others.

Significantly, Paul writes of the same sufferings. It is unlikely the Corinthian Christians were suffering in exactly the same way as Paul did. Probably, not one of them could match the list Paul made in 2 Corinthians 11.23–28. Yet, Paul can say they are the same sufferings, because he recognizes that the exact circumstances of suffering are not as important as what God is doing and wants to do through the suffering. Christians should never get into a 'competition' of comparing sufferings. There is a sense in which we all share the same sufferings. The New Testament idea of suffering is broad and not easily limited to persecution.

1.8–9. The affliction we experienced in Asia: Paul goes on to mention, without details, the afflictions he and his companions experienced. Paul makes no parade of his trials here. The Corinthians were aware of the trial of which he speaks. Paul feels that he had a death sentence on himself, but he uses the language of resurrection to describe his deliverance. Paul is saying that God snatched him from the jaws of death. Only divine intervention rescued him. Suffering is not incidental or accidental to the Christian life. We do not know the exact nature of this trouble. It was probably either some type of persecution or a physical affliction made worse by his missionary work. At least five suggestions for this trouble have been given:

1 Fighting with 'wild beasts' in Ephesus (1 Corinthians 15.32);

2 Suffering 39 stripes after being brought before a Jewish court (2 Corinthians 11.24);

3 The riot at Ephesus (Acts 19.23–41);

4 A particular persecution shortly before he left for Troas (Acts 20.19; 1 Corinthians 16.9); and

5 A recurring physical malady.

Whatever the problem Paul and his companions encountered was, it was bad: they were burdened beyond measure, above strength, to the point of despairing even of life.

1.10–11. He who rescued us . . . through the prayers of many: In the midst of his troubles, Paul the apostle exudes an unflinching confidence in God. Paul's confidence in God's deliverance not only is rooted in his personal faith but also is linked to the intercessory prayer of others. Paul was not an individualist or 'Pastor do-it-alone'. He never acted as a superman in ministry. Not only did he request the prayers of many people, he also relied heavily on those prayers. The Corinthian Christians were really helping Paul when they prayed for him. We often think of the great things God did through Paul, and we are right to admire him as a man of God. But do we think of all the people who prayed for him? Paul credits them with much of his effectiveness in ministry.

1.12–14. We have behaved in the world with frankness and godly sincerity: The Corinthians were probably so accustomed to dealing with ministers who were calculating and manipulative, they probably thought that Paul was acting the same way. Therefore, when Paul said he was coming to them but he did not (1 Corinthians 16.5), they figured he was just manipulating them. The Corinthians slandered him because of the change in his travel plans. In defence, Paul maintains that he and his companions have conducted themselves to the world and especially towards the Corinthians in 'holiness [NRSV margin; 'frankness', NRSV], and godly sincerity, not by earthly fleshly wisdom but by the grace of God'. He is not a chameleon kind of Christian who adapts himself to the moral and spiritual proclivities of the people with whom he associates.

1.15–17. I wanted to come to you first: Paul had planned to visit Corinth twice after he left Ephesus, during his trip to Macedonia and upon his return before going to Judea. However, for reasons which he later explains, he did not go directly to Corinth but first went to Macedonia. His enemies seized his change of plan and charged him with fickleness and unreliability.

They criticized him as a man who couldn't decide on a plan, or who could not carry through on a plan. They also equated Paul's change in his travel plans with diminishing affection. Paul denies the characterization which they have attributed to him. The Corinthians were not wrong in being disappointed that Paul did not come and visit them. But they were wrong in trying to blame Paul for the disappointment. They needed to see Paul's heart and God's hand in the circumstances.

1.18–20. Our word to you has not been 'Yes and No': Paul's first argument is that his ministry of Christ requires him to be reliable. He emphatically declares that his word – his statement of plan and message – was not at the same time yes and no. He supports this declaration by appealing to God's faithfulness and by referring to his previous ministry in Corinth. Sad to say, the world in which we live places little value on words. Politicians retract campaign commitments once they take office. And people swear in court to tell the truth but, nonetheless, some resort to falsehoods for self-preservation. It seems that for many people, promises are simply made to be broken. It is difficult to know whom we can trust. But God's promises reveal his character. He carries out every commitment he makes. The Son of God, whom Paul and his associates preached among the Corinthians and whom these believers received, was not 'yes' and 'no' but an emphatic 'yes'. This was demonstrated in their salvation and sequential spiritual experience. The character of Christ and his work is so vivid to the apostle that it permeates his own life and ministry. Paul is dependable.

1.21–22. It is God who establishes us . . . by putting his seal on us and giving us his Spirit: Paul's second argument for his reliability is his awareness of God's work in their lives, both the Corinthians' and his. He calls attention to what God is doing with them now and to what he did at their conversion. At the present time God is establishing them in Christ. Paul elsewhere describes several things which the Holy Spirit does in believers' lives. The Holy Spirit anoints, or empowers, believers for Christian living and service. The Holy Spirit also seals the believer. 'Seal' (Gk. *arrabon*) or 'stamp', as the word suggests, is a mark of ownership. Moreover, the Holy Spirit becomes a pledge or guarantee of future blessings which lie beyond this life. Paul's awareness of these divine works causes him to be reliable. Both the reliability of Christ in fulfilling the gospel promise and the faithfulness of God in his operation in the lives of his people fashioned the apostle's character. They also fashion ours when we contemplate their significance.

1.23–24. We are workers with you for your joy: Paul completes his argument for his reliability by giving two reasons for his change in plan. Though he decided that it was best not to visit Corinth first, this was not because he had lost interest in the church. They were still his children in the faith, and he felt responsible for them. His first reason for changing his plan is that he might spare them apostolic discipline. He wanted to give them the opportunity to work out the problem themselves rather than give them added sorrow. He confirms his statement with an oath, for he has no way of proving his motivation. He explains that he took this course of action because neither he nor his associates are lords over the Corinthians' faith. Rather, they are promoters of their joy. This means that their ministry is to promote the Corinthians' spiritual well-being by directing their faith to Christ and to his Word. Paul, though an apostle, does not want to dominate their faith. Such right belongs to Christ alone. Pastors and Christian workers must beware of the temptation to usurp this right.

 ## STUDY SUGGESTIONS

Word study

1 In 2 Corinthians 1.1, Paul uses the word *ekklesia*.

   (a) What is the usual meaning of this word?

   (b) How does Paul enhance the meaning of this word?

Review of content

2 Paul refers to the Corinthians as 'saints'.

   (a) Why could this term (being used for the Corinthians) seem out of place to us today?

   (b) To whom does the word 'saints' refer? What is a prerequisite for being considered a 'saint'?

3 What is the situation which has caused the Corinthians to think and speak badly of Paul?

   (a) What two arguments does Paul offer in defence of his character?

   (b) What two reasons does Paul offer for the change in his plan?

4 In vv. 21 and 22, Paul states three things which the Holy Spirit does for us. What are these three things, and why is each vital in the life of a believer?

Bible study

5 In vv. 8–11, Paul mentions an affliction that he and his fellow travellers had experienced. We do not know the exact nature of this affliction. What are five suggestions for the nature of this affliction?

   (a) Read Acts 19.21–41, which portrays the riot at Ephesus.

(b) For what reason were Paul and his travelling companions being ridiculed?

(c) How was the situation resolved?

Discussion and application

6 Why is suffering a necessary part of the Christian life? Has there been a time when you were in the midst of suffering where you knew that God was working in the midst of the circumstances? How did this play out? What methods (e.g. other people, God's Word, etc.) did God use to bring you comfort?

7 Do you think we are too quick to judge the actions of our leaders and ascribe negative motives to their actions? Why is it hard for us to give leaders the benefit of the doubt in situations where confusion or hurt has ensued? In light of Paul's change of his travel plans, what should be the guiding factor in decision making for Christians, particularly those that are in positions of leadership?

8 What did Paul do in times of trial? What characteristics did he exhibit that are of utmost importance to those undergoing trials today?

9 We are called to be saints. How can believers live up to their exalted calling in view of the moral pollution with which they are surrounded? How can we maintain integrity even in situations where suffering is a reality?

2.1–17: Paul's defence

 Summary

2.1–4: Paul's motivation

2.5–11: Discipline and forgiveness

2.12–17: A triumphal ministry

 Introduction

The change in Paul's travel plans stirred up some criticisms of Paul. His opponents questioned his integrity and portrayed him as someone who could neither be relied on nor trusted to keep his promise. These critics were members of the church in Corinth. It is sad but true that Satan uses many members to stir unrest and cause dissatisfaction in a church. Members quarrel over such issues as flower arrangements, the order of service, the colour of and location of the notice board, etc. Others find fault with the preaching style of the pastor. Even a deviation from the printed Sunday bulletin will elicit cries from some members. Thus, church business meetings are filled with hassles over points of order, and there is no room for the Holy Spirit to prompt or guide the leaders to changes. Certainly, church programmes should be run in an orderly fashion, but Christians must not forget that there are times when God may lead in another direction from what has been pre-planned. Obviously, the Corinthians failed to grasp this possibility.

 ## Interpretation and notes

2.1. I made up my mind not to make you another painful visit: Paul continues to defend his change of plans and gives another reason why he did not come to them as intended. Paul's last visit was a painful one. Another visit would have provoked more trouble because the Corinthians were still rebellious. There were those who were still opposing him, and Paul would have had to take strong disciplinary action. As such, Paul is not willing to visit Corinth until they change their attitude.

2.2: Paul's change of travel plans is also a matter of personal interest. Not only did he change his plans for the sake of the Corinthians, but it was also for his own sake. He determined not to come again and cause sorrow to his friends who had made him glad. If they became sorrowful no one would be left to make glad. Their joy was his joy. In everything, Paul is motivated by his love for the Corinthians.

2.3–4: Paul assures the Corinthians that his previous Letter was to deal with the problems while he was away from them so that when he came he would not be distressed. It was not to vent his anger. The Corinthians might have been wondering, 'If Paul really cared that much for our joy, why has he written such a severe letter and judged the sinner so harshly?' He insists that his correction was not something that was done lightly. He is troubled by the harm that the Corinthians did to themselves. He acts out of a heart filled with love for the Corinthians.

Growing up in a paternalistic African culture, both as a young boy and later as a Christian convert, it was unimaginable to me to see an adult crying. Things must be awfully bad. In fact, the members of the Apostolic Faith Church were derided and labelled as the weepers' church. Do we need to hide our emotions? Paul does not pretend or hide his emotions. He wept for the Corinthians because they had allowed impurity in their midst. Here is a preacher who on the one hand displays his humanness in his 'worry' and 'anxiety', and on the other hand his care and compassion for the Corinthians. Though the Corinthians have caused him pain, he still loves them dearly.

2.5. If anyone has caused pain, he has caused it . . . to all of you: Paul shifts his attention to a particular painful event that took place during his previous visit to Corinth. He addresses the one in the congregation who has erred and has caused sorrow not only to him but also to the entire congregation. There is much anguish in Paul's heart concerning the need to discipline the Corinthian church. Paul does not want the Corinthians to think that the troubles they have experienced were all about him. People sometimes ask, 'How does that affect me personally?' And, 'If it does not affect me, why bother?' Paul shows that the sinner was as much a problem to them as he was to him.

2.6–7. Forgive and console him: The offender, whose identity remains unknown, has been punished, and it does appear that the majority of the Christians have distanced themselves from him. Here is a lesson we must learn: we live in days when the word 'discipline' not only evokes various kinds of images but also elicits various reactions. It is sometimes frowned on at home as being antiquated and it is also fast disappearing in the Church. Yet it is one of the key elements in parent–child relationships. But we live in a permissive society where people are left alone to do as they please. It sounds like Corinth. Both Titus' report and Paul's present Letter indicate that the church had responded favourably to Paul's instruction. Now the apostle urges the church to extend forgiveness and comfort to the offender lest he be overwhelmed with sorrow.

2.8. Reaffirm your love: Indeed they should confirm their love toward the offender, perhaps by publicly reinstating him in their fellowship. These directives were a test of their obedience. Paul was not interested in the offender getting his 'just deserts' and did not use discipline as an opportunity to exact vengeance. As the African saying goes, 'when you rebuke a child with the left hand, you draw him/her closer to you with the right.' This is what Paul does here. The ultimate goal of discipline is redemption and to foster better relationship.

2.9–11: Someone offended Paul during his previous visit to the Corinthians. Although it was a personal offence, Paul saw it as an offence against the church. The Corinthians had disciplined the offender and Paul was satisfied with their response. For Paul, forgiveness is now in order and he is willing to forgive whomever they forgive. However, insofar as he has forgiven, it is before Christ. What exactly does it mean to forgive, and why should there be forgiveness? For Paul 'forgiveness' consists in the restoration of the offender to the Christian community; thereby the offender is freed from the threatening grip of Satan.

137

Special note E

Lessons on church discipline

One must admit that discipline in first-century Christian communities, in cities in which there were few 'congregations', was different from discipline in contemporary society in which congregations exist on every corner, particularly in the West. Nevertheless, there are important lessons to be learnt from this episode.

1   Discipline is necessary for the health of the Church. Many churches neglect to discipline sinning members. It is easier to ignore this unpleasant duty with the hope that things will right themselves, but this does not happen. When this happens, the local church is corrupted and loses God's blessing and power.

2   Forgiveness and restoration must be extended to a repentant brother or sister. When discipline is meted out and when offenders repent of their sins, then the church must be quick to forgive and to encourage these repentant ones. The Church must be a living demonstration of forgiveness in a community.

3   It is not an expression of Christian love to remind people of their past sins and to treat them as second-class members. They should be given an opportunity to make a new start and to make useful contributions to the church's life and ministry. We have no right to limit them beyond what God does in his Word. Paul assures the Corinthian church of his forgiving anyone whom they forgive (2 Corinthians 2.10).

4   We must be mindful of Satan's malicious designs (v. 11). The adversary is too alert to take advantage of all who do not walk in Christ's love and forgiveness.

5   Paul understands the sorrow that a congregation feels when a member errs. It is difficult to forgive and once again love that person back into the community. Thus, it is a test of obedience for the congregation. But Paul also understands that forgiving and affirming their love for someone that has erred is the best way to restore him or her to the body of Christ.

2.12–13. When I came to Troas . . . my mind could not rest because I did not find my brother Titus there: Paul now explains what happened in his journey to Macedonia. He did stop at Troas for the gospel of Christ, and he was welcomed but, not finding Titus, he could not find rest in his spirit, and so he took leave. These verses provide us with a window into Paul's heart: his mind could not rest, that is, he found no relief in his spirit ('mind', NRSV) from hopes and fears for his spiritual children at Corinth. Though he had opportunity to preach in Troas, he was too restless in his spirit to concentrate on his service. His foremost thought lay with the Corinthians. Would they reject his authority again, or would they listen to him and do what he had written? What a true pastor Paul is! He has genuine love for the people God has committed to his care. Every minister of the Gospel ought to be constrained by such love and concern.

2.14a. But thanks be to God, who . . . leads us in triumphal procession: 'Like cold water is to a thirsty soul, so is good news from a far country (Proverbs 25.25). Titus' report was good, and the apostle's spirit was refreshed. The good news that Titus brought evokes an outburst of praise by Paul. The apostle goes on to compare his ministry, by way of analogy, to that of a war captive who is led in the triumphant procession of a victorious general. He has in mind the graphic picture of a Roman triumphal parade. However, in this case, the apostle sees himself as a soldier of the victorious general sharing in his triumph. In every place that Paul reaches he gives off the fragrance of the gospel of Christ.

2.14b–16. The fragrance that comes from knowing him . . . For we are the aroma of Christ to God: Also, the apostle likens his ministry to the fragrance that filled the air during triumphant processions. The gospel is an aroma of life to those who are being saved, and an aroma of death to those who are perishing. This verse shows the importance of one's reaction to the gospel message. Perhaps we all can think of someone, a relative or a neighbour, who is known for a particular perfume she wears. Even without seeing her, we know when she's nearby. Without uttering a single word, her fragrance diffuses into her company like that from the broken alabaster box of oil. Every Christian should also be known for wearing a particular perfume – the fragrance of Christ. But it can neither be bought at a cosmetic counter nor sold by the Church. It rises always and only out of our intimate relationship with Christ and wafts a subtle yet noticeable influence toward others. Someone said about a Christian in his small town, 'That man never crosses my pathway without my being better for it!' Another remarked of him, 'You need only shake his hand to know that he is full of God.' What a testimony! What an incredible task such a ministry is: victory through suffering! Who is sufficient for these things?

2.17. We speak as persons of sincerity: This verse does not directly respond to the last question but continues Paul's statement in vv. 15a–16b. Paul and his companions consider themselves different from those who sell the word of God like merchandise. But from sincerity, as from God, they speak in Christ in the sight of God. God therefore is their witness. Paul asserts that his ministry is characterized by sincerity and as being of God. Furthermore, he ministers with the continual awareness of being under God's searching gaze and of his exalted position in Christ. This kind of perception of the ministry keeps the Lord's servants in their proper, useful place. Have you such a perspective of your service? What savour does your life emit?

STUDY SUGGESTIONS

Word study

1 Our word 'discipline' comes from a Latin word, *disciplina*, meaning 'instruction, knowledge'.

(a) In light of this, what must be a key component to any form of discipline?

(b) Thinking of the word used often in the New Testament, 'disciple', which is from the Latin word, *discipulus*, meaning 'learner', what should be our goal of discipline? Are we aiming to put someone in his or her place, or is there something more holistic to this endeavour?

Review of content

2 In 2 Corinthians 2.1–4, Paul gives a third reason why he did not come to visit the Corinthians as planned. (Recall two reasons that were given in 2 Corinthians 1.) What was this reason?

3 Paul had previously instructed the Christians at Corinth to discipline a member of their congregation. What are his instructions now regarding this individual? Does this mean he has changed his mind, or could his new instruction be a part of discipline? Explain.

4 In 2 Corinthians 2.12–13, Paul states that he had an opportunity to minister in Troas, but could not. What hindered Paul from ministering there? What does this say about Paul's character?

Bible study

5 Read Matthew 6.7–15.

(a) Here, Jesus gives us a model of how to pray. What key elements do you see in his prayer? Do your prayers contain those same elements?

(b) After the prayer, Jesus gives us a word of caution. Upon what is God hearing our prayers contingent? What does this say about the importance of forgiveness in our lives?

Discussion and application

6 Why is church discipline so important? What could be the dangers of a church not practising discipline in love?

7 Have you ever been in a situation where you needed to confront a friend or where a friend needed to confront you? What emotions did you feel in either situation? How could things have been done more effectively? What was the result of the confrontation?

8 Have you ever heard or said the phrase, 'I can forgive you, but I will never forget'?

   (a) Is this the correct attitude that Paul is propagating in this chapter?

   (b) It is true that we do not forget many bad things that happen to us, but we can choose to remember them differently. Have you ever experienced a time when you noticed a change in your emotions when remembering a situation where you had been wronged? Discuss.

9 Who is responsible for taking disciplinary action in a local church? What is the church's responsibility after effecting discipline? Does your church have a formal process of discipline and restoration? If so, what is it, and have you ever seen it in action?

10 In v. 11, Paul talks of not being 'outwitted by Satan'. How should the congregation avoid giving Satan an advantage in the matter of discipline in a local church? How should individuals avoid the same thing in regards to friends, family, etc.? Why is this such a difficult task at times?

3.1–18: A ministry of the new covenant

 Summary

3.1–6: Paul's sufficiency for ministry

3.7–18: Sufficiency for a glorious ministry

 Introduction

Who is a minister? What are the marks of an authentic ministry? What qualifies a person for ministry? These questions are as important today as they were at the time Paul wrote 2 Corinthians. If you have ever sought a job, you are likely to have been asked to provide names of persons whom the prospective employer might contact to request letters of reference concerning you. Letters of recommendation were used in the early

Church as a means of establishing the credentials of itinerant preachers (cf. Romans 16.1–2; 1 Corinthians 16.10–11; Philemon). Some people at Corinth questioned the lack of a letter of recommendation by Paul. However, Paul did not need letters of recommendation for his ministry to the Corinthians. The true credentials of the ministry are changed lives, living epistles. Paul's work and commission have been confirmed by the results of his ministry. For Paul nothing is more pleasing to him than the success of his ministry as evidenced in the lives of the Corinthians among whom he has laboured. The lives of the Corinthians are a clear testimony to the success of his ministry. God approves his work. So he can forcefully rebut all the criticisms that are hurled at him. As Paul argues in this chapter, he is a minister of the new covenant.

 ## Interpretation and notes

3.1. We do not need . . . letters of recommendation: In 2 Corinthians 2.17 Paul has just set himself apart from 'many' who are peddlers of God's word. Paul continues in his attempt to establish in the Corinthians' minds not only the sufficiency of his ministry but also its superiority. Today, analogies to the letter of recommendation might include such things as a certificate of ordination, an academic degree in theology, eloquence or personal charisma. Many people think that a certificate of ordination or having a degree in theology means that you have the credentials of ministry. While those things are important and have their place, it must be realized that a piece of paper in itself is never a sufficient credential.

3.2–3. You yourselves are our letter: Paul makes a bold statement, calling the Corinthians his letter. They are the greatest tribute to the success of his ministry. Paul's effective ministry among them bears witness to the validity of his calling. Three things are to be noted about the letter.

1 It is a letter written on Paul's heart. Paul's opponents seek to undermine his ministry and to win the affection of the Corinthians. Paul states that he carries them in his heart everywhere he goes. He cannot forget the way the Spirit worked in their lives through his proclamation of the gospel.

2 The Corinthians are a letter from Christ. As such, Paul makes it clear that the source of the Christian life is the power of Jesus Christ. Although the Corinthians are the fruit of Paul's ministry, Christ was the author of their salvation. Moreover, in as much as a letter must reflect the thoughts and the heart of the writer, the Corinthians should reflect the heart and mind of the Saviour. Believers today must realize that we are letters of Christ, not only in places of worship but also in the various social contexts, such as schools, offices and workplaces, in which we may find ourselves. Together, the entire Corinthian con-

gregation constituted just one letter. Although saved personally, they were to reflect collectively the life of Christ. What an important lesson for local congregations and Christian denominations today! We are, together, the letter of Christ.

3 The Corinthians were a letter written with the Spirit. The Holy Spirit is the facilitator of life and the dynamic of Christian living. As Christians, the Holy Spirit helps us to keep the laws of God because they are now written on our hearts.

3.4–6. Such is the confidence that we have through Christ: Paul has shown that his letter of recommendation is far superior to those of his critics. His critics' letters were humanly authored and written on paper. What of Paul's ministry? Was he self-appointed? Was his ministry a result of his personal strength? *No*. His ministry is also verified by his unwavering confidence toward God. It is God who empowers him for service. So Paul can say that it is Christ who makes him and his co-workers **competent to be ministers of a new covenant**. Their confidence does not arise from an attitude of self-sufficiency but one which is through Christ. Paul understands the Lord working through his proclamation of the gospel as a validation of his ministry. Yet he quickly disclaims any self-adequacy in his ministry. He does not consider any part of his ministry or its results as coming from himself. He gives all credit to God. His sufficiency is of God. The fact that God wrote on the hearts of the Corinthians shows that Paul and his co-workers were competent as ministers of the new covenant. Paul carefully makes a distinction between the old and new covenants. The old is of the letter and the new is of the Spirit. The letter kills, but the Spirit gives life. The law of Moses was not intended to be a way of salvation as Paul's opponents might have argued. For Paul the empowerment of the Spirit through the new covenant is the only way to eternal life (cf. Galatians 6.8).

3.7–11. The ministry of death . . . the ministry of the Spirit: Using the imagery of two covenants, Paul continues to show the superiority of his ministry to that of his opponents. Beginning from here Paul contrasts the ministry and the effectiveness of the two covenants and observes that the new covenant is more glorious on both counts. He acknowledges that the old covenant, although a ministry of death, was glorious. However, the new covenant is more glorious than the old covenant in its ministry. Though the law was holy and served a divine purpose, it could not save sinners. The law pointed the Jews to what sin was and what they needed to do. But the inability of the Jews to keep the law pointed to their need of something greater, namely, Christ and the Spirit. The new covenant, based on Christ's death and resurrection, offers sinners divine forgiveness and eternal life (Ephesians 1.7). The contrast between letter and Spirit is, as a matter of fact, a contrast between the law and the gospel. Paul reasons that, if the law which condemned and which eventually passed away was glorious, how much more glorious is the new covenant which ministers righteousness and continues to be a force to the present day. The glory of the gospel is permanent. The gospel is God's last word.

3.12–13. Since, then, we have such a hope, we act with great boldness: In contrast to Moses' veiling his face, the effectiveness of this new covenant in the lives of all who receive the gospel encourages Paul to have confidence and to speak with boldness. Believers today are in such a better situation now than anyone under the old covenant. Paul alludes to the story of Moses after he met God to receive the law (Exodus 34.29–35). Moses' face shone because of the glory of God, and the Israelites were afraid to come near him, so he veiled his face until he returned to speak to the Lord.

3.14–15: Paul interprets and applies the story of Moses that he has just cited. Though Israel saw the glory of God reflected in Moses' face and were afraid, they did not obey God's law. Israel's basic problem was not a failure to comprehend the law but a failure to obey it (Romans 2.17–29; Galatians 6.13). They suffered from a moral deficiency that prevented them from seeing and believing, hearing and understanding. They were blind to the truth. Even to this day the law, which holds its observers in bondage, is unable to lift this veil from their hearts. Paul insists that the people remain in that same condition when the law is being read to them today.

3.16: Paul interprets the action of Moses as an example for unbelieving members of the nation of Israel in his own day. If they turn to the Lord, the veil of disobedience that sheaths their hearts and minds will be removed. On the one hand, the turning indicates that there is a sense in which Israel must itself act to remove the veil. On the other hand, turning to the Lord applies also to Gentile believers (cf. 1 Thessalonians 1.9; Galatians 4.9). In the new covenant every Christian can enter the presence of the Lord. However, it is only by virtue of the Spirit who removes the heart of stone and writes God's law on our hearts that any can enter safely.

3.17. Where the Spirit of the Lord is, there is freedom: Paul points out that the ministry of the new covenant is attended by the liberating power of the Spirit. This freedom is a release from bondage to former spiritual masters in order that we might serve God. It is not a freedom to sin (Romans 6.1–2, 15). The chains of guilt that bind unbelievers are now removed. This freedom takes place when we are saved; it is experienced in daily life as we yield ourselves to the control of the Holy Spirit. It is a freedom to serve the Lord. The purpose of freedom is service, which promises love and reconciling care of one another. Now through the Spirit believers have the ability to serve the Lord in holiness and righteousness.

3.18. All of us . . . are being transformed into the same image: The people under the law, the believer with unveiled face behold the glory of the Lord as it is manifest in God's Word and are divinely transformed into his image from glory to glory. This transformation is a continuous process throughout the Christian life and will be perfected with the redemption of our bodies at Christ's return. As Moses radiated God's glory when his face was uncovered, so we, believers today, reflect the glory of God.

 ## STUDY SUGGESTIONS

Word study

1 The word 'commend' is from the Latin word *commendare*, which is a combination of two Latin words, *com*, which expresses intensive force, and *mandare*, which means to commit or entrust. In light of this definition, why would letters of recommendation be so important?

Review of content

2 Paul asks the Corinthians if he needs letters of recommendation. What, to Paul, is his true letter of recommendation?

3 How is Paul's letter of recommendation superior to that of his critics?

4 What imagery does Paul use to show the superiority of his ministry to that of his opponents?

(a) What is the new covenant and how does it compare with the old?

(b) What two important points does he make using this imagery?

Bible study

5 Read Romans 16.1–2; 1 Corinthians 16.10–11 and Philemon.

(a) Of what are these examples?

(b) If Paul is writing in such a fashion, is he opposed to using letters of recommendation as a reference?

(c) What should be the primary role of letters of recommendation? Are they the sole measure of a person's worth in ministry? How does Paul use them?

Discussion and application

6 What are the most important aspects of a letter? Since, according to Paul, we are 'letters' of Christ, do you see those aspects on display in your life and in your church for others to see easily?

7 Throughout Paul's writing, you will find a tone that relays the message that Paul is above all a servant.

   (a) How is this different from what we sometimes see from well-known ministers on TV or elsewhere?

   (b) How can realizing the importance of the lives of those to whom we minister as being our letter of recommendation counteract the tendency to become self-reliant or even conceited in ministry?

8 Is there a tendency to pay more attention to a minister if she or he has a degree, is ordained or has some other formal certificate? Is there a tendency to pay more attention to ministers who have more of a natural talent in speaking, singing, etc.? What is the danger in this? What should we consider as the greatest credentials a minister could have?

9 Is it only ministers who should have 'letters' of recommendation in the people that they have impacted? How significant is the believer's testimony to the furtherance of the gospel?

10 Have you ever been through a time at your church where a new pastor had to be chosen? How does this process work in your church? What letters of recommendation are required of the applicants? How, throughout the selection process, can one discover the true letter of recommendation of which Paul speaks in this chapter?

4.1–18: Treasure in jars of clay

 Summary

4.1–4: Sustained by divine mercy

4.5–7: Substance versus eloquence

4.8–12: Catalogue of hardships

4.13–18: Basis of Paul's endurance

 Introduction

It is not uncommon for the Lord's people to experience opposition from Satan, times of discouragement, pressures of need and of sin. But do these adversities give us sufficient reason for quitting? What keeps a Christian worker going in the midst of pressures and adversities? There is a growing concern among denominations about the number of people who are leaving the pastoral ministry. What accounts for this attrition of grassroots leadership? A part of this is what Paul describes in this passage as fainting, losing heart, giving up (2 Corinthians 4.1). Here, Paul continues to develop and defend the view of his ministry in contrast to that of his opponents, doing so particularly by recourse to the gospel message. He opens by asserting that he has 'this ministry'. He then adds the qualification, which sets him apart from his opponents – his ministry is a result of God's mercy. The adversities that Paul faces in his ministry are not sufficient reasons for him to quit. In spite of his experiences, Paul triumphantly declares that he is not fainting or quitting. He then continues to argue that, as a minister of the new covenant, he has renounced all dishonesty and deceit. Instead he continues to commend himself to every person's conscience by openly proclaiming the truth. He denies that he falsifies the gospel message and has already stated that his opponents do. Paul uses images, figures of speech and paradoxes to make his point. He contends that his sufferings and weaknesses, rather than being a proof of lack of apostolic calling, manifest a ministry which is derived from a suffering Lord and which has its ultimate purpose in God's glory.

Interpretation and notes

4.1. We do not lose heart: Paul resumes the theme of 2 Corinthians 3.6, concerning his divine appointment as a minister of the new covenant. Paul regards his ministry as a gift from God, not some personal achievement. With this gift comes the formidable responsibility to spread the gospel faithfully and to speak the truth forthrightly. He calls attention to the fact that he received the gospel, not only as a personal way of life, but also as a ministry. As a result, he does not faint, or lose heart. One cannot but wonder aloud: what makes Paul tick? What keeps him going in the face of all adversities? Part of the answer is in this verse. The glory of the commission Paul received far outweighs all the distressing experiences he might face in fulfilling or discharging it. For Paul, the commission is worth all the trials that go with it. He is filled with a great hope that eclipses everything that is capable of driving him to despair. This will be picked up later in v. 16.

4.2a. We have renounced the shameful things: Here Paul lists three dishonourable practices he disowns and then states what he does. First, he affirms that 'we have renounced the shameful things that one hides'. Paul does not suggest that he used to engage in them. He never did resort to them. He fends off the accusation of deceptive behaviour that has been previously levelled against him in 2.17. He contrasts his own boldness with those who attempt to cover up their true intentions. Those who act

147

honourably, as Paul does, do not need to cover their deeds in secrecy but are open to the view of their immediate community and entire world, Christians and non-Christians. Paul draws a parallel between the nature of the gospel that he preaches and that of his personal character. In the same manner that the new covenant is open, his own methods are also open. He has not manipulated the message.

Second, Paul says that **we refuse to practise cunning**. If the character of the messenger is in question, the integrity of the message also becomes questionable. He repudiates all deception. The noun 'cunning' translates the Greek word *panourgia* that literally means 'readiness to do anything'. In an unfavourable sense, it applies to someone who is crafty, deceitful and tricky. Such persons will employ any trick to accomplish their shameful purposes, and they usually resort to secret plots and manoeuvrings. Paul is a forthright person. In this we must learn that to proclaim the gospel is just as important as to live in a manner that befits the gospel.

Third, Paul says that they do not **'falsify God's word'**. Paul does not preach for personal gain. He does not tamper with God's message. Paul is not like those who use the preaching of the gospel to advance any secular or carnal purpose. Those preachers explain away the force of Scripture so as to excuse sin and generalize its precepts so as to excuse their hearers from obedience, especially in that which goes against their inclinations. Today there are many who pose as Christian ministers; persons who shy away from preaching what they know and believe as truth because not only would it make them unpopular, but also it would help them to secure a larger audience and more extensive financial support. For such preachers, sin is no more than a 'mistake' and sexual aberration an 'alternative lifestyle'. In a word, they turn with the tide and shift with the wind of popular opinion, prejudice, fashion, lifestyle, etc.

4.2b: Having stated what he does not do, Paul now turns to what he does. He states that **by the open statement of the truth we commend ourselves to the conscience of everyone in the sight of God**. Paul presents the truth plainly and openly to everyone, whether learned or unlearned, friend or foe. He commends the sincerity and truth of his preaching. His life and motives are open. He has nothing to hide. Hence, he does not fear scrutiny of his message, motives and methods.

4.3–4: Despite Paul's claim that he has preached the gospel openly, some of Paul's critics still maintain that his message is veiled, perhaps suggesting that he is an eloquent but ineffective preacher and overbearing by letter (10.10). If Paul is truly a faithful messenger, should not everyone understand and believe his message? Or does he fail to make the gospel message clear? Paul maintains that the veiling has nothing to do with his message or method. Instead, the fault lies in two areas: the audience and the source of blindness.

First, to those who are perishing, the gospel neither makes sense, nor is it valuable. The gospel is made plain in Paul's preaching. So it is the hearts of those perishing that are veiled, not the gospel itself. It is their response to the message that shuts out the gospel light.

Second, Satan, the god of this world, has blinded the minds of those who are perishing. Those who persist in rejecting the gospel become victims of Satan. These are people who deliberately choose to continue their dispute against God. Although Satan has been defeated by the cross of Christ (Colossians 2.15), he still has the strength to besiege human minds and to incite them to embrace and exalt evil rather than God (cf. Mark 4.15). He continues to try to blind people to his defeat by leading them to despise the cross of Christ and to look for glory elsewhere (1 Corinthians 2.8). He does all in his power to prevent humans from knowing the one true God whose image can be seen in Christ. Humans make themselves susceptible to his wiles with their preoccupation with the transient, unspiritual, earthly realm. The mind blinded by Satan cannot think straight, and it rebels against God's truth (2 Corinthians 3.14). How many times do we hear criminals confess that 'a voice in their minds made' them commit the crimes? Such voices are not from God.

4.5. We do not proclaim ourselves: As faithful heralds of the gospel, Paul and his co-workers do not draw attention to themselves. Although his ministry is more glorious than that of Moses, it is not concerned with personal glorification. Paul does not advertise or preach himself. He has previously told the Corinthians in 1 Corinthians 2.1–4 that he did not come to them with persuasive words of human wisdom. Moreover, Paul defines his role as that of a servant. Although he could command their obedience, he chooses not to. There is no place in true Christian ministry for self-exaltation, self-glorification. Although the world says, 'Exalt yourself,' Christ says, 'Humble yourselves.'

In media-oriented twenty-first-century society, the preacher is pressured to use the pulpit to display his or her eloquence and oratorical skills. The congregation, in its appetite for entertainment and desire for amusement, adds to that pressure. When ministers are introduced, we are accustomed to hearing such words as 'international', 'great' or 'awesome' used in describing them. In Paul's time, the challenge was rhetorical prowess. But Paul would not succumb to such pressure. Rather, he explains the basic thrust of his preaching: Christ as our Lord; ourselves as his slaves.

4.6: The starting word 'for' in v. 6 indicates that the sentence introduced here explains or reaffirms the implication of what Paul has just said in v. 5, that is, why he humbles himself and preaches Christ exclusively. It is related to his experience as new creation. God has acted incredibly toward him. Unlike those who had been blinded by Satan, God has illuminated Paul's heart. God's light dispels darkness in every form – whether it be the physical darkness of night or the spiritual darkness of human ignorance. The light that dispels darkness is to be found in the face of Jesus Christ. For Paul, to know Christ is to know God. The corollary is true: not to know Christ is not to know God.

4.7. Treasure in clay jars: Paul carries the treasure of the gospel in a clay jar. In the Old Testament the image functioned to show the fragility of humans (Jeremiah 22.28). Specifically the image of 'earthen' vessels or jars is used in the context of suffering as punishment for Israel's sins (Isaiah 30.14; Jeremiah 19.1, 11; Lamentations 4.2). For Paul his suffering is that of apostolic service. The point of the contrast in the verse is the paradox between the inestimable value of the message and the suffering of the messenger. Behind Paul's statement is an allusion to the attack on Paul by his opponents that he is weak and fails to show that he possesses divine power. For Paul, however, divine power is God's possession alone and, paradoxically, it is present in his sufferings as an apostle. Paul shows that his bodily weakness and sufferings do not constitute evidence of lack of apostolic commission but rather manifest an apostleship that is derived from a suffering Lord and that has as its ultimate purpose the glory of God. What a sharp contrast to the 'prosperity gospel' message where suffering is often equated with God's disfavour!

4.8–9. We are afflicted in every way, but not crushed: To develop his point further, Paul turns to what is generally called the 'catalogue of hardships'. Here one finds the list of trials that Paul endured. The list of hardships is meant to instil courage in the Corinthians and to show that God's power is present precisely in Paul's suffering and deliverance. Paul emphasizes the weakness and insignificance of the apostles in vv. 8 and 9 in a manner that is reminiscent of 1 Corinthians 4.9–13. However, Paul here draws a vivid contrast between their sufferings and preservation.

4.10. Carrying in the body the death of Jesus: Paul states that he bears the dying of Jesus in his body, expressing the dangers and sufferings to which Paul and his co-workers are constantly exposed for Christ's sake. It is such dangers that constitute their sharing in his sufferings. His suffering, as one who is under Christ's rule, shows that God's power was present in the dying of Jesus and is present in his own sufferings. Similarly, Paul states that the purpose of bearing the dying of Jesus is to manifest the life of Jesus in his person.

4.11–12. Death is at work in us, but life in you: Verse 11 clarifies the previous verse by repeating its thought in slightly different language. That Paul is given up to death because of Jesus demonstrates his faith and willingness to conform himself to the pattern of existence found in Jesus, even his death (Philippians 3.10). There is an important lesson to learn here. The Corinthians, like many Christians today and especially Pentecostals, believed that sufferings and adversity were inconsistent with the Spirit-filled life, let alone with what is generally termed as 'victorious' or 'successful' Christian living. Paul sees it differently. It is his hardships that validate his ministry. In Paul's day, and for many Christians around the world today, the life of the Christian is a life of suffering. In some places, to become a Christian is to receive a sentence of death.

4.13-15. We also believe, and so we speak: Paul explains why he continues to speak, turning to the ultimate reason why he should act as an apostle and thus submit himself to the sufferings that he went through. His suffering and message are for the sake of the Corinthians and for the purpose of reaching out to more Corinthians. Paul speaks boldly because his faith reveals to him that beyond the earthly tribulation lies the assurance of resurrection. Paul's faith has an objective content. It consists in the knowledge that God has raised Jesus from the dead, that he will raise Paul at the end of time to be with Jesus, and implicitly that he will also raise up other believers. Paul concludes that his ultimate goal as Christ's apostle is to bring glory to God. The basis of all his action has been his converts and not to increase his own stature. His aim is that God's grace may spread to more people as the gospel is preached.

4.16. We do not lose heart: Paul restates what he previously said in v. 1, 'We do not lose heart.' He both summarizes the preceding section and picks up the theme of v. 1. He proceeds to draw a distinction between the outward and inner person. The outward nature is a whole person as seen by others or that aspect of one's humanity that is subject to various assaults and hardships such as are listed in vv. 8 and 9. The inner nature is the unseen personality known only to God and oneself. The Corinthians need to understand that despite Paul's bodily weakness, his inner person is being transformed daily. He then turns to the contrast between the present and the return of Christ, this life and the life to come. For Paul's opponents the present is a time of glory, but for Paul it is a time of suffering.

4.17-18. What can be seen is temporary, but what cannot be seen is eternal: The life to come is a life of glory. Contrary to the position of his opponents, Paul can say that according to God's surpassing gift his present momentary suffering will be followed by eternal glory. Paul neither minimized nor glorified his sufferings. Instead he had an eternal perspective. He took his pain in his stride, looking at everything in light of eternity. He fixes his gaze not upon the things that belong to this age but upon the things that belong to the coming age. As Christians we must be careful not to base our hopes on the things we see. The unseen will endure when all else fails.

 ## STUDY SUGGESTIONS

Word study

1   The word beginning 2 Corinthians 4.6 is a small word, 'for'. Even though the word is small it has large implications.

(a) What are the implications of the word 'for'?

(b) What metaphor does this word introduce?

2 Paul talks of carrying the treasure of the gospel in 'clay jars'. How was this term most commonly used in the Old Testament? What is Paul's purpose in using this metaphor?

Review of content

3 Why does Paul not lose heart even though he has endured a lot of sufferings in his ministry? What was the basis of his confidence in the midst of suffering and persecution?

4 In v. 2, against what accusation is Paul arguing, and what metaphor does he use in this argument?

5 What two arguments does Paul give against the accusation that his gospel is veiled (in vv. 3–4)?

6 From v. 16, describe the distinction Paul makes between the 'inner' and 'outer' natures.

Bible study

7 Read 1 Corinthians 4.8–13 and compare/contrast with 2 Corinthians 4.8–12.

(a) List some of the sufferings found in either passage.

(b) What is the purpose of Paul listing his sufferings?

(c) In the 1 Corinthians passage, Paul seems to be hinting that true disciples of Christ experience hardship. Is this true? Why or why not? If so, what can we learn from Paul to help us manage the sufferings we will experience?

Discussion and application

8 We have seen that if the character of the messenger is in question, the integrity of the message also becomes questionable.

(a) Has there ever been a time when you doubted the sincerity of a message (or just words spoken) you heard due to the lifestyle of the person speaking?

(b) Does the converse hold? That is, if someone does not preach from a balanced array of topics, including the tough-to-tackle questions regarding sin, should the character of the messenger be in question? Why or why not?

9 What could be the danger of a ministry which is performance-driven?

(a) How does the behaviour of a congregation contribute to pressure on the pastor to perform?

(b) What does Paul's response to this same pressure tell a pastor in this situation?

(c) What could individuals in the congregation do differently to avoid such pressure?

10 Does Paul teach that suffering goes hand-in-hand with the Christian life?

(a) Is that the overarching message that we hear from Christian media? Is that the message you hear in your church?

(b) What is the danger of not talking of suffering as part of the Christian life?

(c) If suffering is such a large part of the Christian life, why, according to Paul, should we not give up?

5.1–21: Ambassadors for Christ

 Summary

5.1–8: The new body

5.9–10: The future judgement

5.11–17: Motivated by God's love

5.18–21: The ministry of reconciliation

 Introduction

Why do we do what we do? In other words, what is our motivation for what we do? These questions are particularly relevant for ministry today. It is important not only to do what is right but also to do it for the right reasons. Despite the numerous troubles that Paul faces, he is relentless in pursuing the ministry to which he has been called. His zeal remains unabated. The key is motivation. Paul has the right motives. In 2 Corinthians 5 Paul builds upon the conclusion in 4.17–18 and provides further details of his motivation for ministry. First, Paul is fully convinced of a future life that is devoid of suffering and pain. It is a life without change or death. He has an abounding hope of resurrection and of heaven (5.1–8). Second, Paul is sure of future divine judgement (5.9–10). In the face of the coming judgement he has incredible confidence, for his relation with God is already right. Third, Paul is persuaded that the reconciliation of humanity

153

to God is God's initiative, motivated by love and manifested in and effected by Jesus Christ.

 Interpretation and notes

5.1. For we know that if the earthly tent we live in is destroyed, we have a building from God: Paul starts on a note of confidence. 'We know' implies that the Corinthians had knowledge of what Paul is about to say. But it is more than that. It indicates Paul's unwavering conviction and settled belief that the Christian will eventually be done with the frailty and suffering of his or her present existence. We know, Paul says; not 'we think', 'we hope' or 'we assume' but 'we know'. What a bold statement! As Paul has previously said in 2 Corinthians 4.1–15, believers can face any trial in this life because of the hope of future resurrection.

Thus 2 Corinthians 5.1 shows that possibly for the first time in his apostolic ministry and career, Paul deals seriously with the possibility of his death before the return of Christ (cf. 1 Thessalonians 4.17; 1 Corinthians 15.51). This is probably because of his encounter with death spoken of earlier (2 Corinthians 1.8–11). Remember that Paul was a leather worker, and he made tents. He uses imagery that comes from his own social location. He is saying, 'After all, I might be dismantled at any time.'

5.2–4. For in this tent we groan, longing to be clothed with our heavenly dwelling: He likens the present human body to a foldable tent that is to be replaced with a building, a clear allusion to the resurrection body that Paul mentioned previously in 1 Corinthians 15.38, 40, 42, 44, 46, 48–49, 52–54. The present tent-body that gradually ages and wears out will be taken down and folded up when we die. At the return of Christ and the resurrection of the faithful, we will receive our new bodies, and our salvation will be complete.

Table 1 Contrasting 'now' and 'not yet'

'Now'	'Not yet'
Tent	Building
Earthly dwelling	Heavenly dwelling
Destructible	Eternal
Human-made	God-made

Paul does not define for us the precise nature of groaning. But when one looks at Romans 8.19–20, Paul is saying that our human mortal existence is limited. Paul sought liberation from the imperfection of our present embodiment. He had another home in view. The believer's present existence is punctuated with sufferings and pain. The present age is characterized by groaning, and believers are not exempt from the groaning of the whole created order (Romans 8.22–27). Thus, Paul says, we groan. But we do not groan as hopeless people. It is a groaning that is accompanied with a longing. It is not a longing for death. Paul's hope and groaning are not for death. Death is not the hope of the Christian. Many of us are not earnestly longing for heaven. Is it, perhaps, because we are so comfortable on earth? It is not that we should seek out affliction, but neither should we dedicate our lives to the pursuit of comfort. There is nothing wrong with earnestly desiring heaven! There is something right about being able to agree with Paul and say we groan!

5.5. The Spirit as a guarantee: While Paul speaks of the transformation of the mortal body in v. 4b, it is the last part of v. 5 where he indicates how the preparation takes place. God has prepared the Christian believer for transformation by giving us the Spirit as a guarantee (Gk. *arrabona* – pledge or guarantee), which is different in kind from the final payment. How can the Spirit be God's pledge? It is clearly through his empowering the Christian's daily re-creation or renewal. In other words, what the Spirit does in the present not only prefigures but also guarantees his future completion of that work which he began (cf. Philippians 1.6).

5.6–8. We walk by faith: The word translated 'walk' in v. 7 means 'conduct our total life'. C. K. Barrett explains Paul to be saying, 'We conduct our lives on the basis of faith, not by the appearance of things.' While Paul (as is true of all Christians) is in the physical body, he is away from the Lord (v. 6). However, even in this life Christ lives in him, and he looks for the day when he can see the risen Lord face to face.

In v. 8, Paul talks about being away in the body and being with the Lord. This is still an idea of permanence. So you find a corollary – residence in the body is absence from the Lord, absence from the body is residence with the Lord. What did Paul understand to be involved in being at home with the Lord? The preposition 'with' (Gk. *pros*) suggests location, but when you use *pros* to describe the interrelation of two persons, it implies a fellowship (both active and reciprocal). It is more than location (cf. John 1.1 – 'with God'; Mark 6.3 – 'with us'). At home 'with the Lord' depicts Christians' eternal destiny. 'We will be at home with the Lord' means not only that we will be where he is, but also there will be a higher form of intimate relationship with Christ that we will experience.

5.9–10. We make it our aim to please him: Unlike many who are people-pleasers, Paul considers nothing to be more important than pleasing the Lord Jesus Christ who has commissioned him. Although Paul is not completely devoid of the hope of being honoured by the Corinthians, his proclamation of the gospel and his entire life are devoted to pleasing the Lord rather than winning honour from people. That is his supreme ambition. For him, to live is Christ and to die is gain (Philippians 1.21). At the heart of Paul's desire to please the Lord is the awareness of an awaiting future judgement. So he declares, **For all of us must appear before the judgement seat of Christ** (2 Corinthians 5.10). While 'in the body' we must act in such a way that we will be pleasing to God at judgement.

We shall all be seen for what we are. All believers will be stripped of all disguises, masks and pretensions before the judgement seat of Christ. What we do in the body has moral significance and eternal consequences. To be conformed to Christ's glorious body in the next life, we must be conformed to his image and character in this life. What a sobering thought.

5.11f.: Once again, the focus shifts back to Paul's ministry as he reveals his third motivation for ministry. He first talks about his ministry of proclamation and then expounds in greater detail the content of his preaching.

5.11–14. The fear of the Lord: Paul reiterates what he has first stated in 1.12–14. He sees the fear of the Lord as the basis of faithful and diligent service. It is said that 'One serves the most the person one fears the most'. It is not a slavish fear but a reverential awe. Such fear of God excludes self-reliance. So Paul does not vainly try to rely on his own wisdom and paltry resources. Some of Paul's critics must have accused him of being beside himself (v. 13a). So it is today. We live in a society that is not only suspicious of Christians but also often thinks that Christians are at least a little crazy, too. However, we can say like Paul that Christ's love for us, as well as our love for him, motivates us. To live for Christ is to live for others. Furthermore, for Paul and for believers today, our convictions are rooted in the death and resurrection of Christ.

5.15–17. Therefore, we regard no one from a human point of view . . . if anyone is in Christ, there is a new creation: Paul now highlights the first consequence of what he stated in vv. 14–15. He no longer judges by human standards (v. 16). Prior to his conversion Paul had a negative view of Christ as the Messiah. So do many today. Judging Christ from a human point of view continues in various forms both in society at large and within the academic world. But such judgements are just as wrong as that of the Pharisees of Christ's day who saw him as no more than a carpenter's son or as an ordinary prophet. Apart from Christ, people are also evaluated by human standards. Today, people are treated based on what region of the world they come from: nationality, ethnicity, educational standards, wealth and so on. Sadly, the Church is not exempt. Such standards do not promote reconciliation; they engender only strife and divisions. Christians must shun all superficial human standards. The second consequence is in v. 17. It is an emphatic statement that describes the radical transformation that takes place when one places one's faith in Christ. To be a Christian is more than a mere show of hands and 'accepting' the Lord without a corresponding change of life. Instead it is a transformation that is brought about as a result of union with Christ. One must remember that Jesus did not bring a new religion but a new creation.

5.18. All this is from God, who reconciled us to himself: 'All this' refers to what Paul has written in vv. 14–17, particularly to the redemptive work of Christ in vv. 14–15. God reconciled Paul and others to himself. It was not something they could do by themselves. God took a decisive step in Christ to bridge the gulf between God and humanity. All people were alienated from God and undeserving of God's favour, but he brings into personal fellowship with himself those who come to faith in Christ.

5.19. In Christ God was reconciling the world to himself: This verse is the heart of the gospel. First, the initiative was with God; he bridged the gulf of separation created by our sin and rebellion. Second, the mediator was Christ. Reconciliation centres on the death of Christ at Calvary through which Christ stood in the breach for us. Third, as a result of Christ's death, God opens the way to reconciliation. God has now committed the message and ministry of reconciliation to believers (5.19b–20). This is every Christian's ministry. It is not for a selected few. It belongs to all, not to some.

5.20. We are ambassadors for Christ: Paul provides one of the clearest expressions of his calling and mission. He is an ambassador. So are Christians today. As ambassadors, Christians have a grave responsibility. What is our message? 'Be reconciled to God.' God offers reconciliation but it has to be accepted by those to whom it is offered.

5.21. He made him to be sin who knew no sin: Paul concludes the chapter by referring back to the death of Christ and its goal. He became a sin offering in order that we might have the righteousness of God imputed as well as imparted into us.

 Special note F

The new creation

In Charles Dickens' story, *A Christmas Carol*, Ebenezer Scrooge, that wrinkled, cynical, embittered, greedy old man, encounters death in a dream on Christmas Eve. His late partner, Jacob Marley, appears to him, dragging his chains, to tell Scrooge that his death is certain and looming. All his life long, Marley had worked on forging every link in his chain through hatred, greed and unrighteousness. Scrooge is taken on a tour of Christmases past, present and future, and sees his own name carved on a gravestone. The dreadful nearness of death finally has the effect of changing him. He awakens on Christmas morning a different man. When Scrooge awakens the next day, everything looks different to him – the weather, the light, the people, his relationships, and his lightness of step – everything, literally! Awareness of his impending death and the possibility of being different has made his outlook on life new and vital.

Dickens makes no mention of the gospel in his story, but it provides a good portrait of what takes place in us when we contemplate the death of Jesus and truly see it for what it is. When, by faith, we enter into the death of Jesus on the cross and his resurrection from the grave we have new life, become a new creation, and everything changes for us. In a much more profound sense, the death of Christ on the cross makes each of us a new creation. We are utterly new and, like the pilgrim in John Bunyan's *Pilgrim's Progress*, freed from all the baggage that held us down in the past.

Paul is not talking about reincarnation. That is the best that non-Christians can hope for – that people get another shot at this life. But could anyone hope to do better if another chance were given? I'm not so sure. We would probably make just as bad a mess of it the second time around. Paul is talking about a new creation, a life filled with the presence of God.

 ## STUDY SUGGESTIONS

Word study

1 God has prepared the Christian believer for transformation by giving us the Spirit as a guarantee (or pledge). What word is translated as *guarantee*? How is this different from a final payment? How can the Spirit be God's pledge?

2 What is the actual meaning of the word translated 'walk' in v. 7? How does reading v. 7 with this meaning in mind change the way someone may interpret this verse?

3 In v. 8, how is the preposition *pros* translated? Is this merely a reference to location or does it mean more than that in this instance? Explain.

Review of content

4 At the beginning of 2 Corinthians 5 Paul uses a metaphor created from his own social situation – his job – to capture the reality of our present bodies.

(a) Describe that metaphor.

(b) Compare and contrast the bodies we have now with the ones we will have in the future.

(c) What does Paul mean when he says, 'For in this tent we groan . . .'?

(d) Create a metaphor (describing the reality of our present bodies) of your own using your social situation.

5   In v. 11, what does Paul give as the basis of faithful and diligent service? Is this a slavish type or reverential? Explain. In light of this, where does self-reliance fit in?

Bible study

6   Read Galatians 3.23–29.

  (a) In light of 2 Corinthians 5 and the newfound lens which characterizes the new creation into which believers are brought by faith in Christ, what divisions of people (if any) should exist in the minds, relationships, etc. of believers? Explain.

  (b) Locate passages in the New Testament where we see in action what Paul is teaching concerning those who are in Christ. Discuss how these passages eclipse lines of worldly divisions to show the power of restoration found in Jesus Christ.

Discussion and application

7   Are you earnestly anticipating and longing for heaven?

  (a) If so, how does this affect your actions throughout your everyday situations? If not, why?

  (b) Does our society contribute to a longing for heaven? In what ways?

  (c) Does our society detract from a longing for heaven? In what ways?

8   In v. 17 Paul speaks of those who are in Christ being a new creation.

  (a) Is it natural to view someone who has just been saved as a new creation? Is this supernatural? Explain.

  (b) What can the Church do to guard against viewing new converts 'from a human point of view' (v. 16)?

9   In vv. 19–20, we see that God has committed the message and ministry of reconciliation to believers, so that we are to be ambassadors for Christ. Is this a responsibility of all believers or only of those formally called to ministry? If all should be sharing this responsibility, why do you think only a small percentage of congregations are actively involved in ministry? How would a church based on this exhortation by Paul actually look?

10   What are the characteristics of the body that awaits the believer after death? What are some of the rewards that await the believer? How should this impact our life now?

Applied theology essay 3
Reconciliation

DARYL BALIA

When Paul wrote that 'in Christ God was reconciling the world to himself' (2 Corinthians 5.19) he probably did not anticipate that such a statement would become for many a summary of the teachings of the Christian faith. Some say that the theme of reconciliation is at the centre of all Paul's writings. The great theologian, Karl Barth, gives it a central place in his books to show how Christ as mediator brings God and human beings together. It is important to make God the focus when the subject of reconciliation comes up. We can speak of reconciliation among people in our day and age on the basis of what God has done in Christ. God took the initiative as an act of love. He sent Christ into the world so that through him men and women might be reconciled to God. Reconciliation relates to Christ's entire life, his incarnation, ministry and death. It is not possible for us to understand fully the reason why God has acted in such a way. Billy Graham once preached a sermon where he said that God was lonely and wanted a relationship with us. Sin on our part, however, was a barrier which made us turn against God. It is this state or condition, of being an enemy, which Christ had first to remove through his work of reconciliation. We can now have fellowship with God again because of what Christ has done.

South Africa is often mentioned as an example of a country where reconciliation has been achieved between races of people who were previously divided. The Church in South Africa is regarded highly for its 'ministry of reconciliation' which contributed to the ending of apartheid. Yet, a hundred years ago, social justice and human rights abuses were not matters that the mainline churches worried about. Instead, they drifted with the political climate of the time and offered no active opposition to government policies which were exploiting Blacks. When the first ecumenical gathering took place in 1904, the concerns expressed related to building more churches, proclamation of the gospel, medical missions and education for black people. By 1942, when an ecumenical council was in place, black Christians were still finding it difficult to see a positive role for the churches in ending apartheid. This was because churches remained racially segregated and divided on many issues. Apartheid became entrenched when the National Party came to political power in 1948. Afterwards, stronger voices of protest against the injustices of apartheid were heard. These were still mainly white and male. Beyers Naude was one such prophet. He resigned his position as minister of a 'Whites only' church to work for peace, justice and the freedom of all citizens of South Africa.

The political turning point came in 1976. Soweto, a black township outside Johannesburg, erupted in protest. Christians were rudely awakened to their sombre silence in the midst of a gathering storm. The need for black leadership gained recognition at last. Desmond Tutu emerged as an ecumenical leader capable of steering the churches into challenging the status quo. He once wrote an open letter to the white Prime Minister as follows:

> I write to you Sir, because like you I am deeply committed to real reconciliation with justice for all, and to peaceful change to a more just and open South African society in which the wonderful riches and wealth of our country will be shared more equitably.

Tutu went on to become Archbishop of Cape Town. He won the Nobel Peace Prize for his commitment to reconciliation and justice. For many Whites, Tutu was too radical in calling for economic sanctions to destroy apartheid. For many Blacks, his ministry of reconciliation was too forgiving and open-ended. Two important theological responses were generated in 1985. They showed how sharply divided Christians were over political change. One was the Kairos Document. It arose from the struggle to discover a Christian response based on social analysis to the ongoing crisis in South Africa. The other was a 'Statement of Affirmation' put out by evangelical Christians. It offered Jesus Christ alone as the most viable option for the country's future. The first placed no hope in the government of the day to change course. The second assumed the government could still work towards the common good.

Nelson Mandela became South Africa's first democratically elected president in 1994. He appointed Desmond Tutu to head a Truth and Reconciliation Commission (TRC). This was after Tutu had decided that,

> I wanted to get out of the limelight and to enable the church as a whole to contribute in a quiet and effective way to the healing of the nation. I continue to believe that this is an area of ministry which the church has neglected through the apartheid years. We need to empower people to rise above their circumstances, to reclaim their full humanity and to seize the moment in which we live in South Africa. Blacks and whites need to rise to the challenge which God is offering us.   (Charles Villa-Vicencio, 'Tough and Compassionate: Desmond Mpilo Tutu', in *Archbishop Tutu: Prophetic Witness in South Africa*, eds. L. Hulley, L. Kretzschmar and L. L. Pato, p. 38. Cape Town: Human & Rousseau, 1996)

The TRC's purpose was to unearth past events where human rights were abused, to pardon those guilty of such abuses, and to restore dignity to the victims. Telling the truth, often through individual stories, is important when old enemies are trying to bury the past. But you cannot forget the structural evils of a system that must also be held accountable. If in a public meeting you tell the truth of an evil deed committed, does this mean that you should now be free? What about justice and compensation to the victim? To benefit the victim, reconciliation should always include truth, justice and reparation. It is seen as an alternative to revenge, which left to itself will only continue the cycle of violence.

Blacks and Whites were moving towards a new democratic future as South Africans. They wanted to be united as one nation, undivided and passionate for a better life for all citizens. This was to be the new society built on the ruins of apartheid, free from all forms of racial segregation. With such a common future as a goal, people were able to support the work of the TRC and collectively say 'never again' to apartheid.

Giving victims a public space to tell their stories of suffering promotes reconciliation. It helps to prevent a repetition of past horrors and allows for acknowledgement of transgressions. Other institutions, such as the courts, police, political bodies or defence formations, might not be neutral. In a truth commission, composed of men and women of honour and integrity, we are better able to hear evidence of crimes against humanity. Such a commission can pursue matters of truth and justice more objectively. It can contribute to personal healing, including the healing of memories. Tutu believed his vision of reconciliation for South Africa's future was secured through the work of the TRC despite the evil nature of human beings. Once Tutu broke down in tears after hearing stories of pain and anguish. He illustrated the public's own experience of the memory of past suffering. Some Whites felt the TRC process was not impartial. Some Blacks refused to accept that the liberation struggle also included some acts of human rights violations. When reconciliation is pursued on a national level it will not be possible to please everyone. However, it produces national healing and remains a better alternative to punishing people through criminal trials.

Reconciliation is not only a national or communal experience. For it to be real, reconciliation must take place at the individual level and is often shaped by willingness to forgive. If there is no healing in personal relationships, no transition from the past to the future, talk of reconciliation will remain only talk with no walk. Some think of it as a goal towards which one should work. It is a process that unfolds over time, not an event. A person wanting to be forgiven for some crime should not barge into the victim's life without checking to see if he or she would be welcome. In a situation of oppression, it is easy to lose a sense of personal identity. It is important that there is mutual respect and a commitment to end any feelings of superiority over the 'other' person.

Not all cultures deal with the experience of reconciliation in the same way. In some cultural traditions, ancestors must first be consulted before one forgives someone. Among some honour-and-shame cultures, saving face means never forgiving. This would be a sign of weakness or betrayal of solidarity with one's family or group. The forgiveness that Jesus preached challenges this way of thinking.

One of the most powerful stories to come out of South Africa's struggle for reconciliation concerns a young American student named Amy Biehl.

She came as an exchange student during apartheid. She had a passion to achieve social justice for those less fortunate than her. On a visit to a black township, she was killed by political activists Ntobeko Peni and Easy Nofemela. After the country became democratic, her parents came to South Africa to ask for these two young men to be given a second chance in life. They were forgiven for their misdeeds and released from prison. They began to work for the Amy Biehl Foundation Trust in promoting goodwill among all citizens.

Even when a political struggle turns violent, it does not mean that those involved are not open to a peaceful resolution of conflict. The person who shoots the gun is affected by violence as much as the person who gets shot. Both are therefore capable of being reconciled. They can change from being enemies of one another to becoming friends. Of course, it is much better if reconciliation takes place before there is any violence or loss of life, but this is not always possible.

South Africa as a country understood the meaning of reconciliation because it had been experienced elsewhere before. The Second World War has left a deep scar on the face of the world, and there are still ongoing attempts to heal the hurt suffered by many of its victims. Germany, Poland, Japan and, more recently, Chile, Haiti and Argentina are good examples of places where the need for healing is still being felt. Of course, in Asia, Koreans remain deeply divided by security fences while in Sri Lanka, Tamils and the Sinhala continue to fight each other. The Rwandan genocide is past, but efforts to achieve national unity and peaceful living for all ethnic groups there are ongoing. A breakthrough has been achieved among Catholics and Protestants in Northern Ireland. The journey of reconciliation has just begun in that context. More troubling, however, is the situation in the Middle East where Israelis and Palestinians remain bitterly divided. A giant concrete wall is being erected by the Israelis to separate themselves as a nation from their neighbours. Such a measure might improve the security situation in the short term, but how will it bring peace, reconciliation and a lasting solution for the Middle East conflict? Christians are called to the 'ministry of reconciliation' in the world. Churches should get involved with others in resolving these conflicts which cause us so much harm and hurt.

We learn from life that reconciliation is not something one can experience without some sacrifice. One must be prepared to suffer some pain at a personal level for someone else to experience the meaning of forgiveness. This is not easy to achieve in all circumstances. Paul's message to Christians, and that of the New Testament as a whole, is clear on the subject. It is not an option for Christians but a way of life in Christ – to forgive others and to receive their forgiveness as well. Reconciliation will not become a practical experience if as individuals we do not put this matter to the test in our personal relationships. This is what follows when Paul pleads with us to be reconciled to one another. It flows from the reconciliation that God has made possible between himself and human beings through Christ. Churches have not always taken the ministry of reconciliation as seriously as they have taken the command to preach the gospel. In modern situations torn by strife, some Christian leaders have emerged to make a useful contribution towards peace. They have inspired many across the world by risking their lives to bring people together in harmony. We need to give the theme of reconciliation more space in our reflections on God's message in the Bible. We need to prepare future generations of Christians by healing the memory of past failures and working for a world of justice.

6.1–18: Christian relationships

 Summary

6.1–3: Paul defends his integrity

6.4–10: Paul's sufferings

6.11–18: A call to holiness

 Introduction

The chapter concludes a lengthy section concerning the nature of Christian ministry (2 Corinthians 2—6). The phrases 'ministers of a new covenant' and 'ministers of reconciliation' are described and contrasted with the ministry of a group with the inflated title: 'super-apostles', who preached a 'different gospel' (11.4–5). Here Paul clearly shows that if the Corinthians fail to manifest vital Christianity rather than a shallow substitute – a Christianity of substance, not of style – then they are in danger of receiving God's grace 'in vain', to use Paul's words in 2 Corinthians 6.1. As such, the discussion in the chapter is to be understood in a twofold context, both aspects of which are related to his discussion about ministry and reconciliation in the previous chapters. First is the believers' ministry of reconciliation to those outside Christ. Second, and perhaps more important, is the opposition to Paul from some of the Corinthians. It is to this latter group that Paul urgently addresses his admonition. In both instances Paul shows the relational nature of grace.

 Interpretation and notes

6.1. As we work together with him: Paul continues with his apostolic defence as God's servant focusing specifically on his call. The verb *synergountes* ('working together') has no object. So it simply says, 'working together'. Although Paul could be referring to his working together with others, God is better understood as the object of the phrase 'working together' in light of Paul's statement in 5.20 (see also 1 Corinthians 3.9 and 1 Thessalonians 3.2). Paul perceives his apostolic work as being an integral part of God's mission. So Paul reminds them of his divine commission and authority while he asserts that what he does is God's work, not his own work. Think about this as a minister; you are given an opportunity by God to participate in his divine programme. You are not just a hireling, working 'for God'. You are working together with God. That is, we are in a business partnership.

6.2. Now is the acceptable time: Paul quotes Isaiah 49.8 to make his plea. In the same manner as the Servant in Isaiah, Paul calls the Corinthians to reconciliation with himself as a proof of their salvation. If we fail to put to practical use the details of the spiritual benefits received by the favour of God, even God's favour becomes a useless and empty thing. In the present context, the failure of the Corinthians to reconcile with their apostle with whom they had an estranged relationship amounts to receiving the grace of God in vain. So it is true of us today. In this verse, Paul is concerned about the Corinthians' relationship not only with God but also with him. It is unfortunate that many people behave as if it is only the personal relationship with God that counts, regardless of their relationships with each other. Nothing is further from the truth as well as from Paul's mind. Right relationship with God demands and as a matter of fact should result in right relationship with others, especially believers. Christianity is about restored relationships. Paul's concern for the Corinthians is significant. An unread Bible, a wasted Sunday, and such knowledge of the truth as does not mould our life are the grace of God received in vain.

6.3. We are putting no obstacle in anyone's way: Paul is careful not to offend in anything, lest blame be laid on the gospel ministry. The Greek word translated 'obstacle' means something that makes another stumble or that which puts off someone. We must continually remember that our manner of life either commends or discounts the message that we seek to share with the world. Often it is not the difficult, hard-to-understand truths or somewhat embarrassing things about the gospel that cause people to stumble; rather, it is our misrepresentation of the gospel through our lifestyle that causes problems for unbelievers. When there is a gap between belief and behaviour, doctrine and deeds, people are turned off. Blameworthy conduct brings reproach on Christ and his work. Although each person is accountable to God for his or her own life, nevertheless, believers, especially those in positions of responsibility, ought to serve as positive influences on those who come in contact with them.

6.4. We have commended ourselves: Paul continues to defend his call. He does so by returning to his paradoxical understanding of ministry (cf.

4.7–12). When Paul speaks of himself as a servant (v. 4), it is often in the same context as his descriptions of his suffering (vv. 4–10; cf. 11.23–33). His suffering actually commends Paul as a genuine servant of Christ. A clear parallel exists in Paul's thought between his own suffering and that of Christ. Paul gives the Corinthians another catalogue of his qualifications, in a somewhat more detailed fashion.

Paul begins this list by using the word 'endurance', a word that implies a refusal to buckle under pressure. Afflictions, in and of themselves, do not commend anyone. It is endurance that commends us. Paul is suggesting that the Corinthians follow his example and do not receive God's grace in vain. Paul's ability to endure the sufferings (afflictions, hardships, calamities, beatings, imprisonments, riots, labours, etc.) demonstrates the grace of God in his life.

How do we know that a person is strong? It is in times of pain. It is during such times that we know someone's integrity and calibre. Believers today sometimes experience such sufferings. Things go wrong and they are sometimes beset with hard things. While it is true that these problems are not unique to Christians, it is how Christians respond to them that spells the difference. If believers can handle pressures that crush others, if they can continue to love those who have misused and hurt them, then they have endured. Like those triathletes who, because of their sense of mission, bike 200 miles, swim 10 miles, and run double marathons, demonstrating incredible endurance in the process, there is something about Christians who endure under tremendous pressure, and it is that endurance that attracts the attention of non-believers.

In October 2006, at West Nickel Mines Amish School in an Amish community in Lancaster County, Pennsylvania, Charles Carl Roberts IV took children hostage and eventually killed five little girls. The normal reaction to a situation as devastating as this is for the community to cry out for vindication. This is not, however, what the Amish community did. Instead, they publicly announced their forgiveness of the man who had brutally murdered their little girls. And, in a society where justice, vindication and revenge are the norm, the forgiveness of a man committing such an evil act drew much attention. This was an opportunity for the world to see the love and forgiveness of Christ exemplified in the lives of those who love him. Just as Paul's sufferings spoke volumes to the Corinthians of God's love, so the forgiveness of the Amish speaks of God's love to this man and his family.

6.5: Paul goes on to list some uncommon circumstances such as beatings, imprisonments and riots. In Ephesus, the whole city is in hot pursuit of the apostle because of his faith. The truth is making an impact whether people like it or not.

Today many Christians around the world face various hardships that compare with the apostle's. Recently, in Orissa, India, a mob that comprised about 500 armed Hindu worshippers descended on the village to attack Christians. Christian converts in Somalia face difficulties and, in Northern Nigeria, churches are frequently burned down.

There is a challenging reality about Paul's faith which causes him to suffer such things. So it is with believers today. 'Hard work, sleepless nights and hunger' speak of the discipline to which the apostle subjects himself either deliberately or by the sheer force of circumstances. There are nights when he goes without sleep as well as times when he suffers hunger. Of note, Paul makes reference here to hunger, which is translated elsewhere to mean, 'fasting'. So, this is not hunger as a result of lack of food but hunger as a means of self-denial. Additionally, there was the hard work of studying, preaching and travelling so as to encourage the saints.

6.6–7: Paul changes from referring to hardships to ethical qualities that characterize his ministry. He does not just put up with the troubles associated with ministry. He responds with positive faithfulness, manifested in various ways. Despite troubles he lives in purity. The word 'purity' here means 'guiltless conduct'. He faces troubles with knowledge – knowledge that God is in charge, no matter what happens – and an understanding that his afflictions are part of an honourable service to Christ. Paul's ministry is typified by patience. He is patient with the people to whom he ministers (Acts 20.31). He frequently exercises much kindness as he proclaims the gospel of Christ. He insists that his ministry is conducted in the Holy Spirit ('holiness of Spirit', NRSV). It is not unusual for Paul to link the Spirit to ethical qualities. Paul sees his ministry in 2 Corinthians 3.6–8 as ministry in the Spirit. These virtues are the evidence of the indwelling Spirit. Truthful speech also characterizes Paul's ministry. He does not peddle falsehoods, as tempting as they may be sometimes. Moreover, Paul's proclamation of the gospel is accompanied by the power of God.

6.8–10: As the climax to his apostolic defence, Paul lists a series of paradoxes that contrast appearance with the reality of his life. Paul is talking about how his opponents and the world evaluate him. From his opponents' and the hostile world's point of view, he is no minister from God, only a fraud who preaches foolishness and leads his followers down the garden path to destruction. Although considered to be a deceiver, he speaks the truth. Although unrecognized as an apostle by some, he is so recognized by others. Fixing his eyes on the unseen, eternal glory that awaits him buoys his spirit so that he is always rejoicing. Although undergoing various kinds of sufferings and troubles, he is at the same time full of joy. Notwithstanding poverty, he possesses everything. His ministry keeps him poor, yet he makes many rich through his preaching. Paul models himself after Christ (8.9).

6.11–13: Paul addresses the Corinthians by name and directs their attention to the freedom with which he writes and the large place which they have in his heart. Some of the Corinthians considered Paul to be aloof. The Corinthians are not restricted in Paul's feelings for them, but he senses that he is in theirs (v. 12). Paul speaks freely to the Corinthians and pours out his heart to them. As their spiritual father, he urges them to reciprocate his love for them by giving him an equal place in their hearts (v. 13). It is unfortunate that it can become so difficult, if not impossible, for two parties (individuals or groups) to reconcile when they have 'hard feelings' toward each other. Sometimes, it requires just one of the two parties to take the initiative. This is what Paul does in this Letter, particularly in this place. Paul is seeking for reconciliation, taking a step toward laying aside past grudges. Paul hopes that the Corinthians will reciprocate and unreservedly open their hearts wide to him.

6.14–16a. Do not be mismatched with unbelievers: Paul admonishes the Corinthians to open wide their hearts to him but this will require them to do something: they must not be mismatched or 'unequally yoked' with unbelievers. To do so would hinder the Corinthians having proper affection for him and God. They cannot love as they should as long as they are having wrong associations with teachers who oppose Paul's directives. Paul does not forbid our association with the unsaved. Instead he warns that believers should avoid putting themselves in compromising situations. Jesus mingled with the lost, entering their homes, eating at their tables and listening to their problems. He was known as their friend. Yet, he did not participate in their sins or allow them to lead him into sin. He has sent us into the world in order that we might evangelize the unsaved. We must associate with them so that we may win their confidence and share the gospel with them. While living and serving in the world, Christians must maintain a prophetic distance. The five questions that Paul raises in these verses underscore the importance of being 'in the world yet not belonging to it' (John 17.14–17).

6.16b–18. Come out from them and be separate from them: The Old Testament reveals that separation is essential to consecration (Joshua 3.1–5). So Paul supports his command for separation by stating the new identity of the Corinthians. They are now sons and daughters of God. Furthermore, they are the temple of the living God. This means that God dwells among his people, talks with them and regards them as his own. The temple is set apart from other buildings because of the presence of God. Without the presence of God, the Church is no more than just a social gathering. God's presence among believers is the foundation for Christ-like living. In the Old Testament, the temple of Solomon was what it was because it was filled with God's glory.

 STUDY SUGGESTIONS

Word study

1 In v. 1, how is the verb *synergountes* translated? What are the two options for the meaning of this word? Which meaning is the more probable here? Why?

2   In v. 5, how is the Greek word *nesteiais* translated? Is this a voluntary or involuntary situation? Explain.

Review of content

3   What are some ethical qualities that characterize Paul's ministry? What could be Paul's purpose in including the Spirit in this list of ethical qualities? What are some hardships which Paul faces? How would he have fared through the latter (hardships) without the former (ethical qualities)?

4   List and discuss the paradoxes Paul mentions in vv. 8–10. Are there any paradoxes of your own that capture the reality of the Christian life?

5   What situation in Corinth is Paul addressing when he instructs the Corinthians not to be 'mismatched with unbelievers'? Does this mean that we must never have communication with unbelievers? If so, why? If not, what does it mean (practically) for us today?

Bible study

6   Read Isaiah 53.

   (a) Of whom does this passage speak? What do you think about the Suffering Servant in this passage?

   (b) Compare and contrast Paul's suffering in 2 Corinthians 6 to the Suffering Servant in Isaiah 53.

   (c) In light of Isaiah 53, why would Paul place such an emphasis on his own sufferings?

Discussion and application

7   Understanding that we are working together *with* God rather than simply *for* God, how should this impact our work? What implications does this have on ministry and service in the kingdom?

8   Can you think of some times when you or people you know have received the grace of God in vain? Is this easy to recognize when you are in the midst of the situation? What was the result of this? How could the local church have helped keep you (or them) from receiving God's grace in vain?

9   In the same vein as Paul's declaration of his love for the Corinthians in vv. 11–13, how important is it for us to express our love to other members in our community of faith? How might it be detrimental to withold this communication for fear of rejection or betrayal? How would Paul respond to such fear?

10 How is it that we find our identity from the community of which we are a part? What are the implications of this statement? In light of being a part of a community, what responsibilities does this add to the individual? To the community?

7.1–16: Urgent appeals

 ## Summary

7.1: A call to cleansing

7.2–4: An appeal to open hearts

7.5–7: The coming of Titus

7.8–11: Godly sorrow

7.12–16: The vindication of Paul's confidence

 ## Introduction

At the time of writing, the Corinthians did not have confidence in Paul and were estranged from the person who had brought them to Christ through the proclamation of the gospel. Paul makes a great effort to restore their confidence, knowing full well that a lack of confidence in his person would result in a lack of confidence in his message. In this Paul continues to act as an agent of reconciliation. A change of heart among the Corinthians resulted in an abundance of joy for Paul. Today also there is a dearth of confidence among some Christians and many factors tend to drive wedges between us. But the Church must continue to be a community of reconciliation, a communion of saints that is characterized by mutual love and shared trust.

 ## Interpretation and notes

7.1. Making holiness perfect: Having appealed to his readers to avoid unequal yokes, Paul now expresses his command for separation in 2 Corinthians 6.14 in terms of cleansing from defilement of flesh and spirit, a way of referring to the total person. With this, Paul lifts the notion of separation to a higher dimension than externals. The call to cleansing is an appeal to the Corinthians, who are both God's temple and people, to live as befits their calling. Sin, whether physical or psychological, leaves the residue of guilt and spiritual pollution. How can we remove this from ourselves? By appropriating the provision which God has made for our cleansing. We deal with our sins with repentance and confession; God applies the value of Christ's death and shed blood for us and forgives us. Because the Corinthians, as members of the new church of God in Christ Jesus, have now become recipients of these promises from God, they are likewise confronted with the responsibility to effect complete ethical and religious renewal in accordance with the directives of God. Every aspect of the Corinthians' lives must be affected in the Corinthians' efforts to make themselves clean. In doing so, they will increasingly become like Christ.

7.2–4. Make room . . . for us: Paul returns to his appeal for reconciliation. He urges the Corinthians to receive him, to open their hearts to him (v. 2). He longs that they show him the same unbroken love which he has for them and that they give him a place in their hearts just as he has given them a place in his. But why should they receive him? He asserts that he has not wronged anybody; he has not ruined anyone and has not taken advantage of anyone. In short, he has not hurt anyone with reference to morals, finances or doctrine. Because of his integrity of life and ministry, there is no reason for the Corinthians to have shut him out of their hearts. His own attitude toward them serves as an example of what theirs should be toward him. Rather than feeling resentful toward them for their lack of affection, he still has them in his heart and regards their lives as being entwined about his so that whatever happens to them happens to him. Because of the feeling of intimacy that he has for them, he has spoken out freely and boldly as a friend, not as a stranger. He declares that his boast on their behalf is great. Titus' report brought good news that anticipates better things for Corinth. Hence, the apostle overflows with joy in the midst of distress. In spite of the difficulties of ministry and the resistance of Corinth, Paul continually rejoices in what Christ has done and is doing.

7.5–7. God . . . consoled us by the arrival of Titus: Paul had sent Titus to Corinth and the apostle anxiously awaited Titus' return and report. Having to leave Ephesus early, Paul went to Troas and then over to Macedonia, hoping to meet Titus there. While he was waiting for Titus in Macedonia, Paul was troubled on every side by conflicts without and anxieties within (v. 5). He was downcast and depressed by adverse circumstances. Paul has no wish to dwell on his past troubles. He only wants the Corinthians to be aware of the severity of his trials. He is all too human as we are. Today ministers hardly admit to their inner struggles lest they appear to their followers as weaklings. Paul moves to emphasize God's comfort in the midst of troubles. Paul's description of God contains a great promise for those who are miserable and those who are downcast. Titus was used of God to comfort Paul in a way which only a true friend and a faithful, sympathetic associate can do. Titus also had news for the apostle (v. 7). Not only had the Corinthians received him but they also dramatically displayed a change of attitude toward Paul. Titus spoke of their earnest longing, mourning and fervent mind toward their father in the faith. This added to Paul's joy. Do we find joy in our friends? As friends, do we bring joy to others? We can help lighten the burdens of others and bring them joy by pleasant acts of friendship and of cheerful news.

7.8–9. I made you sorry . . . your grief led to repentance: Paul had written a letter to the Corinthians that dealt with a sensitive issue involving one of the members of the Corinthian congregation (2.4). The letter was probably disciplinary in nature and caused temporary pain to the congregation. Apparently, the letter produced godly grief among the Corinthians and, consequently, repentance. The imposition of discipline or the suffering of pain that does not lead to repentance is not godly. Discipline must serve a redemptive purpose. If it does not lead to repentance, it will cause irreparable harm.

7.10. Godly grief . . . worldly grief: Paul contrasts the type of grief the Corinthians exhibited with worldly grief. Whereas godly grief produces **repentance that leads to salvation,** worldly grief produces only remorse. When a person has 'godly' sorrow for his or her sins, he or she will take the appropriate action of repudiating them and confessing them to God. Genuine contrition or sorrow for sin is a turning away from sin and a turning toward God for the forgiveness of sins. This results in salvation, something that no one ever regrets. Many people are sorrowful for being caught in their sins instead of realizing the sinfulness of sin and its eternal consequences.

7.11: The Corinthians have been diligent, something which Paul now commends. Their sorrow for sin has led to repentance. Paul gives a sevenfold description of their diligence.

1 Earnestness, referring to the Corinthians' care for Paul.
2 Eagerness to clear themselves.
3 Indignation against the offender. The Corinthians have now changed their lethargic and apathetic attitude to the disciplinary matter about which Paul wrote.
4 Alarm.
5 Paul mentions their longing for his return, which signals that they want the relationship to be fully restored.
6 Zeal. The Corinthians are now ready to defend Paul.
7 Punishment. They are now ready to see justice done.

Paul concludes that the Corinthians, apart from their initial inaction against sin and their support for him, were always guiltless in the matter. They have now further proved their innocence by their reaction to his letter and their reception of Titus.

7.12: Paul points to a more important reason for writing the severe letter. He does not really deny that he wrote because of the problem relating to the offender and the offended, but he emphasizes a deeper, spiritual cause – that their care for him in the sight of God might be made manifest. This underscores the importance of the manner in which the Corinthians responded to his letter. The letter gave them opportunity not only to deal with the offender but also, more importantly, to show them that they were indeed devoted to him. He wishes to make clear that healing their strained relationship and restoring their friendship was of greatest importance to him. Their inaction in the face of the offender's defiance may have concealed temporarily their true loyalty to Paul. Paul's reprimand therefore was not aimed only at an individual but at the whole church. Paul's rebuke of the Corinthians, although painful, worked by stirring them to action. Their zeal to punish the offender showed their devotion to Paul and to the gospel. Paul's explanation for the letter shows that a minister of reconciliation is not intent on making sure that punishment is meted out to those who may deserve it (to strike back) or to protect the honour of his person or his office. He is interested only in resolving the wrong and ensuring that reconciliation occurs.

7.13. In this we find comfort: Paul's confidence in the Corinthians is also vindicated by their reception of Titus. We can imagine the apprehension with which Titus travelled to Corinth. But whatever fears he had were dispelled, and he was confident and encouraged (v. 7). The Corinthians not only welcomed him but also refreshed his spirit.

7.14: The Corinthians proved themselves to be everything about which Paul had boasted. Paul had expressed his confidence in them to Titus and it turned out to be justified. Otherwise Paul's good opinion about them would have put him to shame.

7.15–16: Indeed, the love of Titus overflows toward the Corinthians whenever he remembers the respect that they showed him and the obedience that they gave to Paul's letter. They accepted Titus as Paul's representative and, in doing so, showed their obedience to Paul's apostolic authority. Paul concludes the section as he expresses his confidence in the Corinthians. This prepares the way for the discussion about Christian giving in the next two chapters.

 STUDY SUGGESTIONS

Word study

1 Look up the definition of the word 'repentance'.

(a) Which of the following words (if any) carry the same connotations as 'repentance': regret, sorrow, remorse, penitence, atonement, shame, contrition? Explain your choices.

(b) Do our churches adequately teach the meaning of 'repentance' and create an atmosphere where such a change is probable?

Review of content

2 What is the purpose of 2 Corinthians 7.1? How does it relate to the previous chapter? What does Paul mean by 'making holiness perfect'?

3 In vv. 5–7, what had Paul sent Titus to do?

(a) What was the result of this venture?

(b) Considering Paul's relationship with the Corinthians, why was Paul worried about the relationship and how was Paul reassured?

(c) In v. 11, what did godly sorrow (grief) produce in the lives of the Corinthians? Is Paul rejoicing here in their sorrow? If so, why? If not, in what is he rejoicing?

Bible study

4 Read Matthew 26.47–56; 27.3–5.

(a) What actions in Matthew 27 support the statement that Judas repented?

(b) What actions do not support that statement?

(c) Do you think Judas repented of his betrayal? Why, or why not? If he had asked Jesus for forgiveness, what do you think the outcome would have been?

(d) Can you think of an instance where you were almost too ashamed to ask God for forgiveness? How did you overcome those emotions? What was the result? Describe how you felt when you knew you had been forgiven and had experienced true repentance.

Discussion and application

5 Does sorrow necessarily imply repentance? How does regret differ from repentance? Do you know some biblical examples of sorrow without repentance? Have you experienced the difference in these two in your life or in the life of a family member or friend? What was the result of sorrow/regret in each circumstance?

6 What is the danger in discipline which does not have a redemptive quality? How can the Church guard against delivering such discipline? What are some ways to encourage a redemptive quality in disciplining your children?

7 Even though the Corinthians had hurt Paul, when he sent Titus to them, he boasted to Titus of them. In the midst of a situation where he is hurt, how is Paul able to boast of those who hurt him? Have you ever been in a situation where you were able to do the same? How?

8 How can we refresh the hearts of believers we know? Does your response to your pastor (while he or she is preaching and in everyday conversation) give him or her occasion to rejoice and be encouraged?

9 Examining how holiness is described in this chapter, is holiness an individual thing, that is, just 'between me and God'? Explain. How can the actions of an individual affect the church community, and how should the church community influence the actions of an individual?

2 Corinthians 8.1—9.15

The collection

8.1–24: Grace of giving

 Summary

8.1–9: An example of giving

8.10–15: An appeal based on equality

8.16–24: Titus and the other brothers

 Introduction

A famine had ravaged the Judean area in the mid to late 40s and the Jerusalem church had been hard hit. Although Paul did not solicit personal financial support, he spent about 10 years soliciting funds among the Gentile churches for the Jerusalem church. The account of the collection, something which played an important role in his apostolic ministry (cf. Romans 15.25–32; 1 Corinthians 16.1–4; Galatians 2.10; Acts 24.17), is provided in 2 Corinthians 8—9. Paul does not write about the collection until he is sure that some of the outstanding issues between him and the Corinthians have been resolved, the result of which is the confidence that he exudes in 7.16. Mutual confidence has now been restored. The purpose of the collection is twofold. First, it is designed to alleviate the needs of the Jerusalem church, thus constituting an expression of the interdependence of believers worldwide (8.14). It is a way the Corinthians can minister to the needs of the poor Christians in the Jerusalem church. Giving, although never a substitute for personal involvement in the ministry of reconciliation, is fundamental to it. Second, it is to demonstrate the nature of the Church as a body that transcends national and geographical boundaries.

 Interpretation and notes

8.1–5: As Paul begins his appeal he brings to mind a great example of Christian giving. In a very tactful manner, Paul begins with an example, not a plea. Although the Macedonian churches (Philippi, Thessalonica, Berea)

were facing a severe ordeal that included persecution (1 Thessalonians 1.6; 2.14), they still contributed generously in spite of the hardships and difficulties. There are three phrases in v. 2 that seem incompatible: **abundant joy**, **extreme poverty** and **wealth of generosity**. The word for poverty could be translated 'penury' – scraping the bottom of the barrel. This is extreme poverty. Paul challenges the Corinthians to emulate their example of the Macedonian churches and lists specific aspects that the Corinthians should consider.

1 *It was an evidence of grace* Paul cites the generosity of the Macedonians as an evidence of the grace of God that was operative in their midst. Giving is participating in the work of God.

2 *It was during a severe ordeal of affliction* One would have thought that people in extreme poverty would have extreme sorrow; but joy is not conditioned by what we have outwardly. Their poverty did not impede their generosity. Their tribulation did not diminish their joy. Christians can experience joy in the midst of sufferings and persecution (Matthew 5.10–12; Acts 5.41; Philippians 1.12–18; James 1.2; 1 Peter 1.6–7). We must refuse to become creatures of circumstances. This is true of the Macedonians; hence Paul holds up their supreme sacrifice as a motivation for the Corinthians. Sometimes out of our own sympathy and affection for people, we want to excuse them from giving. To do so is to deprive them of their blessing.

3 *It was liberal* In spite of the extreme poverty of the Macedonians, they gave generously. They did not give only according to their ability but they gave until it hurt. What mattered to Paul was not the amount or the quantity of what they gave. It was the spirit in which they did so. With God, a couple of 'cents' sacrificially given can far outweigh billions of dollars. This was the reason Paul used them as an example for the Corinthians to emulate.

4 *It was voluntary and insistent* Paul describes the emotional state of the Macedonians as they gave. It seems likely that Paul at first declined their support, reminding them of their own poverty. But they would have none of that; they urgently pleaded (v. 4) with him to take the money. They begged with much entreaty to give. They considered it a privilege to give. Others would have made their own situation an excuse not to give. As a matter of fact, Paul would have gladly excused them, but they refused. Despite their own needs they were not going to be denied the opportunity to minister grace to others through their giving. The eagerness of the Macedonians to participate allows Paul to use them as a model for the Corinthians.

Having worked in the Philippines for many years as a missionary, I have seen the example of the giving of the Macedonians replicated on countless occasions.

5 *It was a testimony of their commitment to Christ* Paul puts the giving of the Macedonians in the context of their commitment to God and their loyalty to him as their apostle. So intense was the desire of the Macedonians to serve the Lord that they would not allow their economic hardships to keep them from being involved in the ministry opportunity that was open to them. To the Macedonians, this was no prideful competition with the other churches for honour. Their giving was first to the Lord (v. 5), an act of consecration, and it was from him that they took their cues. The Corinthians are left to draw the inferences.

8.6–8: The initial zeal of the Corinthians in the project evidently sagged. They had made a beginning and should have finished it. Unlike the Macedonians, they were not facing persecution and were not in financial straits. They should have contributed willingly. So Paul prods the Corinthians to complete what they previously started. Rather than scold the Corinthians for lack of completion, Paul praises them for their initial enthusiasm. Paul appeals to their desire for status and honour by pointing to their spiritual riches – their faith, speech, knowledge and diligence (zeal). He announces his plan to send Titus to supervise the endeavour. Paul's world was an honour-and-shame world in which shaming was a regular motivational technique. People would prefer to retain rather than lose honour. Paul has bragged to the Corinthians about how good an impression they had made on Titus (7.13). The warm reception that the Corinthians gave to Titus made him an ideal candidate to carry out the task. So Paul's appeal is to the sense of honour and shame that the Corinthians might possess. Paul is quick to say that he is not issuing a command to the Corinthians on the basis of his apostolic authority. The collection is to be a free work of love. So Paul would prefer the love of the Corinthians to be no less than that of the Macedonians, and the example of the Macedonians provides a basis for testing the reality of the Corinthians' love for him and their fellow Christians.

8.9: Paul provides a stronger reason for the Corinthians to participate in the project. **For you know the generous act of our Lord Jesus.** He tells the story of Jesus who, although rich, became poor in order that they, though poor, might be rich. Paul sees in Christ the greatest example of showing eagerness and generosity. If the sacrificial giving of the Macedonians does not stimulate the Corinthians to give, then the selfless example of Christ should at least do that! Unlike the Macedonians who gave out of their extreme poverty, Jesus gave when he was extremely, incalculably rich. Just like the Macedonians, Christ gave himself, and the Corinthians would do well to emulate those two examples. Christ's decision was voluntary. In his incarnation, Christ surrendered his riches so that humanity could share in his spiritual riches of salvation. Christ's sacrifice, rather than competition with either a local church, group or denomination, must be the real motive for giving.

8.10–12. Completing it according to your means: Paul continues with a direct application of all that he has said so far. He encourages the Corinthians to complete the effort they had begun a year previously. Once again, Paul does not issue a command. Instead, he reasons with them that though their original intent was good, they need to carry it out, otherwise their good intentions will amount to nothing. He exhorts them to complete the action since he presumes that the will is still present, and he wants them to act according to their will. He concludes by saying that the readiness of will is more important than the amount. Paul is asking them to give according to their means. Although the Macedonians contributed even beyond their ability, Paul tells the Corinthians to contribute according to their means (v. 11), not beyond their ability. Paul does not tell them to go as far as the Macedonians. What does Paul mean by 'according to your means'? He explains that in v. 12. Provided a gift is willingly given, its acceptance is determined on the basis of what we have. God assesses the value of what we give not in terms of the amount that we give but by comparing what is given to the total amount of the finances of the believer. Jesus gave us an example in Mark 12.41–44 of the widow's mite. Jesus said she gave more than the other, because she had a mite, and she gave all.

8.13–15: There is a change in the appeal. Some of the Corinthians probably raised objections to the 'collection project'. Paul does not intend to alleviate the need of some by impoverishing others. Among God's people, giving is to be according to the principle of equality where those who enjoy affluence share with those in need (v. 14). This principle serves as a guideline for equalizing the distribution of the necessities of life among God's people so that all will have sufficient provision. Paul illustrates this by the daily ration of manna which the Israelites received during their wilderness journey (v. 15; Exodus 16.14–22). At this time, Corinth was one of the few cities of Greece which was experiencing material prosperity. If the Corinthian believers were willing to share their affluence with the poor saints in Jerusalem, perhaps later the Jerusalem saints would be in a position to help the Corinthians when they experienced recession (v. 14). Paul is not attempting to set up a form of socialism by equalizing property, but he is seeking to relieve the acute distress of believers who are suffering material need. When the opportunity to exercise some kind of self-sacrifice presents itself and the Lord would have us to act, we too must take appropriate action as God directs. This action may involve our time and strength as well as money and goods.

8.16. But thanks be to God who put in the heart of Titus the same eagerness for you that I myself have: Although the affection of Titus for the Corinthians developed as a result of his interaction with them Paul can trace the interest of Titus to the working of God – 'Thanks be to God.' So, Paul is simply saying, 'Well, I want you to understand that your relationship with Titus is a great help, but understand it is not only your relationship with him that engendered this. God is involved in it!' Paul traced Titus' affection to the providential working of God. That meant the Corinthians would understand that the affection of Titus and Paul was based on concern for *them*, not for their money. That is the point.

8.17. He is going to you of his own accord: When Paul says that Titus is 'going of his own accord', he uses the word *authaireytos* ('going on his own initiative'). **For he not only accepted our appeal** – this refers to v. 6. But Paul says that in addition to the urging of Paul that Titus should complete the collection. Titus himself was very earnest and was going on his own initiative. The intensity of Titus' affection is not based just on Paul telling him to 'go and do it'. Titus may have sometimes worked independently of Paul. There is a hint here that even though Paul is the apostle, he does not 'drag everybody by the nose' and make everybody do his will. Rather, there is a kind of liberty in their working relationship.

It is a liberty that many leaders do not want to allow today, especially among Christian leaders in Africa. We must not kill the initiative of our members. If the Church is the Church *of God*, then we should not limit God as bringing about good things in the Church only by the initiative of the pastors or leaders. Otherwise, it is not a 'body ministry'. Each member should contribute to the welfare of the entire body.

8.18–19: Along with Titus is an unidentified Christian 'brother' that Paul is sending. Whoever the brother was, he was a person in good standing of influence. This unidentified Christian brother had two qualifications. First, he was well known and highly praised in the churches for his service to the gospel. Second, he was selected and commissioned by an unspecified number of churches to travel with Paul to administer the collection. As if to underscore the brother's integrity, Paul says that the brother sought not his own glory but the Lord's and to prove his eagerness to help.

8.20–21: Although Paul is organizing the collection, the money is to be collected by Titus and two messengers appointed by the churches. Paul and his companions are going to great lengths to avoid being accused of even the appearance of bad dealings. Later a delegation will take the gift to Jerusalem.

Here is a valuable lesson: there should be strict honesty in the handling of church money. As the old saying goes, 'Caesar's wife should be above reproach.' So should those who handle church finances. The manner in which church finances are handled should be above board. The testimony of Christ has suffered because trust has been violated. Yes, it is true that God knows when our intentions and motives are honest. But it is also necessary they appear honest and proper to fellow believers and the outside world. Christians should avoid shoddy handling of finances.

8.22–23: Here we find a second anonymous representative who is to travel to Corinth with Titus, and he is also identified simply as 'our brother' He has been tested, his zeal has been proved, and Paul and his companions have great confidence in him. Paul knows that he is very susceptible to misrepresentation. Paul could have laid himself open to a slanderous charge (cf. 12.16–18), and he wants to avoid that. In v. 23 Paul uses the word *apostoloi* (literally and NRSV margin, 'apostles'; 'messengers', NRSV). Paul states the credentials of the people he has sent. He draws a distinction between Titus, who is his partner, and the two other delegates that he is sending. Titus is a partner, a colleague and a personally appointed representative; whereas the other two are the representatives of the churches. It is important that he calls them *apostoloi* of the Macedonian churches. By life and service they bring credit to Christ.

8.24. The proof of your love: Paul's letter of commendation ends with a warm appeal. He simply enjoins the Corinthians to give evidence of their love for Christ and for the members of his body. How were they to do that? They were to do that by extending warm hospitality to the delegates and co-operation with their efforts to supervise the final arrangements for the collection. All was to be done in a very good way, as if in the presence of the churches. They were to do things transparently.

 STUDY SUGGESTIONS

Word study

1   In 2 Corinthians 8.17, Paul uses the word *authaireytos.* How is this word translated? To what/whom does Paul attribute this good relationship between Titus and the Corinthians?

Review of content

2   For whom was Paul taking up a collection in this chapter? What occurrence had caused this need? What was the twofold purpose of Paul taking up the collection?

3   What three churches are included in the phrase 'the Macedonian churches'?

   (a) Why would Paul mention their giving to the Corinthians? What does Paul allowing them to give tell the Church about its poor today?

   (b) Does Paul command the Corinthians to give? Why or why not?

   (c) Does he ask them to give to the same extent as the Macedonians? Explain.

4   Compare and contrast the giving of the Macedonians with the giving of Jesus. Why might the example of Jesus be a more effective example for persuading the Corinthians to give?

Bible study

5   Read Mark 12.41–44.

   (a) Why did Jesus say that the widow had given more than anyone else?

   (b) What does it say to you that Jesus noticed this woman's sacrifice?

   (c) Has there ever been a time when you sacrificed and felt no one noticed or cared? What does this passage speak to you regarding that?

Discussion and application

6   The Macedonians not only gave but also were eager to give. Describe the attitude of the Macedonians while giving. Does this challenge you? Is your attitude towards giving always eagerness? How can we teach our children that giving is a privilege?

7   In vv. 6–7, when Paul is asking the Corinthians to give, he does not browbeat them with the fact that they began something and did not finish it. What does he do instead? What implications does this have in the Church today?

8   Christ gave when he was extremely, incalculably rich. He gave so much that he became poor. How does this example speak to you today? Why do you think that the poor traditionally have less of a problem with giving than the rich? Discuss.

9   Paul did not force his own initiative on Titus, although Paul was the 'apostle' and Titus was working for him.

   (a) How should this affect the way those in positions of leadership in the Church treat the other workers in the Church?

   (b) Have you ever worked under someone who wanted his or her way without allowing input from others? What was the result?

   (c) Have you ever worked for someone who had more of a community mindset for leadership? What was the result?

10 Have you experienced a situation where the handling of money in the local church was not above reproach? Did this cause irreparable harm? What can we learn from Paul's example (especially v. 21) about the handling of money?

9.1–15: More about giving

 Summary

9.1–5: Giving without compulsion

9.6–7: Giving: an act of pleasing God

9.8–11: Giving: an empowering act

9.12–15: Giving: an expression of thanksgiving

 Introduction

The Church's need and handling of money is as sensitive now as it was at the time Paul wrote to the Corinthians. It deserves to be handled with utmost sensitivity, graciousness and dignity. Fiscal responsibility and the question of how to motivate people to give is a difficult task even when the circumstances seem right and perfect. Paul's lengthy discussion in 2 Corinthians 8—9 shows how important planning and administration are to the success of any ministry, particularly giving. Generosity is not something that is innate to human beings. As such, people must be taught how to give and receive. Paul is not about to leave anything to chance so he intensifies his appeal for help. He is very much interested in securing the co-operation of the Corinthians instead of coercing them.

 Interpretation and notes

9.1–5. Achaia has been ready since last year: In 2 Corinthians 8 Paul appealed to the example of the Macedonians as well as Christ as a means of motivating the Corinthians to participate in the Jerusalem collection project. Here, he appeals to the past performance of the Corinthian Christians, reminding them that he has spurred the Macedonians by their eagerness.

Paul's readiness to see the Corinthians in the best possible light has caused him some embarrassment. He wants to avoid further embarrassment, both to himself and to the Achaians. Hence, Paul has sent representatives in advance to prepare the collection. His objective is twofold: First, he wants to make sure that his boasting to the Macedonians about the Corinthians' eagerness to help is not found to be unsubstantiated. Second, Paul wants to make sure that when the delegates of the Macedonian churches arrive at Corinth with Paul on his forthcoming visit, the Corinthians will still not be unprepared.

183

As a further reason for their arrival Paul suggests that thereby the collection may be prepared as a **bountiful gift** rather than a demand by the apostle. Twice in v. 5, Paul uses the word *eulogia* (it was generally used in Greek for 'fine speaking'; from where we get the word 'eulogy'), which in biblical Greek refers to the act of blessing or consecration whether by God or human. Here Paul uses the word *eulogia* for the offering. It is an act that produces a blessing, thanksgiving to God. It is also a means by which God bestows blessing upon its recipients. Paul basically says, 'If I come to you and you are just then preparing the money, it looks like an extortion rather than a willing gift; and what we want from you is a willing gift, so you need to get everything ready before we get there.' If the gift is to have a spiritual dimension, it is essential that it should be a genuine 'bountiful gift', a free offering, not an extortion against their will.

9.6. Sow sparingly . . . reap sparingly: Paul sums up the benefit and principle of giving by means of a proverb. The principle of the proverb is clear: we reap in proportion to our planting. God will reward according to one's generosity. Caution must be taken not to translate Paul's words here into some sort of prosperity gospel in terms of possessions and material wealth.

9.7: In this verse Paul provides three important guidelines of giving.

1 Giving is a personal matter. 'How much' one gives is a question each person must answer for himself or herself. There must be no sense of compulsion or any kind of reluctance.

2 Giving requires resolve. It is to be done as one has *purposed* in one's heart. The verb translated **made up your mind** or 'purposeth' (AV) is found only here in the New Testament and means 'to choose deliberately' or 'to make up one's mind about something'.

3 **God loves a cheerful giver**. The word translated 'cheerful' here literally means to be *hilarious*. Giving must be done personally without fanfare and coercion or manipulation, and it must be joyfully done. Giving must be done out of conviction rather than out of constraint.

9.8–9. God is able to provide you with every blessing in abundance: Paul spells out the implication of the proverb in v. 6. God gives to us so that we can give more. When Paul talks about **every blessing,** he is talking about spiritual grace and material prosperity. Nevertheless, prosperity does not mean being a millionaire. It simply means that God meets our needs as they arise. But Paul goes further. He says that God will make all spiritual grace abound to us so that we will be able to bless others. Paul again resorts to Scripture to support his view, quoting Psalm 112.9, a passage that ascribes praise to those who give freely to the poor (2 Corinthians 9.9). We must beware of what Paul does not say. Paul neither insinuates nor suggests that wealth or surplus income is a sign of God's approval or blessing, although such an idea was a common view among some of Paul's Jewish contemporaries. It is not giving per se that Paul applauds. What is at stake here is a lifestyle of generosity.

9.10–11: Paul shows that divine providence is behind the whole process of sowing and reaping. In an allusion to Isaiah 55.10 and Hosea 10.12, Paul assures the Corinthians that God will not ignore their generosity but will enlarge their **harvest of . . . righteousness** (v. 10). The Corinthians' return will be a spiritual harvest. Paul then goes on to describe what the Corinthians can expect if they participate in the collection for the saints at Jerusalem. They will be **enriched in every way,** that is, both spiritually and materially. Paul is too well aware that faithful believers may be poor as the Jerusalem saints were at the time. The purpose of God's enrichment is not just for the benefit of the Corinthians but so that it will **produce thanksgiving to God** as they minister to others including Paul and his companions.

9.12–15: Paul ends his appeal by pointing out the threefold effect of the offerings. First, it is a means of supplying **the need of the saints. This ministry,** as Paul describes giving, will relieve the distress of those to whom the benefits accrue. Paul then introduces another word to describe the collection. It is the Greek word *leitourgia* from which the English word 'liturgy' is derived. Giving is service to God. It is part of the believers' worship experience. Second, giving leads to an overflow of thanksgiving to God. Paul has in mind the thanksgiving by the Jerusalem church that will result from the offerings. Third, the collection is a test of true commitment in faith to the gospel of Christ by the Corinthians. The completion of the collection will show that they have passed the test, and its acceptance by the Jerusalem church will lead those Jerusalem Christians to glorify God for the spread of the gospel. The acceptance of the collection will indicate fellowship with all Jews who have accepted Christ. Paul adds that in their prayers the Jerusalem Christians will express their longing for the Corinthians as Gentile Christians. The racial barrier between the Jews and Gentiles will be overcome. For Paul, the success of the collection manifests God's redemptive act in Christ, particularly his reconciliation of Jew and Gentile by means of the gospel. God's **indescribable gift,** Jesus Christ, was the greatest example of the self-giving God and the inspiration of all Christian giving. As such whenever we have the opportunity to give, our thoughts should focus on God's indescribable gift.

Special note G
Paul's vocabulary of giving

In 2 Corinthians 8—9, Paul uses various words to describe the collection project. Although these words describe the same activity, each nevertheless provides the reader with a unique perspective of how one should view giving as an integral part of Christian living and ministry. Apart from words such as love, partnership, earnestness, undertaking and other phrases that describe the attitude and process of giving, Paul describes the act itself with the following words:

1 *Charis* 'Work of grace' (8.1, 4, 6, 7, 19; 9.14). The word here means generous giving on the part of Christians, which is considered as a gift of thanksgiving.

2 *Diakonia* 'Ministry' or 'service' (8.4; 9.1, 12–13). It is used for supplying the needs of the poor.

3 *Eulogia* 'Blessing' (9.5). The giver of the blessing is God (or Christ; Hebrews 6.7; Galatians 3.14), even where the blessing is pronounced by a person (Hebrews 12.17). Paul calls the collection for the Jerusalem church a blessing, which includes the Old Testament sense of generosity, abundance in gifts and proceeds.

4 *Leitourgia* 'Service' or 'worship' (9.12). Its usage here is similar to Philippians 2.30 as the fulfilment of the true Christian 'worship' and the church's offering of 'sacrifices' pleasing to God.

For Paul, giving meant far more than a response to human need or simply delivering aid to poor people. It had major theological and spiritual consequences and was something he was prepared to risk his life to carry out. Hence it cannot be adequately expressed with business language or in transactional terms.

 ## STUDY SUGGESTIONS

Word study

1 In 2 Corinthians 9.5, what two Greek words does Paul use for the 'collection'? Describe the significance of each. Why would Paul use those words in this situation?

Review of content

2 In vv. 6–7, what three principles does Paul teach regarding giving? Do you practise those three principles when you give? Which ones are difficult for you? Why?

3 According to Paul, what is the reason why God gives to us? What are the implications of this in your local community of faith? Does this mean that wealth is a sign of God's approval or poverty a sign of God's disapproval? Why or why not?

4 At the end of this chapter, Paul points out two main benefits of the Corinthians supporting the Jerusalem Christians beyond supplying their needs. What are these benefits? Have you reaped such benefits in your life, church, community, etc.?

Bible study

5 Read Psalm 112.

   (a) List and discuss some of the blessings of the righteous that are named in this passage.

   (b) Have you experienced these blessings? In what ways?

   (c) Verse 9 declares that the righteous 'have distributed freely, they have given to the poor'. Is this a requirement for 'righteousness'? Explain.

Discussion and application

6 While 2 Corinthians 9 is focused on giving, Paul is not merely applauding giving for the sake of giving. Paul is applauding a lifestyle of generosity.

   (a) What is the difference between these two concepts?

   (b) Which is harder, that is, which requires more effort?

   (c) Is this necessary in the Christian life, or merely something that would be nice for Christians to do?

7 Why was Paul, whose ministry was to the Gentiles, so interested in collecting money for the saints in Jerusalem (Jewish Christians)? How does this speak to the relationship between Christians of different denominations? Are we following Paul's example in helping brothers and sisters who are in different churches, denominations, countries, etc. from our own?

8 Have you ever experienced a situation where you had a need that you could not meet on your own? How did you feel in that situation? How did God help you through that situation? Were other Christians involved in that help?

9 Does giving affect other areas of our lives than just finances? What could be the danger to himself or herself for a Christian of not giving freely? How does this affect the Christian community?

2 Corinthians 10.1—13.14

Paul's self defence and preparation for visit

10.1–18: Paul's apostolic defence

 Summary

10.1–6: Meekness and firmness

10.7–11: Paul responds to the charge of weakness.

10.12–18: Paul responds to the charge of ambition.

 Introduction

In an attempt to deride and ridicule the great missionary, William Carey, someone told him that he had learned that Carey was a 'shoemaker'. But being the humble person that he was, William Carey told him that he was not even a 'shoemaker' but an ordinary cobbler or mender. The point seems to be that an ordinary cobbler was the least qualified to be a missionary. Something of the same dynamics is to be seen in Paul's life. Paul was well educated (Acts 22.3). However, he willingly gave up whatever privileges he had as a Jew and lowered himself for the sake of the Gospel (Philippians 3.3–8). Although called as an apostle he worked as a tent-maker. This was repulsive to some of Paul's accusers. They thought that an apostle would not have to work for a living. He would be above that, it appears that some of them were saying. Paul was meek and gentle but his opponents misconstrued those qualities and equated them with weakness and timidity. They argued that he was a weakling when he was with others and was bold only when he was far off and writing letters. He barks more than he bites, they would probably have said. The false teachers at Corinth caricatured Paul in this manner. So, starting from 2 Corinthians 10, Paul defends his apostleship and ministry against various misrepresentations by false teachers who had infiltrated the Corinthian church. They vilified Paul's authority and apostolic commission. They mischaracterized his godly virtues and misinterpreted his wise purposes. But how seriously mistaken they were! To be meek does not mean that one is flabby, indolent or easygoing. As Paul writes, we see that his meekness is not incompatible with the firmness and reality with which he must deal with his opponents and his readers.

Interpretation and notes

10.1. I myself, Paul, appeal to you by the meekness and gentleness of Christ: Paul begins his defence with an emphatic *I myself, Paul,* probably to underscore the seriousness of the issue he is about to address in the rest of the Letter. It is about Paul's apostolic authority. His enemies accused him of being humble when he was present with the Corinthians and being bold when he was absent from them. They implied that Paul was really a coward who acted boldly only at a distance. They confused humility with cowardice. The pomp and show of his opponents are absent from Paul's ministry. In contrast, Paul's ministry is marked by the 'meekness and gentleness of Christ'. He will not allow the Corinthians to force him to adopt a different attitude but is eager to follow the example of Jesus and live as a genuine demonstration of Christ-likeness.

10.2: Although Paul desires to remain meek among the Corinthians, he is not about to take the accusations of his opponents 'lying down'. He has decided to pay a visit to Corinth to deal with the estrangement. He wants the Corinthians to respond appropriately, otherwise he will be willing to show boldness to those who oppose him and think that he and his colleagues are **acting according to human standards**. These people will need sharp rebuke or discipline and Paul is willing to act accordingly. He will confront their errors gently but firmly too. Paul assures his readers that although he is meek, he can also be bold and courageous. His boldness will not be limited to his letters. To be meek does not require one to surrender to the enemy. Meekness is compatible with firmness.

10.3: Paul's opponents have charged him with walking according to human standards, or literally, according to the flesh (See Special note A: The flesh). He admits that he and his companions **live as human beings** but do not **wage war according to human standards**. Paul does not wage spiritual warfare after the flesh as his enemies do.

10.4–6. The weapons of our warfare are not merely human, but they have divine power: The apostle asserts that his weapons are not merely human. The conflict between God's forces and those of Satan is spiritual and must, therefore, be fought with spiritual weapons (2 Corinthians 6.7; Ephesians 6.11, 13–17; 1 Thessalonians 5.8). As such, victory is not possible through the use of the theatrics and gimmicks of the world. What are these human weapons? John Chrysostom describes them as 'wealth, glory, power, loquaciousness, cleverness, half-truths, flatteries, hypocrisies and so on'. The weapons of the believer have divine power to destroy the enemy's strongholds, destroy arguments, destroy every proud obstacle raised up against the knowledge of God, and able to take every thought captive to obey Christ. Paul describes the conflict in terms of spiritual warfare not waged against people as such but against philosophies, views, tactics, theories and thought patterns, and against the world's wisdom that resists, rejects and substitutes itself for the knowledge that God has been pleased to reveal through his Word.

10.6. We are ready to punish every disobedience: Paul says that he will punish those who deserve it when he arrives, but he first wants to make sure that the Corinthians bring their own obedience to his authority to completion. Paul is patient. He wants to try to persuade as many as possible to amend their ways.

10.7. Just as you belong to Christ, so also do we: What exactly did Paul want the Corinthians to consider? Paul now urges his readers to face the reality of things as they actually are. Many have been duped by the deceptions and lies of his opponents who have claimed that they **belong to Christ**. He wants them to see the facts clearly. As to facts, Paul gently reproves his readers for being superficial in their judgement. They have too readily accepted the teachings and the allegation of his enemies without evaluating them in the light of the facts regarding his ministry. If they would look behind the false picture painted by his opponents, they would see the facts that certify the genuineness of his apostleship and the falsity of these teachers' claims. Whatever special appointment others may have had, Paul and his co-workers belong to Christ just as much.

10.8–11: The Corinthians will also find that Paul received his apostolic authority from Christ (v. 8). Ordinarily the apostle does not boast of his authority, but necessity forces him to do so now. He will not be put to shame by remaining silent as though he were a fraud, as his enemies have alleged. Though writing as a meek man, the apostle could glory in his authority, for it was given to him by Christ for beneficial purposes – for the edification of others. Meekness requires us to look at the facts and accept them. Since our sufficiency is of God, we must give him credit for all that is accomplished.

Paul implies that the false teachers are exercising their self-appointed authority for destruction. Their teaching and conduct are destroying the church. A true apostle would never exercise his authority to this end. For instance, it is not Paul's intention to throw his apostolic weight around by his correspondence so as to intimidate or frighten his readers (v. 9). The Corinthians will also find that another charge that his enemies have made against him is not true (vv. 10, 11). They have accused him of writing weighty and powerful letters and being ineffective in physical presence and speech (v. 10). But Paul warns that his deeds, when he is present, are as powerful as his letters when he is absent (v. 11). He has written strong, disciplinary letters to the Corinthians, not because he is more courageous at a distance, but because it is better for them to put their house in order themselves. He does not want to go to Corinth with a rod unless it is necessary.

10.12. Those who commend themselves: Paul's opponents set themselves up as the standard of excellence, and they credited to themselves the achievements of others. Their behaviour stood in contrast to that of

Paul. He would not stoop to their level or degrade himself by comparing himself to them. To do so would be to participate in their manner of measuring and comparing themselves among themselves, a practice that would confirm that **they do not show good sense**. In the competitive culture of our day it is a natural thing to make comparisons. Children are constantly comparing age, height, grade and abilities with each other. Adults compare achievements – education, positions, houses, cars and material acquisitions. Sadly enough, ministers compare the size of congregation, attendance at meetings, property, etc. And without doubt, we like to compare ourselves with someone who makes us look good. We can always find somebody who does not match up to us. We think we are building ourselves up when in actual fact we are knocking others down. Paul's opponents had set up standards by which they looked good – themselves. Paul didn't match up to their standards.

10.13–16. We will not boast beyond limits: In contrast to his opponents who have credited themselves with the labours of others, Paul says he and his companions will not boast beyond proper limits. Instead, they will restrict their boasting to what God has established through them – **within the field that God has assigned** to them. God has assigned to Paul a field of ministry – a field that included the Corinthians. He was the first to go as far as Corinth with the gospel of Christ. Refusing to boast of things beyond his appointed sphere of labour, Paul does not claim the labour of others for his own (v. 15). Paul wants to preach the gospel in places beyond Corinth, even west of Rome, because he does not want to violate the same principle by which he criticized others. He would not boast in or take credit for the work that has already been done by someone else.

10.17–18. Boast in the Lord: Paul appeals to the Old Testament to sum up his outlook (Jeremiah 9.23–24). Christians must not boast of their wisdom or abilities. Instead they must give the Lord credit for all that is accomplished through their lives, for they know that they cannot do anything apart from the Lord. Therefore, all boasting must be in the Lord and what he is pleased to do through us. The Lord does not accept those who commend themselves according to their own standard of excellence, as did the false teachers at Corinth.

 Special note H
Spiritual warfare

Much has been written about spiritual warfare, leaving the average Christian in a quandary over what is true or not true. Spiritual warfare means different things to different people. On the one hand, many Christians in the Western world attribute various problems to rational causes. Hence it is common to attribute a natural or human explanation to most problems and leave it at that. On the other hand, in places such as Africa and Asia, where there is a palpable reality of the spirit world and demons, believers are often aware of other causes. In some cases, spiritual warfare is no more than 'exorcism' or 'casting out of demons'. What is needed today is a balance in Christian lives. We must recognize that there is not one area of Christian ministry that has not become a battleground. What is often lacking is a discernment that some form of spiritual resistance is taking place. The one who has a spiritual warfare perspective will be inclined to test the situation to ascertain whether or not there is something more than natural influences involved. Spiritual warfare is a proactive approach to our faith. We actively resist the devil when his hosts harass us. We actively pursue spiritual disciplines that will make us stronger and better prepared. We actively engage the enemy when people are in spiritual bondage. Spiritual warfare is the putting aside of passive attitudes towards faith, which keep us from commitment and cause us to pursue only those things that will benefit us. Here are some useful tips for carrying out spiritual warfare.

1   *A biblical world view* Christians must take very seriously the biblical warnings to God's people about an enemy that is real. They must know their inheritance in Christ, know God's promises and not become easy prey to the lies and deceptions of the enemy. They must know and understand the enemy's strategy and constantly fortify themselves in an understanding of God's truth.

2   *Prayer* Prayer is an indispensable weapon in spiritual warfare. How true is the saying that 'a prayer-less Christian is a powerless Christian'. Believers must utilize prayer as a weapon to penetrate strongholds that cannot be breached in any other way.

3   *Vigilance* During the Nigerian–Biafran war (1967–70), part of the signature tune of Radio Biafra was 'eternal vigilance is the price of liberty'. That phrase underscores the importance of vigilance and alertness in a time of war. As soldiers, Christians must never let down their guard but must be alert to the activity of the enemy. Such alertness is by no means fear or paranoia. Christians must not go around crediting Satan and his hosts for everything wrong under the sun. Paul is a good example of a spiritual warrior. He does not go out of his way to look for demonic activity, but when he encounters it, he quickly recognizes it, and then he confronts it with spiritual authority, victoriously.

4   *Personal discipline* Christians must discipline their thoughts and actions. If these areas are compromised, they will not be effective in resisting the enemy. They must take sin very seriously, because sin always gives the adversary an advantage. They must always be on guard against comparing themselves with others and being entrapped by

the subtlety of religious pride. True warriors know that they can do nothing that is effective in their own strength. Their strength, authority, wisdom and discernment are dependent upon their close walk with their Lord and the power of the Holy Spirit.

 STUDY SUGGESTIONS

Word study

1 Look up the definition of 'meek'. What does Paul mean by saying that he is meek? Is this an acquiescence to the will of others? Describe the godly meekness that Paul is advocating.

Review of content

2 What accusation against Paul is he addressing and refuting in 2 Corinthians 10? How does Paul show his godly character while boldly standing against the false teachers?

3 Why does Paul boast about his apostolic authority being from God? How does he use this to contrast with the authority of his accusers? In v. 8, what important element does Paul reveal about true apostolic authority in relation to community?

4 In what two ways were the boastings of Paul's accusers without foundation? Compare and contrast this with Paul.

Bible study

5 Read Acts 9.1–22.

   (a) Paul claims that he is an apostle appointed by God. Do you see evidence of that here?

   (b) Given Paul's extreme conversion, why is he so careful about the manner in which he approaches the Corinthians and his accusers?

   (c) Paul is careful to boast only in the Lord. Do you think his conversion experience has anything to do with this? Why or why not?

Discussion and application

6 In a world where 'the end justifies the means', does Paul advocate such a mindset? Do our methods really matter? Why or why not?

7 What should be the believer's standard of evaluation of success? Are churches 'successful' when they have more people coming to church on Sunday morning than will fit in the pews? How would Paul define a successful church?

8 Why is comparison with others often evil? In a society that teaches children to be competitive, how can we counteract this? Instead of comparing ourselves with each other, what is a healthy substitute? In what ways have you been guilty of comparing yourself to others?

9 What is the value of boasting in the Lord? Should we never boast, so that we can avoid doing so in a manner that puffs us up? What is the possible danger in not boasting in the Lord?

10 Have you ever been in a service where testimony has been given? Did the testimony boast in the Lord? How did the testimony encourage you?

11.1–33: Paul's foolish boasting

 ## Summary

11.1–4: Paul's motive

11.5–6: Paul's ministry

11.7–12: Preaching without charge

11.13–15: The character of the false teachers

11.16–20: Foolish boasting

11.21–33: Paul's apostolic credentials

 ## Introduction

Paul's opponents in Corinth were proud and pretentious. Claiming to be superior to Paul, they had entered the community and propagated some false teachings, thereby undermining the authority of Paul, the apostle and founder of the Corinthian church. They not only boasted but also beguiled some of the believers at Corinth. A few had listened to these false claims and, in so doing, were endangering their spiritual well-being. The spiritual welfare of the church was at stake, and Paul must take whatever steps necessary to salvage the Corinthian believers from the adverse influence of the false teachers. Therefore, Paul too is forced to boast, not because of pride of accomplishment; rather it is because of a jealous affection for the Corinthian church. He loves them and wants their love in return.

 Interpretation and notes

11.1. Bear with me in a little foolishness: Although Paul himself has earlier condemned human boasting as worthless, he himself now engages in it. Forced to do so by the tactics of his enemies, Paul shows their allegations are false by indulging in 'a little foolishness'. He asks the Corinthians to bear with him in his foolishness, and he is confident that they will. Paul calls the defence of his apostleship folly because he knows that the things he believes to be honourable about his apostleship will be regarded as foolish by some of the Corinthian Christians. Unlike that of his opponents, who were indulging in self-praise and trying to show that they were something more than they actually were, Paul's boasting is not an ego trip. Paul realizes that the present situation demands it if his converts at Corinth are to be preserved. It is for the preservation of the church. It would seem that the Corinthians were sympathetic to self-praise.

11.2. I feel a divine jealousy for you: Paul is concerned not only about the loss of the Corinthian community from him but also, more importantly, for their loss from the gospel. His opponents seem to have had some success. He describes his concern as 'divine' jealousy. As one scholar notes, 'Human jealousy is a vice, but to share divine jealousy is a virtue.' One reason for Paul's godly jealousy is for the exalted relation that the Corinthian believers have with Christ. Paul likens himself to a father who gives his daughter to her future husband in betrothal and at the wedding. His preaching the gospel in Corinth and the people's response in salvation is analogous to the betrothal act. By his ministry, Paul gave the Corinthian believers to one husband, to Jesus Christ. He also anticipates the time when he will present them as a chaste virgin to Christ. For Paul the problem is more than that of loyalty to one apostle or the other. It is loyalty to the gospel and to Christ that is at stake.

11.3–4. But I am afraid: Paul recounts the story of Eve in Genesis 3 to underscore his fear about the danger that the Corinthians face. They are in danger of drifting away from their devotion to Christ. In the same manner as Satan perverted Eve's sincere faith in God, so the false apostles attempt to persuade the Corinthians to jettison their whole-hearted allegiance to Christ. Paul has every reason to be jealous and afraid. There is a danger of deception. Paul's fear is justified. Apparently, some missionary intruders were wooing the Corinthians to abandon Christ whom Paul preached. The new missionaries insisted that where Paul introduced them to Christianity, they could lead them to experience Jesus, the Spirit, and the gospel, in a fuller way. To his dismay, Paul says, **you submit . . . readily enough**. Understandably Paul is alarmed and very much disappointed.

11.5–6. Super-apostles: For the first time Paul names his opponents. They are 'super-apostles', or at the least so claimed. Although they accorded themselves the highest dignity, they were not apostles at all. They were false apostles (11.13–15). Whoever these most eminent apostles are, Paul will not claim to be less than they. Later Paul will explain how he (in an unlikely way) is greater than these supposedly most eminent apostles. The apostle notes two differences between himself and his opponents. First, he is not a trained speaker. In Paul's day, the ability to speak in a polished, sophisticated, entertaining way was popular. Others, such as the super-apostles, were able to speak in this manner. It does not matter to Paul, because he is not concerned with meeting people's standards for a 'polished' or 'entertaining' speaker, he is concerned with faithfully preaching the gospel. Paul, although clearly rhetorically skilled himself, knows as we do that the Holy Spirit can work through those who are unskilled or unlearned in polished oratory. Second, he is not an amateur in the knowledge of the truth of the gospel. For Paul that knowledge is to be found in the message about Christ crucified and risen. That was the knowledge that saved the Corinthians when Paul first preached to them.

11.7–9: Paul did enjoy hospitality from the Corinthians (Romans 16.23), but his refusal to accept financial remuneration did not sit well with them. Paul does not intend to shame them by refusing any financial support from them. Rather it is to honour Christ. Furthermore, the Corinthians could not understand why Paul would voluntarily accept humiliation for their sake and how his humiliation would lead to their exaltation. The Corinthians' failure to understand why Paul behaved this way shows a failure to understand their apostle fully but, more seriously, a failure to understand the gospel that exchanges self-exaltation for self-sacrifice in service to others. In short, it seems that their basic problem is that they have allowed their socio-cultural environment to shape their understanding of their Christian faith and community practice, and they lack the knowledge of God that exposes those values as foolish. In the culture of that day it would have been considered a demeaning thing for Paul to work, particularly as a craftsman. Craftsmen were held in low regard by the leisured class in the ancient world.

Furthermore, for Paul to receive support from the relatively poverty-stricken Macedonians (2 Corinthians 8.2) while he turns it down from the relatively well-off Corinthians also would have insulted them. They gladly would share what is theirs with him (12.13–14), but he refuses to accept. Refusing gifts was considered a dishonour to the giver. The Corinthians interpreted his refusal to accept their support as a sign that he did not love them (11.11) but desired instead to shame them. They thought he judged them less worthy than others, and they were therefore less favoured (12.13) since they were excluded from the charmed circle of Paul's partners in the gospel. In many cultures today, particularly in Africa and Asia, refusing to accept a gift from others can easily be construed as an insult. The social practices of Paul's time made his refusal to accept their gifts a major factor behind their hostility toward him. Paul needs to set the record straight.

11.10–11: Paul asserts that he will continue to preach without financial support in Asia. If it is a sin to preach the gospel free of charge, accepting no financial support (11.7), then it is one of which Paul is proud, and he will continue to boast about it. He explains that his practice is his boast and that he does it because of his love for them. His boast is that he proclaims the gospel free of charge, and their complaints will not cause him to modify his firm policy.

11.12: Paul provides another reason for refusing their financial support. It is the claim of his rivals and charges of his opponents. They have boasted that they are his equals and sought an opportunity to validate their claims. They apparently have succeeded in gaining the support of the Corinthians at the expense of Paul. He undercuts their boast by serving the church without accepting their money. If they want to attain Paul's status, then they need to adopt his position on boasting. If they want to operate on his level of ministry, let them abandon their self-serving ways and take the humble role of a slave (4.5). Unless they adopt his practice of preaching for nothing, they cannot classify themselves with him.

11.13–15: The second part of Paul's strategy is flatly to describe and identify these intruding super-apostles. Paul has earlier made it clear in this Letter that appearances can be deceptive (4.18; 5.12), and this is particularly true when dishonest persons put on a religious appearance to further their selfish ambitions. Paul's rivals' claim to apostleship has been so convincing that some of the Corinthians have been tricked. In this section Paul launches a frontal assault on his rivals. These so-called super-apostles are in reality **false apostles, deceitful workers, disguising themselves as apostles of Christ**. They were probably missionaries. These are not unbelievers who maliciously plot to infiltrate the church as undercover agents. They may deceive themselves and others that they are doing God's work, but their narcissism and superior air reveals that they serve someone other than God. They only masquerade as apostles in the same way that Satan masquerades as an angel of light. Paul ties his opponents to the serpent who deceived Eve (11.3). Satan can pose as an angel of light. Satan is seductive and insidious. It should not be surprising then if satanic evil infiltrates a church and deludes it. The argument runs, if Satan disguises himself with the raiment of righteousness, then so will his minions. The rivals are no different from the master they serve. Disguising their true identity, these agents of Satan had invaded Corinth, wearing the garb of righteousness. They probably were personable, suave, sophisticated and convincing to the unwary. They may have been meticulous in speech or dress. But they were deadly foes of the church, and their end will be as their works.

The greatest weapon the devil has in his arsenal to test us is praise and flattery. The Corinthians, who want to become rich and reign as kings (1 Corinthians 4.8), are particularly susceptible to a false gospel dispensed by jaunty, diamond-studded apostles that appeals to their innate human pride and desire to be special. Paul next accuses these rivals of disguising themselves as **ministers of righteousness**. In 2 Corinthians 3.9 he describes his own ministry as a 'ministry of justification' ('the ministry that brings righteousness', NIV). The rivals pose as participants in this same ministry that leads to righteousness and is undergirded by the Spirit. They are frauds. Paul does not pinpoint the particulars of their false theology but focuses more on their boasting beyond measure. It is their demeanour and behaviour that reveal them to be ministers of Satan rather than of righteousness. Ministers of righteousness are those who live righteously, not those who purport to be righteous or to preach a righteous message. Ministers of righteousness remove the veil of hard-heartedness and, by the Spirit, lead God's new covenant people to be transformed into the image of Christ – to be Christ-like (3.12–17). They renounce shameful things and deceitful practices (4.2). They also repudiate all fleshly boasting and boast only in the Lord. These persons are therefore not simply deceitful rivals of Paul. As servants of Satan, they are rivals of God (cf. Acts 13.10). 'To follow them is to risk damnation.' Such language may sound harsh, but Paul judges the situation to be perilous, calling for sharp warnings to jar the Corinthians awake. God will judge them according to their works (2 Corinthians 5.10) and not according to appearances that so easily fool humans.

11.16–19. I too may boast a little: Paul returns to the idea of foolish boasting earlier mentioned in v. 1 as he prepares them again for his fool's speech. He does not want them to be fooled by his fool's disguise and mistake it for true apostolic speech. The Corinthians have willingly tolerated the foolish boasting of Paul's rivals. Paul uses biting sarcasm: if they are wise enough to put up with so many fools, surely they can listen to Paul for a while! They can probably endure a little boasting from their own apostle. Paul's rivals **boast according to human standards**. Paul is willing to do the same, although reluctantly, if that will enable the Corinthians to listen to him (12.11). Still for Paul it is below the dignity of an apostolic discourse (11.17). It is that of 'worldly persons' trying to outshine their rivals, itself a 'foolish' ambition. Paul adopts his rivals' ways to show how ultimately foolish they are. He speaks as a fool because it will allow him to boast about himself, which is foolish, and not something that the Lord would approve. By explicitly saying that this is what he is doing, he undermines the boasting of his rivals. It shows it to be foolish and contrary to what the Lord would have them do. They are fools who engage in worldly discourse that has nothing to do with 'speaking according to the Lord'. The Corinthians have no trouble with those who glory in themselves because that is exactly what they expect them to do. By contrast, they have been put off by Paul's abject humility.

If they will not bear with him when he is wise and speaks according to the Lord then, Paul mockingly says, perhaps they will bear with him when he acts the fool and boasts in the same manner as the rivals they so esteem. He ironically appeals to their extraordinary tolerance of fools, **You gladly put up with fools, being wise yourselves!** (v. 19). What Paul does here is to destroy the so-called wisdom of the wise by embracing it himself and in the process showing it to be the folly of the fool. Even when he descends to the level of his rivals in boasting, he transcends them. Paul will boast about the visible things. What is visible, however, points to his weaknesses – part of the problem as far as the Corinthians were concerned. His boasting in his weakness allows him to expound on God's grace.

11.20: The Corinthians put up with the speech of fools and the despondency of tyrants. How inconsistent they are! They pretend to be wise but bear with fools! They claim to be followers of a meek Christ and yet willingly submit themselves to teachers who masquerade as servants of Christ, when they, as a matter of fact, are tyrants! Here is Paul, who is meek and weak and whose life looks like that of Christ, and here are people who look like tyrants and they at the same time claim to be followers of Christ. The meekness and gentleness of Christ (10.1), which characterize his demeanour toward them, are interpreted as a sign of weakness.

11.21: Ironically, Paul confesses, **To my shame, I must say, we were too weak for that!** Paul and his companions would not take undue advantage of the Corinthians as his opponents have done. For Paul, if being 'strong' means doing what his rivals have done, then he is unquestionably weak. Yet it is a weakness that God approves. God never condones the tyranny, arrogance and meanness that church leaders have inflicted on the Church across the ages. Paul goes on to say that his weakness allows God's power to work more powerfully in him (1 Corinthians 2.3; 2 Corinthians 12.9; 13.4). He repudiates the weakness that some Corinthians accuse him of, and 'dares' to boast with the best of his rivals; although, as he understands it, it is with the worst of them. He continues to remind the Corinthians that boasting in this manner is utter foolishness.

11.22: Paul's rivals have apparently touted their Jewish heritage to prove their supreme qualifications as servants of Christ. **Hebrews** may refer to Jews who originated from Palestine or may simply denote those who spoke Hebrew. Paul probably uses the term as an archaic title of respect for his nation. It recalls that God set this people apart from all other peoples of the earth in descent (see Genesis 11.14), language, faith and practice. **Israelites** denotes membership in a people and religion. **Descendants of Abraham** refers to the people of the promise (Genesis 12.7; 13.15; 15.5; 17.7; 22.17–18; 24.7; 28.4) for whom the messianic blessings were destined (John 8.33, 37; Hebrews 2.16). These terms affirm that Paul and his rivals are full-blooded Jews. But Paul has redefined the ultimate significance of these categories in Romans and Galatians. The people of God, according to Paul, now includes Gentiles who believe in Christ and who become joint heirs with him of the glory to come (Romans 8.15–17). Such ethnic and religious distinctions make no difference in light of the new creation in Christ. But if his rivals still find such things to be impressive, then he is no less Jewish than they.

11.23: Paul's opponents also apparently claim to be 'servants of Christ'. But as Jesus warned of false prophets who will come saying all the right words, 'Lord, Lord', but who are inwardly ravening wolves (Matthew 7.15–21), not all who lay claim to this title are true servants of Christ. Paul's rivals have arrogated the title 'servants of Christ' to themselves understanding it to confer on them a lofty status which makes others their inferiors, if not their servants. They may think of themselves as men sent on mission. Yet their mission is not 'to preach the gospel where Christ was not known' (Romans 15.20) but to enhance their own reputation and following by building on another's foundation. Their arrogant, boastful attitudes betray whom they really serve. Paul now enumerates how he eclipses his rivals. First, he has undertaken far greater labours. This statement recalls what he told the Corinthians earlier. He worked harder than the first disciples, he said, but he qualified this statement by saying that it was not he but the grace of God that is with him (1 Corinthians 15.10). Here he simply asserts that his labours are greater. Next, he claims that he has had far greater hardships, more imprisonments, more beatings, more scrapes with death. His language reveals that these were typical, recurring situations. **Exposed to death again and again** (NIV) reads literally 'in deaths often'. Paul must have come close to death on several occasions.

11.24: Paul refers to the synagogue discipline of scourging (cf. Matthew 10.17). The number of lashes prescribed depended on the severity of the crime. The 40 lashes are prescribed in Deuteronomy 25.1–3 as the maximum number that may be given before the punishment degenerates into a cruel humiliation. For Paul to submit to this punishment five times testifies not only to his physical stamina but also to his commitment to his people, Israel. Submitting to this discipline also may have allowed him continued access to Gentiles on the fringe of the synagogue who were more disposed to the gospel's message.

11.25. Beaten with rods: a specifically Roman punishment meted out in public by an officer attending the consul or other magistrate, bearing the fasces, and executing sentences on offenders. As a Roman citizen, Paul was technically exempt from such punishment, but citizenship did not accord one an iron-clad guarantee against injustice, only the right to certain formal procedures. A heavy beating with rods was generally imposed by earnest officials on members of the lower classes who could not afford to pay a punitive fee. It was, however, considered an appropriate punishment for those causing civic disturbances (Acts 16.22). Once, Paul says, he received a stoning (Acts 14.19). Three times Paul was shipwrecked and once he spent a 24-hour period in the sea before being rescued. Paul's shipwrecks in carrying the gospel to other lands testify to the truth of this statement.

11.26: Paul's travels exposed him to endless dangers and hardships. He next lists dangers from having to ford rivers, presumably swollen by floods, to danger from bandits. The danger from kinsmen reflects Jewish hostility to Paul (Acts 9.23, 29; 13.50; 14.5, 19; 17.5, 13; 18.12). He has also faced danger from pagans. Acts states that Gentiles, threatened by the gospel's message, posed serious threats to Paul. They made false charges that Paul was a troublemaker intent on causing social unrest throughout the world, and they branded him as an enemy of Roman law and order (Acts 14.15; 16.16–24; 19.23–41). **In danger in the city, in danger in the country, in danger at sea** (NIV) sums up almost everywhere Paul has gone. In the city he barely escaped an angry rabble in Ephesus and a dragnet to capture him in Damascus. In deserted areas and mountainous regions he faced dangers from robbers, kidnappers who sold their victims into slavery, and wild beasts. The startling mention of **false brothers** (cf. Galatians 2.5) implies that his fellow Christians were intent on harming Paul. He does not expand on what they tried to do to him, but the context suggests some kind of betrayal and possibly direct physical violence.

11.27: Paul now refers to physical deprivation he has suffered from his devotion to his calling and the toil and moil that comes from his arduous labour as a craftsman. The sleepless nights probably were voluntary and connected to his mission campaign. **Hungry and thirsty** is followed by **often without food**. With the 'nakedness' that follows, it is likely that the fasts were forced upon him by his poverty. Paul talks about how he is held in contempt for being hungry and thirsty and poorly clothed in 1 Corinthians 4.11. Being **cold and naked** caps his list of hardships. The catalogue of woes portrays an apostle lacerated by beatings, shadowed by enemies, worn down by exposure and deprivation, in shreds and tatters, and with no place to lay his head. It also shows an apostle unbent by all the hardships in his devotion to Christ's cause and his calling.

11.28: Paul has other things in mind that he could say but he decides to omit them and turn his attention to what he considers of great importance. So, **besides other things**, there is the stress of caring for the churches. They place a daily pressure upon him. As if all the physical things were not enough, he has agony of heart because he loves his children. The word translated 'anxiety' (Gk. *merimna*) could mean 'worry'. It makes his heart burn that they should lose their way or that Christ should not be formed in them. What a great pastor Paul is! It is much easier to pastor those who love their shepherd. It is a quite different story when friction and suspicion mar that relationship as it was in the case of Paul and the Corinthians. Yet Paul continues to feel responsibility for them and the other churches that he has founded. It is this sense of responsibility for the spiritual welfare of his churches that stokes his anxiety for them.

11.29: Paul concludes his list with two examples of his anxieties for his churches: concern for the weak and for those who stumble. Paul knows that anyone might fall (1 Corinthians 10.12), but the 'weak' are particularly vulnerable. His anxiety for his churches is an expression of his godly jealousy (2 Corinthians 11.2), which can flame into a divine fury. He does not casually accept a member of one of his churches falling into sin or being caused to stumble. It makes him burn inwardly.

11.30. I will boast of the things that show my weakness: Paul now leaves his comparison with the super-apostles and his catalogue of endured hardships and moves on to demonstrations of his weakness in 11.30—12.10. It is odd to boast about one's weakness, but Paul's declaration in 12.10 becomes the key for unlocking the purpose of this peculiar tactic. His weakness has a 'revelatory function'. He will therefore tell tales of battle skirmishes, heavenly journeys with divine revelations, and miraculous cures – but turn them on their heads. They do not show how brave and wonderful he is, but how great and wonderful the grace of God is that sustains him in his weakness. Then he finally summarizes this caricature he has created by saying what he boasts the most about is his weakness. Paul says he works harder and is constantly on the move, and he experiences deprivation; his reward is usually more hardship! The evidence of God's approval is not higher standing or the goods of this earth – none of the things the Corinthian opposition would have pointed to as evidence of the favour of God. For Paul, very often doing the best meant raising the hatred of those who were dug in against Christ and his truth.

11.31–33: Paul invokes God's name to verify what he is about to say concerning the account of his escape from Damascus. He relates it as an example of his weakness. He emphasizes the manner of his escape rather than the seriousness of the threat. Hiding in a basket is not something that someone with power would do. The incident occurred at the very beginning of his ministry, serving as a paradigm, as it were, for what was to come. Paul's escape parallels similar escapes in the Bible: Rahab and the spies (Joshua 2.15), and David with the help of Michal, who let him down through the window (1 Samuel 19.12). These examples show a pattern in which an ignoble escape on one day leads to victory on another (Joshua 6.1–25; 1 Samuel 23.1–14), and what appears at first to be a humiliating escape in fact leads to the manifestation of God's power. In sum it is clear that Paul is not simply engaging in self-mockery. His point is that God's power has worked in him in such a way that his weakness becomes strength, the conclusion in 2 Corinthians 12.10.

Special note I

Further reflection on 2 Corinthians 11.21–33

As we read this section, William Shakespeare's story of the murder of Julius Caesar by Brutus comes to mind. At the funeral, Brutus stands up to say that

Julius Caesar was an overly ambitious person. Brutus and his accomplices loved Rome so much that, although they hated to kill Caesar, they had to do it. Mark Antony also stands up to make the now familiar speech.

> Friends, Romans, countrymen, lend me your ears;
> I come to bury Caesar, not to praise him.

But then he goes on in this speech to subtly and cleverly begin to praise Caesar, to unfold the greatness of his friend and undermine the words of Brutus.

> He was my friend, faithful and just to me.
> But Brutus says he was ambitious;
> And Brutus is an honourable man . . .
> When that the poor have cried, Caesar hath wept;
> Ambition should be made of sterner stuff.
> Yet Brutus says he was ambitious;
> And Brutus is an honourable man.

Antony continues in this manner, talking about the 'honourable Brutus' who has just slain this noble person, and at the end he has turned everybody against Brutus. Claiming he will not praise Caesar, Mark Antony actually elucidates the greatness of his friend. Paul's fool's speech is somewhat similar in its intent. He speaks as a fool and, in boasting as his opponents do, he turns their boasting on its head. Paul's rivals wanted others to speak well of them and argued as to who had the greater name among their friends. So Paul says he will boast like they do, but then, having begun like Mark Antony who said, 'I have come to bury Caesar, not to praise him', his boasting is all of his weakness. Paul's boasting unmasks the foolishness of his opponents.

 STUDY SUGGESTIONS

Review of content

1   At the beginning of 2 Corinthians 11, Paul starts to boast. Why does he do this when he knows boasting is worthless? How is his boasting different from that of his opponents?

2   In vv. 5–6, what two differences does Paul give between himself and his opponents?

   (a) Given these differences, why do you think some of the Corinthians were willing to listen to the opponents?

   (b) Are there times you have experienced when the false seems more entertaining than the truth? Describe the situation and outcome.

3   What does Paul mean when he tells the Corinthians they have allowed someone to make slaves out of them? In what ways were they enslaved?

4   In vv. 21–33, what two important claims of Paul's opponents does he address? How does Paul dismantle both claims?

5   What does Paul boast most about? What does Paul see as the true mark of discipleship?

   (a) How is this different from his opponents? To what would his opponents have pointed as evidence of the favour of God?

   (b) How is this counterintuitive to what we see today?

Bible study

6   Read Romans 5.1–11. Here Paul is teaching us how to boast and about what we should boast.

   (a) What three things does Paul say in Romans 5 that 'we boast in'?

   (b) In 2 Corinthians 11, how does Paul exemplify his teaching from Romans 5?

   (c) If you were asked to give a record of all the good you have ever done in order to obtain some office or reward, what would you boast in? How does this compare to Paul's instruction and example?

Discussion and application

7   In view of all its imperfections, how could the Corinthian church be considered a 'chaste virgin'? What was threatening the holiness of the Corinthian church? Are there things that threaten the holiness of the Church today? How do we guard against such evils?

8   What relevant principles may ministers draw from Paul's financial practice and teaching? Does Paul's practice of preaching without charge suggest that Christian ministers today should not be paid by the organizations where they serve? Why or why not?

9   Do you know of any people who, like the opponents of Paul, know how to behave as 'righteous' (i.e. they know all the right words, the right way to dress, etc.) but who are merely 'peddlers of the word'?

   (a) Why do false teachers normally appear as good people?

   (b) Why are they so dangerous to the Church and the lives of Christians?

(c) How can we detect these false teachers and guard against them infiltrating our communities?

10 Are there any people or causes for which you and the Church ought to have godly jealousy? How should we react to experiencing godly jealousy? Following Paul's example, what steps should we take to prevent opponents from discrediting us during the process of confronting the things/situations which have caused such jealousy?

12.1–21: Foolish boasting and heavenly visions

 Summary

12.1: The necessity of boasting

12.2–10: Paul's visions

12.11–21: Paul's commendation and trust

 Introduction

The false teachers at Corinth boasted of their special experiences in which the Lord appeared to them. Their claim must have impressed the Corinthians, making them wonder if Paul could measure up to the intruders. The chapter continues Paul's boasting that started in 2 Corinthians 11. However, it contains more. Paul shows the power of grace in both his life and ministry. He speaks frequently about grace in 2 Corinthians (1.2, 12; 4.15; 8.1, 7, 9; 9.8, 14). He recognizes that the believer has nothing to boast of apart from what he or she receives from the Lord (1 Corinthians 4.7). God's grace is what makes Paul's hardship and constant sufferings bearable. We need the grace of God today!

 Interpretation and notes

12.1. It is necessary to boast: Paul begins a discussion about visions and revelations with a similar introduction to those found in 11.30 and 12.6, 'it is necessary to boast'. Although Paul knew that boasting was unprofitable, foolish and unbecoming of an apostle of Christ, it was

205

necessary to counteract the false claims and destructive influences of the interlopers. The situation in Corinth compels Paul to boast to deflate the pride of his enemies and remind the Corinthians of the genuineness of his apostleship. However, he is careful to do this in a way that exalts the Lord. He immediately hints at the subject of visions and revelations, which, in all likelihood, his opponents have hammered on.

12.2–5. Caught up to the third heaven: Paul has previously spoken of a humbling experience that he had (11.31–33). Here he speaks of an experience above anything that his foes can claim. He was caught up into Paradise! While at first the reader may wonder whether Paul is talking about someone else, v. 7 makes it clear that Paul is indeed referring to himself. He describes this unique event in the third person in order to avoid the appearance of exalting himself (v. 2). It happened 14 years ago. Though he is not sure whether it was in or out of body (vv. 2, 3), he was caught up to the third heaven or Paradise (vv. 2, 4). There he heard inexpressible words, which he is not allowed to repeat. Paul interrupts his account of this experience to say that he will boast of this man's experience, but he will not boast of himself except of his weaknesses (v. 5).

12.6: Although Paul will boast, he will not speak foolishness but will rather speak the truth. Paul will boast only of his weaknesses. He will also refrain from speaking more about his translation to heaven lest anyone should think of him more highly for this than for what they see in his conduct or what they hear from his teaching. Paul, unlike many ministers in the twenty-first century, knows that validation as God's minister does not come from one's self-commendation, endorsement or from other-worldly and ecstatic experiences. The opponents of Paul elevate revelations and visions as signs of true apostleship. However, Paul wants the Corinthians to evaluate him according to the observable facts of his life and ministry, his obedience and faithfulness in proclaiming the gospel, not by his account of mystical experiences.

12.7–8. A thorn . . . in the flesh: Paul's revelations were of an exceptional character. However, his reference to them is to show the reason for one of his most humbling experiences – his continuing 'thorn in the flesh', that **messenger of Satan** which buffets him constantly. What is Paul's thorn in the flesh? Its exact nature has prompted much speculation. Paul does not go into any detail in describing it because the Corinthians apparently are well familiar with what he means. In all likelihood, it refers to a physical ailment. This 'thorn' irritates him so much that he has prayed three times for its removal, but God has not granted this request. Although his request has been denied, his prayer has been answered. The answer he received, however, is quite different from what he expected. It is simply different from what Paul wishes. We must learn an important lesson here. God did not chastise or rebuke Paul for asking again and again. But, once Paul had a sense of God's answer, he stopped asking. God asks us to ask until our joy is full (Luke 18.1–8; John 16.23, 24). Nevertheless, there is a time when we must accept God's answer and rely on his strength for our weakness. From his suffering and the Lord's denial, Paul has learned two reasons for the 'thorn'. One is to keep him humble. Twice he says that it was given to him lest he be exalted above measure (v. 7). It is to be a continual reminder of who and what he is and how dependent he is upon the Lord.

12.9–10. My grace is sufficient: Whatever the 'thorn' was, the other reason for it was to keep Paul in a state which would allow the Lord to work effectively through him. In answer to Paul's prayer, the Lord has assured him that his grace will be enough for Paul and his power is perfected in the sphere of human weakness. Paul's life and ministry are proof of this glorious fact. In the same way as the divine presence rested upon Israel of old, so too the power of Christ rests upon Paul now. The very essence of Christian life and service is Christ living and working through us. As we abide in him, he produces this fruit. Paul boasts in his weaknesses and takes pleasure in his woes. Paul proceeds to offer a catalogue of trials which he endures for the sake of the gospel. In contrast to his opponents Paul can assert, in a rather paradoxical manner, that it is precisely through these sufferings for the sake of the gospel that he demonstrates the presence of Christ as Lord.

12.11–13: Paul almost apologizes for his boasting, but it had to be done. The Corinthians should have commended him, for they knew well his apostleship (v. 12). But they failed him by listening to his critics. Because the Corinthians – Paul's spiritual children – did not take his side, he was forced in his own defence to commend himself. Even though Paul insists, though he is the least of the apostles, that his apostleship is second to none, here he says, 'I am nothing.' This is probably Paul's honest evaluation of his status before God (cf. 1 Corinthians 15.9–10; 2 Corinthians 3.5; Philippians 3.12–16). He knows that whatever he is comes from God. But there is an implied sarcasm in the affirmation. If indeed Paul is nothing, so are the other superlative apostles. The difference is that they are ignorant of their real status, do not recognize that they are nothing before God and prance around as if they were kings. The Corinthians should have known that Paul's apostolic credentials were from God. His apostolicity was visible as he founded churches, including the one at Corinth. Paul continues to press his case with irony. He wants to know how they could have considered themselves to be **worse off than other churches** except that he does not burden them with financial obligations to him. Surely the Corinthians do not believe that refusing to exploit them like his opponents (12.17) somehow disqualifies him as an apostle? If they count this a wrong or sin, he mockingly begs their forgiveness.

12.14: As Paul indicates his readiness to make a third visit to Corinth, he is still determined not to be a financial burden to the Corinthians. If the Corinthians thought that Paul was after their money, they were totally wrong. He will continue his previous financial policy of not receiving gifts from them. His motivation is quite simple – he wants not only to silence the false charges of his enemies but also to show the purity of his love for the Corinthians and his desire to promote their spiritual well-being. He does not want their money; he wants their moral reformation and renewed commitment to Christ. As Victor Furnish rightly notes, Paul wants them to know that 'it is the gift of their lives to Christ, not of their money to himself, that he covets'.

12.15. I will most gladly spend and be spent for you: Driven with paternal, godly love, Paul will very gladly spend and be spent for them. The Corinthians' failing love for Paul does not lessen his love for them. In fact, he loves them more abundantly. His love for them is so great that he willingly imposes upon himself the discipline of self-deprivation and of earning his way, which the financial policy he has charted for himself requires. This means that he has to get along on less and work his hands more in order to keep body and soul together, but it is a small price for the edification and perfection of his children in Corinth. This same spirit of sacrifice motivated his Master to become poor that others might be made rich in him.

12.16–18. I did not burden you: Paul comes back to his main point. He did not burden the Corinthians. Paul's opponents had claimed that his collection for the Jerusalem saints was a clever ploy to obtain support for himself. To settle the matter, Paul asks a series of questions. He has not taken advantage of them through Titus and the brothers that he sent to them. Paul further challenges the Corinthians to consider the fact that he and Titus acted in the same spirit and followed the same course of selfless service. There is no justifiable reason to question Paul's motives. If his co-workers are not guilty of some kind of financial impropriety, then how could they think that he is? Why, after preaching the gospel for free and refusing to become a burden to them, would he now try to take advantage of them in a dishonest manner? He could have received their support openly and received their approbation of him. Apparently the Corinthians indeed failed to understand the reasons behind Paul's refusal of their support.

12.19: Could the Corinthians have misunderstood why Paul writes the way he does? He is convinced they do. They think he is excusing or defending himself when he answers the false charges of his enemies and vindicates his apostleship. But Paul wants to make it very clear that he feels no need to defend his own integrity or authority for his own sake. Paul assures his readers that everything that he is doing is for the purpose of edifying them. Since his image has been distorted by the lies and innuendos of his foes, he seeks to correct this for their well-being, not for his. Only as their confidence in his apostleship is restored can he rescue them from certain ruin.

12.20–21: In v. 3 Paul has expressed his fear that the Corinthians have already been deceived as Eve was by the serpent. Now he is concerned that when he comes the Corinthians will be torn apart with disputes and wrecked by immorality. If the Corinthian community is marked by disharmony and immorality, it will be humiliating to Paul. He does not speak of humiliation in human terms. Rather he fears that God will humble him in the sense that God will show him the failure of the Corinthians to live the Christian life as Paul has instructed them. If so he will mourn for many who are still unrepentant of their sexual sins.

 Special note J

Paul's thorn in the flesh

1   God allows thorns. Nowhere has God promised the believer a smooth flight to heaven. It is not only unrealistic and unscriptural but also wrong to assume that the Christian will have no troubles in this life. Afflictions are a part of this life. Thorns or adversities reveal what we think about ourselves. At times, trials and troubles are necessary tools for shaping our character into a more Christ-like image. Without adversity, we would be too quick to praise our own accomplishments and advancements. Therefore, our trials help keep our egos under control.

2   A thorn is not a punishment for past or present sins. To suggest that Paul was afflicted either because of his pre-conversion persecution of believers or due to some present sin in his life is without any scriptural warrant or justification.

3   God has a purpose in thorns. Although we may not realize it, adversity reveals what we truly think about God. Sometimes we get angry with God for our troubles, and other times we excuse him altogether for having nothing to do with them. The fact that God did not remove Paul's thorn is not an indication of God's weakness or non-involvement. Rather, it shows that it fulfils his purposes.

4   God has power over thorns. God can remove the thorns if he chooses to. In Paul's case God chose to demonstrate his power not by removing the thorn but by doing something greater – by giving grace that was sufficient to bear it.

Many times churches fail adequately to prepare their members to face thorns. I know of a young lady who was actively involved in her local church and loved God. Her mother died when she was still in high school. Shortly after that, another member of her family to whom she was very close also died. This caused her much grief and confusion to the point that she left the church. While this is tragic, her story is not an isolated one. Too many people leave the Church when tragedy strikes, but if they really knew what Paul is teaching here, they would realize that God has given them the grace to make it through the situation.

❓ STUDY SUGGESTIONS

Word study

1 Paul talks of a *thorn* in his flesh in this chapter.

  (a) Why is a thorn an apt metaphor of what Paul may be experiencing, regardless of what the 'thorn' actually is?

  (b) Can you think of another metaphor that would creatively yet competently capture what may be a thorn in your flesh?

Review of content

2 In vv. 2–5, what experience does Paul describe? Why does he describe this using the third person, when it is in fact Paul who had this experience?

3 What are four lessons we can learn from Paul's thorn? Do any of these deconstruct erroneous ideas we may have had about God, suffering and prayer? Explain.

4 At the end of 2 Corinthians 12, Paul mentions a fear that he has regarding the Corinthians. What is that fear? Why would this bother Paul as deeply as it appears? What is Paul's purpose in mentioning this fear to the Corinthians?

Bible study

5 Read Luke 18.1–8 and John 16.23–24.

  (a) Does God want us to ask him for what we desire? Is it wrong to ask something of God, even if asking repeatedly?

  (b) How many times did Paul ask for the thorn in his flesh to be removed? What was the result? What were two reasons for the thorn?

  (c) Will we always get exactly what we ask of God? Will God always hear and answer our prayers? Explain.

Discussion and application

6   Paul had an experience far beyond that of his opponents. Does he desire the Corinthians to judge him on the basis of that experience? Learning from Paul's example, when is it appropriate to boast? In what spirit should this always be presented?

7   Have you ever made a request from God and received a firm, 'No'? What is the natural response to this? How was Paul able to accept this answer and rejoice even in his suffering? How can we do the same?

8   In what ways were the Corinthians guilty in tolerating the false apostles? In light of this, how should we handle persons speaking negatively of those in ministry who we believe to be righteous servants of God? Do we have a responsibility to defend them, or should we just allow them to defend themselves?

9   Do you know of a situation where someone has left Christianity due to a tragedy? How would Paul respond to that person? What measures can we as Church take to ensure that this does not happen?

10   Have you ever heard the phrase, 'There is no rose without a thorn'? What do you think this means? Does it describe the reality of the Christian life? Why or why not?

13.1–14: Concluding appeal

 Summary

13.1–4: An apostolic warning and authority

13.5–9: A call for self-examination

13.10–13: Exhortations, greetings and blessings

 Introduction

The chapter concludes the final section of the Letter that began with 2 Corinthians 12.14. It deals with Paul's promised visit, which was soon to take place. Paul is not concerned about money or the possessions of the Corinthians. He has a parent's love for them, desiring to give of himself rather than make a gain from them. Still there are some who question his motives. Even though he loves them passionately, they are not requiting his love. They think he is exploiting them. Paul's opponents have created a divisive spirit in the church, posing the danger of moral disorder. Paul is ready to deal with the problem sternly should the situation remain unchanged during his third visit. Hence he warns his readers that, when he comes, he will take disciplinary action if necessary.

 Interpretation and notes

13.1–4. The third time I am coming to you . . . I will not be lenient: He will deal with the offenders with a strong hand, for there are some in Corinth who do not take his authority seriously. They seek proof of Christ speaking to him (v. 3), that he is really Christ's apostle or agent. To their sorrow they will discover that his dealings with them will be mighty, not weak. It comes about in this way. Though the Lord was crucified because of weakness, yet he lives because of the power of God (v. 4). In like manner, Paul and his associates are weak with him, but they live with him because of the power of God. This power is manifested in Paul's life and ministry, including the discipline that he administers by apostolic authority.

13.5–9: Paul urges his readers to examine or try themselves rather than him. They are to look for a 'proof' not only in Paul but also in themselves. They should regard themselves as being on trial. They should prove their own selves. Do they not fully know their own selves that Christ is in them? Unless indeed they are without proof; that is, if they fail to find the proof of their having him. When they realize that Christ is truly in them they will at the same time recognize that Christ is in Paul – that Paul has not failed the test. The self-examination that Paul urges will reassure them not only of their own salvation but also of the legitimacy of Paul's apostleship. If the Corinthians fail to recognize the presence of Jesus Christ among them, then they must have abandoned the gospel and renounced true Christian existence. So Paul expresses the hope that the Corinthians, after first realizing their own Christian existence, will recognize the validity of his life as a Christian and as an apostle. Paul assures his readers that he is praying that they may quit doing evil. He does not make this request for the purpose of being approved by them but because they should be doing what is good even though he may appear to be without proof of his apostleship. As far as he himself is concerned, he **cannot do anything against the truth**, that is, the truth of the gospel; he can only promote it. Paul wishes to be accepted by the Corinthians but not at the cost of sacrificing the truth. He can do so only on the basis of speaking the truth of the gospel. Without any resentment towards the Corinthians despite their betrayal of him, Paul adds that he is glad when he is weak and they are spiritually strong. He then prays for the restoration of the Corinthians.

13.10: Paul states that the purpose of his Letter is restoration. The Corinthians needed to amend their ways. Although he has authority as an apostle, Paul hopes to avoid the need to be severe. He would rather use his authority for the right purpose – to preach the gospel and build up the community. It is not only the Lord's intention but also Paul's desire.

13.11–13: Paul concludes his Letter with final exhortations. They are to put things in order, listen to Paul's appeal, agree with one another and live in peace, presumably with each other and with Paul their apostle. He assures them that, if they do these things, God who is the author of love and peace will be with them in manifestation of spiritual power and blessing. The final greeting mentions all three persons of the Triune God, highlighting the resources that the Lord's people have and which enable them to act and live according to God's will. However, Paul's emphasis falls on grace, love and fellowship experienced by believers rather than on Trinitarian theology. **The grace of the Lord Jesus Christ** appears in the final greeting in 1 Corinthians 16.23; Philippians 4.23 and Philemon 25. Grace stands for the whole blessing of redemption. It is summarized in 2 Corinthians 8.9. **The love of God** is expressed and seen most clearly in Christ's sacrificial death. **The fellowship of the Holy Spirit** (RSV) implies participation in the Spirit and in the spiritual gifts, and the fellowship created by the Spirit. Paul wishes for the Corinthians a deepening of their participation in the Holy Spirit; he also wishes for the unity which the Holy Spirit gives to the community. Paul calls down God's blessings upon *all* of them, including those who have given him so much trouble in Corinth. The Letter seems to have met with success.

 STUDY SUGGESTIONS

Review of content

1 Why did Paul delay his visit to Corinth until they received this Letter? Why did Paul give so many warnings to the Corinthians? At the beginning of 2 Corinthians 13, Paul gives the Corinthians a warning. What is that warning? Why was it necessary?

2 In v. 7, Paul speaks of his desire for the Corinthians to do no wrong. If Paul had been without proof of his apostleship, would this be justification for the Corinthians to do wrong? Why or why not?

3 In v. 11, Paul gives the Corinthians a prescription to restore themselves to a healthy, spiritual state. What is involved in this prescription? How would these things contribute to spiritual health?

4 Paul closes his Letter by pointing to two resources that the Lord's people have and which enable them to do what God requires.

What are these resources? Are they available even for the Church today?

Bible study

5 Read 1 John 1.

(a) How does John's exhortation to 'walk in the light' correlate with Paul's call for self-examination to see whether the Corinthians are living in the faith?

(b) Notice 1 John 1.7. In view of the rift between the Corinthians and their founding pastor, how might self-examination lead to a restored fellowship with the apostle?

(c) Why is self-examination vital not only to the individual but also to the community?

Discussion and application

6 Since the Corinthians were Christians, why was it necessary for Paul to exhort them to examine themselves? Do we need such self-examination today? Is Paul suggesting that the Corinthians should examine one another or that each person should examine himself or herself?

7 Why is it difficult for us to practise self-examination? What obstacles do you face when you try to set aside time for quiet reflection on your walk with God? What can we do to avoid such obstacles?

8 How important is the community of faith in helping each believer maintain spiritual health? What does a spiritually healthy person/ congregation look like? Do we see this often in our churches? Why or why not?

9 Why must evil be dealt with firmly in the Church? On whose shoulders does the responsibility lie? The lead pastor? The elders? The entire community? Explain.

Index

Adam 115, 117
angels 36, 44, 77, 78
Apollos 15, 27, 28, 29, 31, 32, 34, 35, 122
apostle 4, 5, 9, 10, 12–15, 23, 26–7, 29, 34–6, 62–3, 86, 91, 94, 97, 106, 109, 113, 129, 130–4, 137, 139, 150–1, 164–7, 171, 178, 180–2, 184, 188–90, 193, 195, 196–7, 198, 201, 202, 206–7, 208–9, 211–14
attitude 3, 4, 28, 30, 38, 40, 44, 45, 46, 48, 60, 75, 79, 81, 88, 94, 100, 105, 136, 141, 143, 171, 172, 182, 186, 189, 192, 200
authority 4, 5, 31, 39, 41, 65, 76, 77, 81, 104, 122, 130, 139, 165, 173, 178, 188, 189, 190, 193, 195, 208, 211, 212, 213

baptism 16, 18, 68, 85, 89, 90, 91, 114, 115, 116
believers 1, 10, 16, 18, 24, 28, 29, 31, 41, 42, 43, 44, 47, 48, 49, 50, 52, 53, 56, 57, 59, 60, 70, 72, 79, 80, 82, 85, 95, 97, 100, 102, 106, 107, 108, 109, 110, 112, 114, 116, 117, 118, 121, 122, 123, 125, 130, 133, 135, 142, 144, 145, 151, 154, 156, 157, 159, 164, 165, 166, 168, 169, 175, 176, 179, 180, 185, 192, 195, 197, 209, 213
belongingness 12
blameless 12, 13
boasting 40, 64, 183, 191, 193, 194, 195, 197, 198, 199, 203, 205, 206, 207

body of Christ 13, 30, 44, 45, 46, 47, 70, 75, 78, 80, 83, 84, 85, 86, 93, 105, 107, 110, 138

calling 10, 45, 52, 56, 62, 86, 135, 142, 147, 157, 161, 170, 198, 201
celibacy 50, 51, 54, 56
Cephas 63, 113
character 11, 13, 34, 45, 72, 120, 133, 134, 140, 148, 152, 156, 209
Christ 9, 10, 11, 12, 14, 15, 17, 21f, 29, 40, 47, 59, 62, 65, 79f, 89, 93, 108, 114f, 129, 149f, 168, 174, 178f, 185, 189, 195, 200, 213; the benefits of 18; the cross of 14, 16, 149; the judgement seat of 35, 155, 156; the resurrection of 62, 79, 112, 113, 114, 115, 116, 156, 158; the return of 151, 154; the revealing of 12; the work of 18
clay jars 150, 152
collection for the saints 3, 5, 91, 92, 120, 121, 125, 176–87, 208
comfort 74, 100, 129, 131, 135, 137, 155, 171, 173
community 2, 4, 5, 13, 14, 19, 26, 27, 28, 30, 33, 38, 39, 40, 41, 42, 43, 44, 45, 46, 47, 48, 58, 72, 73, 75, 78, 79, 81, 84, 86, 87, 101, 102, 106, 109, 112, 115, 123, 125, 130, 137, 138, 148, 166, 169, 170, 175, 182, 186, 187, 193, 195, 196, 209, 213, 214
confession 15, 41, 79, 81, 113
conscience 34, 59, 60, 61, 72, 102, 147, 148
consolation 100, 131

Corinth: church in 4, 15, 18, 26, 35, 39, 40, 45, 69, 78, 81, 93, 102, 123, 130, 136, 137, 138, 188, 195, 204; first visit to 20; painful visit to 3, 121, 136

Corinthians: God's building 29; God's field 29; God's temple 27, 47, 170

covenant: new 79, 141–6, 147, 148, 164; old 143, 144

cross 1, 14, 16, 17, 18, 19, 20, 21, 22, 23, 29, 36, 61, 79, 80, 89, 90, 91, 93, 114, 139, 149, 158, 164, 199; the message of 14, 17, 18; the power of 36

crucifixion 17, 21, 23

cultic meal 69, 71

Day of the Lord 12, 32

death 16, 17, 22, 23, 30, 36, 40, 69, 79, 80, 81, 112, 113, 115, 116, 117, 118, 130, 131, 139, 143, 150, 153–62, 171, 200, 213

demons 22, 23, 70, 71, 72, 192, 193

denominations 10, 11, 15, 19, 31, 83, 89, 91, 94, 103, 143, 147, 178, 187

dependable 133

discernment 24, 26, 33, 88, 92, 192, 193

discipline 5, 37, 39, 40, 42, 43, 62, 66, 67, 69, 122, 133, 135–41, 166, 172, 174, 189, 192, 193, 200, 208, 212

disqualification 66, 68, 69, 74, 208

division 3, 4, 10, 14, 15, 16, 18, 19, 26, 31, 45, 78, 81, 94, 122, 156, 159

divorce 39, 50, 52, 53

edification 46, 71, 83, 84, 88, 94, 99–105, 190, 208, 209

endurance 25, 38, 70, 97, 146, 150, 151, 152, 166, 198, 202, 207

Ephesus 109, 122, 132, 134, 166, 171, 201

equality 18, 19, 51, 59, 77, 78, 103, 106, 107, 108, 111, 179

eternal life 115, 143

ethics 4, 11, 12, 51, 112, 130, 167, 169, 171

evangelism 19, 24, 29, 65

evil 41, 44, 59, 91, 94, 105, 124, 149, 161, 162, 166, 194, 198, 204, 212, 214

faith 4, 12, 21, 22, 29, 30, 35, 37, 38, 40, 52, 54, 55, 65, 70, 84, 86, 88, 91, 93, 95, 97, 98, 109, 112, 113, 114, 115, 122, 123, 132, 133, 134, 136, 147, 148, 150, 151, 154, 155, 156, 157, 159, 160, 166, 167, 171, 178, 185, 192, 196, 199, 203, 206, 214

false teachers 121, 122, 188, 190, 191, 193, 194, 195, 205

famine 91, 176

fear of God 156

fellowship 11, 19, 41, 42, 70, 71, 72, 74, 80, 81, 137, 155, 157, 160, 185, 213, 214

financial support. See material support

first fruits 115, 116

flesh 15, 26, 27, 31–2, 40, 117, 132, 170, 189, 198, 206

food sacrificed to idols 4, 58, 62, 71

foolishness 14, 16, 17, 18, 19, 20, 24, 27, 30, 36, 116, 167, 194–204, 206

forgiveness 36, 45, 53, 79, 94, 99, 114, 135, 137–8, 140, 141, 143, 162, 163, 166, 171, 172, 174, 208

fornication 46, 47

foundation 11, 27, 29, 30, 107, 112, 113, 114, 168, 193, 200

fragrance 139

freedom 4, 43, 44, 46, 47, 48, 57, 59, 62, 66, 67, 94, 104, 106, 108, 109, 144, 160, 167

generosity 86, 91, 177, 178, 183, 184, 185, 186, 187
gifts 5, 9, 11, 13, 24, 26, 27, 35, 36, 78, 82–110, 186, 197, 208, 213
giving 5, 25, 61, 69, 72, 91, 97, 106, 107, 117, 121, 125, 176–87
glory 12, 23, 24, 27, 28, 72, 74, 77, 78, 100, 117, 144, 145, 147, 149, 150, 151, 167, 168, 180, 190, 199, 200
gospel 14, 16, 19, 20, 21, 22, 23, 24, 28, 30, 31, 37, 38, 47, 52, 54, 64, 65, 67, 68, 72, 73, 77, 91, 108, 109, 110, 113, 114, 121, 122, 123, 133, 138, 139, 142, 143, 144, 147, 148, 149, 150, 151, 152, 155, 157, 160, 163, 164, 165, 167, 168, 170, 173, 180, 184, 185, 188, 191, 195, 196, 197, 198, 200, 201, 206, 207, 208, 212, 213
grace 9, 11, 27, 30, 36, 44, 46, 70, 78, 83, 124, 130, 132, 151, 164, 165, 166, 169, 176–177, 184, 186, 199, 200, 202, 205, 207, 209, 210, 213
Greeks 16, 17, 18, 20, 57
groan 154–5, 158
guarantee 133, 155, 158

hardships 36, 116, 150–2, 166, 167, 169, 177, 178, 200, 201, 202, 205
harvest 28, 115, 116, 185
head covering 10, 75–8, 81, 82, 108
healing 84, 86, 88, 90, 91, 106, 161, 162, 163, 164
heaven 59, 153, 154, 155, 159, 206, 209
holiness 4, 10, 12, 18, 30, 53, 132, 144, 167, 170, 174, 175, 204
Holy Spirit 10, 11, 20f, 31, 32, 44, 46, 47, 54, 83f, 133f, 155, 158, 167, 169, 193, 196, 198, 213

hope 9, 97, 98, 107, 114, 118, 138, 144, 147, 151, 153, 154, 155
human: nature 24, 27, 31, 94, 102, 116, 156, 159; standards 17, 27, 156, 189, 198
humility 36, 45, 149, 189, 197, 199, 207, 209

identity 11, 19, 46, 65, 162, 168, 169
idolatry 45, 67, 69, 70, 71
idols 3, 4, 57–74, 83
image 77, 84, 109, 117, 144, 156, 198, 209
immaturity 27, 30, 32, 33, 94
immorality 2, 3, 10, 39, 41, 43, 46, 47, 48, 51, 69, 209
individualism 4, 132
inner person 151
integrity 4, 5, 34, 122, 130, 135, 148, 152, 162, 164, 166, 171, 180, 208
Israel 10, 44, 68–74, 83, 144, 200
Israelites 68–70, 74, 144, 179, 200

Jerusalem church 5, 120, 121, 125, 176, 179, 180, 183, 185, 186, 187, 208
Jesus. *See* Christ
Jews 2, 16, 17, 65, 66, 77, 108, 132, 143, 184, 185, 187, 188, 199, 200, 201
Judea 132, 176
judge 12, 24, 27, 29, 30, 32f, 40–4, 71, 78, 80, 83, 84, 108, 115, 135, 136, 153, 155, 156, 190, 197, 198, 211
judgement seat of Christ 35, 155, 156
justification 11, 15, 77, 108, 198, 209, 213

knowledge 11, 17, 18, 26, 27, 29, 57–9, 68, 71, 84, 88, 95, 97, 98, 103, 123, 140, 143, 151, 154, 162, 165, 167, 178, 190, 196

law 39, 44, 63, 107, 108, 115, 143, 144, 201
lawsuit 44, 94
leadership 26–31, 67, 70, 86, 90, 106, 109, 110, 135, 147, 161, 182
letter of recommendation 141, 142, 143, 145, 146, 181
liberty. *See* freedom
Lord's Supper 5, 70, 71, 74, 75, 78, 79, 81, 82, 94
love 37, 42, 53, 57–62, 65, 68, 72, 74, 91, 93f, 104, 106–7, 120, 122, 123–4, 129, 136–40, 144, 153, 154, 156, 160, 166f, 178, 184, 185, 195, 197, 201–2, 203, 208, 210, 212, 213

Macedonia 3, 121, 132, 138, 171, 177–9, 181, 182, 183, 197
marriage 3, 39, 50–6, 68
material support 62, 63, 64, 67, 68
mature 10, 22, 25, 26, 27, 33, 101
meekness 37, 188–90, 193, 199
Messiah 17, 114, 115, 156
ministers 26, 27, 28, 30, 35, 42, 56, 64, 65, 66, 67, 72, 86, 87, 103, 106, 109, 110, 122, 132, 139, 141, 142, 143, 146, 147, 148, 149, 160, 164, 165, 167, 171, 191, 198, 204, 206
ministry 5, 11, 12, 13, 24, 26, 27, 35, 36, 38, 52, 61, 63, 64, 77, 83, 86, 90, 94, 101, 103, 106, 107, 109, 110, 115, 129–75, 178, 183, 185f
miracles 22, 68, 84, 89, 91, 95, 98
mission 10, 13, 21, 28, 38, 90, 93, 157, 165, 166, 200, 201
money 3, 5, 41, 64, 67, 120, 121, 124, 177, 179, 180, 182, 183, 184, 187, 197, 208, 212
Moravians 21, 25
Moses 68, 70, 143, 144, 145, 149
mystery of God 20, 21

new creation 45, 149, 156, 157–8, 200

offence 137
Old Testament 12, 23, 39, 90, 114, 150, 152, 168, 186, 191
opponents 4, 5, 20, 135, 142, 143, 145, 147, 150, 151, 167, 188, 189, 190, 191, 195, 196, 197, 200, 203, 204, 205, 206, 207, 211, 212
oratory 20, 21, 196
order 77, 78, 89, 100, 102–5, 116, 121, 136

Paradise 206
Passover Feast 41
peace 9, 11, 36, 53, 94, 104, 107, 122, 130, 160, 161, 163, 164, 213
philosophy 2, 17, 47, 112
power 11, 16f, 27, 36, 46, 59, 62, 70, 84, 86, 87, 89, 90, 92, 93, 95, 97, 106, 109, 114, 115, 117, 118, 123, 138, 142, 144, 150, 159, 167, 189, 190, 193, 199, 202, 205, 207, 209, 212, 213
prayer 10, 45, 73, 77, 78, 81, 86, 90, 91, 102, 117, 122, 129, 131, 132, 140, 185, 192, 207, 210, 211
preaching 16, 20, 21, 23, 25, 29, 30, 84, 114, 118, 119, 136, 148, 149, 156, 167, 175, 194, 195, 196, 197, 204, 208
pride 3, 14, 27, 30, 35, 40, 178, 193, 195, 198, 206
proclamation 16, 21, 22, 25, 54, 64, 79, 81, 84, 112, 114, 118, 143, 155, 156, 160, 167, 170
prophecy 77, 81, 84, 88, 90, 95, 97, 100, 101, 102, 103, 104
prosperity gospel 150, 184
purity 39–43, 44, 47, 50, 98, 167, 208

reconciliation 4, 5, 45, 94, 121, 153, 156, 157, 159, 160–4, 165, 168, 170, 171, 173
redemption 18, 40, 137, 144, 213
reincarnation 118, 119, 158

relationships: with God 11, 18, 47, 53, 54, 70, 76, 79, 102, 130, 139, 155, 160; with others 3–5, 37, 47, 49, 50, 53, 70, 74, 76, 81, 123, 137, 159, 163, 164–5, 173, 174, 179, 180, 181, 187, 202

remarriage 55, 60

repentance 30, 96, 171, 172, 173, 174

responsibility 34, 41, 42, 48, 60, 63, 74, 103, 125, 141, 147, 157, 159, 165, 171, 183, 202, 211, 214

resurrection 3, 4, 46, 62, 79, 112–19, 131, 143, 151, 153, 154, 156, 158

revelation 21, 23, 84, 95, 98, 122, 202, 206

rhetorical questions 9, 15, 16, 18, 35, 196

righteousness 18, 144, 157, 185, 187, 198

rights 45, 51, 60, 61, 62–5, 68, 71, 109, 160, 161, 162

Rome 2, 109, 191, 203

rulers 22, 23, 25, 76

sacrifices 4, 41, 57f, 163, 177, 178, 179, 182, 186, 196, 208

saints 10, 11, 43, 44, 89, 120, 123, 125, 130, 134, 135, 167, 170, 179, 185, 187, 208

salvation 11, 16, 17, 19, 23, 28, 29, 49, 52, 53, 74, 80, 84, 85, 114, 131, 133, 142, 143, 154, 165, 172, 178, 195, 212

sanctification 10, 18, 85

Satan 40, 42, 122, 136, 137, 138, 141, 146, 149, 189, 192, 196, 197, 198, 206

self-indulgence 68, 69, 70, 103

selflessness 37, 60, 62, 72, 178, 208

servants 15, 26, 28, 29, 34, 64, 67, 139, 146, 149, 164, 165, 169, 198, 199, 200, 211

services 11, 34, 37, 38, 52, 59, 83, 91, 100, 102, 103, 104, 105, 107, 109, 110, 121, 123, 130, 133, 136, 139, 143, 144, 150, 156, 159, 167, 169, 180, 181, 185, 186, 194, 196, 207, 208

sexual immorality 2, 3, 39, 43, 48, 51, 69

sexual purity 43, 44

signs 17, 22, 34, 89, 93, 162, 186, 206

sin 1, 2, 4, 12, 17, 31, 33, 40f, 51, 54, 69, 72, 73, 74, 79, 91, 94, 96, 110, 113, 114, 115, 136, 137, 138, 143, 144, 146, 148, 150, 152, 157, 160, 168, 170, 171, 172, 193, 197, 202, 208, 209

singles. *See* celibacy

spiritual: gifts 5, 9, 82, 83, 86, 87, 88, 92, 93, 94, 95, 97, 98, 99, 109, 213; warfare 192

Stephanas 16, 123

stewards 34, 37

strength 13, 21, 37, 132, 143, 149, 179, 193, 202, 207

suffering 17, 22, 35, 36, 38, 54, 74, 91, 93, 96, 107, 114, 116, 125, 131–2, 135, 139, 147, 150–3, 154, 162, 163, 165–7, 169, 172, 177, 201, 205, 207, 210, 211

super-apostles 164, 196, 197, 202

temporary 97, 108, 151, 172

testimony 5, 20, 40, 115, 139, 142, 146, 178, 180, 194

thanksgiving 9, 72, 129, 131, 183, 184, 185, 186

thorn in the flesh 209–10

Timothy 37, 122

Titus 3, 137, 138, 139, 170, 171, 172, 173, 174, 176, 178, 179, 180, 181, 208

tongues 83–6, 88, 89, 93, 95, 97, 99–105, 106

tradition 75, 77, 79, 85, 89, 92, 108, 113, 162

transformation 117, 144, 155, 156, 158

Troas 132, 138, 140, 171
truth 21, 23, 24, 26, 30, 34, 35, 37,
    40, 58, 83, 96, 113, 122, 133,
    144, 147, 148, 149, 166, 167,
    192, 196, 202, 204, 206, 212

unity 14–15, 19, 45, 67, 70, 74, 81,
    83, 84, 85, 86, 88, 93, 94, 107,
    110, 163, 213

veil 77, 108, 144, 198
virginity 54, 55
visions 205, 206

weakness 16, 17, 21, 25, 36, 93,
    117, 147, 150, 151, 162, 188,
    199, 202, 203, 206, 207, 212

widows 50, 51, 52, 55
will of God 9, 10, 129
wisdom: of God 17, 18, 21, 23, 84;
    human 14, 16, 17, 18, 20–6, 31,
    149
women 5, 10, 22, 54, 75–8, 81, 92,
    103, 104, 105–11
wonders 22
workings 83
world (-ly) 16, 18, 19, 20, 91, 94,
    159, 172, 198, 199, 206
worship 2, 5, 10, 30, 46, 57, 70, 71,
    75–8, 82, 89, 91, 94, 100,
    102–5, 107, 108, 110, 121, 142,
    166, 185, 186

Yoruba 21, 45, 117, 118

Printed and bound by CPI Group (UK) Ltd, Croydon, CR0 4YY

13/04/2025

14656472-0002